'A WALK-OVER?'
THE KAISER. "This is the doormat of our new premises."
EMPEROR KARL. "Are you quite sure it's dead?"

THE LAST YEARS OF AUSTRIA-HUNGARY

A Multi-National Experiment in Early Twentieth-Century Europe

Revised and expanded edition

edited by
Mark Cornwall

UNIVERSITY
of
EXETER
PRESS

First published in 1990 by
University of Exeter Press
Reed Hall, Streatham Drive
Exeter EX4 4QR
UK
www.ex.ac.uk/uep/

Revised and expanded edition published in 2002

British Library Cataloguing in Publication Data
A catalogue record of this book is available
from the British Library.

ISBN 0 85989 563 7

Typeset in 10.5 on 12.5 pt Sabon by Exe Valley Dataset Ltd, Exeter

Printed and bound in Great Britain by
Short Run Press Ltd, Exeter

CONTENTS

MAPS, TABLES AND ILLUSTRATIONS

Maps

Tables

Illustrations

Contributors

Catherine Albrecht is Associate Professor of History at the University of Baltimore. She has published widely on the history of professional economists, economic development and nationalism in the Czech Lands, most recently in *Austrian History Yearbook*. She is currently finishing a monograph on *Economic Nationalism in the Bohemian Crownlands 1848–1918*.

F.R. Bridge is Emeritus Professor of International History at the University of Leeds. His many works on Habsburg foreign policy include *From Sadowa to Sarajevo. The Foreign Policy of Austria-Hungary 1866–1914* (London, 1972) and *The Habsburg Monarchy among the Great Powers 1815–1918* (Oxford, 1990). He is completing an enlarged edition of *The Great Powers and the European States System 1815–1914* (London, 1980).

Mark Cornwall is Senior Lecturer in European History at the University of Dundee. His publications include *The Undermining of Austria-Hungary. The Battle for Hearts and Minds* (Basingstoke and London, 2000) and articles on the creation of Yugoslavia and the Sudeten problem. He is now working on the Czech–German relationship in the Czech Lands 1800–1950, with particular reference to youth and nationalism in the early twentieth century.

Lothar Höbelt is Assistant Professor and Universitätsdozent in the Institut der Geschichte at the University of Vienna. His major monograph concerns the German Liberals of Austria: *Kornblume und Kaiseradler. Die deutschfreiheitliche Parteien Altösterreichs 1882–1918* (Vienna, 1993). More recently he has published *1848: Österreich und die deutsche Revolution* (Vienna, 1998), and contributed a section on 'Parties and Fractions in the Cisleithanian Reichsrat' to *Die Habsburger Monarchie 1848–1918. Verfassung und Parliamentarismus*, vol. VII/2 (Vienna, 2000).

Rudolf Jeřábek is a leading archivist in the Austrian State Archives in Vienna. His doctoral thesis concerned the Brusilov offensive and he is the author of *Die Kämpfe in Südkärnten 1813* (Vienna, 1986) and *Potiorek. General im Schatten von Sarajevo* (Graz, Vienna and Cologne, 1991).

Janko Pleterski is Emeritus Professor of History at the University of Ljubljana. He has published widely on many aspects of modern Slovene and Yugoslav history. His books include *Prva odločitev Slovencev za Jugoslavijo 1914–1918* (Ljubljana, 1971), *Slowenisch oder deutsch? Nationale Differenzierungsprozesse in Kärnten 1848–1914* (Klagenfurt, 1996) and *Dr Ivan Šušteršič 1863–1925. Pot prvaka slovenskega političnega katolicizma* (Ljubljana, 1998).

F. Tibor Zsuppán was formerly Lecturer in Modern History at the University of St Andrews. He has published a range of articles on Hungary during 1918–19, on the Hungarian electoral system and on feminism. Recently he has been working on the Hungarian government's policy towards Transylvania, 1867–1872.

ACKNOWLEDGEMENTS

I would like to thank all the contributors for so readily placing their research and ideas in my editorial hands. Celia Hawkesworth gave valuable advice on my Croatian translation for Chapter 6, while Mike Rouillard and Philip Ford helped in the design of the maps. The Centre for Russian and East European Studies at the University of Toronto proved an ideal environment in which to complete the book. My final debt is to all at University of Exeter Press for their patience in remaining committed to this project.

JMC
Dundee/Toronto, November 2001

Note on Terminology

In the following chapters certain terms and titles are employed which may require explanation. The Habsburg Monarchy by the twentieth century consisted of a range of territories in the eastern half of Europe acquired by the Habsburg dynasty over centuries, either by inheritance, marriage or conquest. In 1867, the dynasty reached an agreement (*Ausgleich*) with the Magyar gentry by which the kingdom of Hungary received semi-independent status within the Empire. From this time the Empire was effectively divided in two with the title 'Austria-Hungary', and the so-called 'dualist system' was thereby inaugurated. In 1868 Emperor Franz Joseph assumed the title of 'Emperor of Austria and Apostolic King of Hungary'. Organs or officials appertaining to both halves of the Empire (such as the Common Army) were eventually designated *kaiserlich und königlich* (imperial and royal—abbreviated to k.u.k.); in turn, the corresponding Austrian title was *kaiserlich-königlich* (k.k.), and for Hungary *königlich-ungarisch* (royal Hungarian or k.u.). While the lands of the Hungarian crown can correctly be referred to as Hungary throughout the period of Dualism, the other half of the 'Dual Monarchy' had no official title until October 1915 when Franz Joseph agreed to the term 'Austria' being used. Until then, these lands outside Hungary were cumbersomely termed 'the kingdoms and lands represented in the Reichsrat' (i.e. in the parliament in Vienna), or Cisleithania for short. In this book, however, the terms Austria and Cisleithania are used interchangeably to denote the same territorial half of the Empire. From 1868, a kind of sub-Dualism existed in Hungary when, following an agreement or *Nagodba*, Croatia-Slavonia was granted, theoretically at least, a degree of autonomy within the Greater Hungarian kingdom. Similarly, in Austria after 1867, the Poles acquired administrative control of the kingdom of Galicia. Lastly, as regards the former Turkish provinces of Bosnia and Hercegovina (occupied in 1878 but only formally annexed by the Monarchy in 1908), their status remained anomalous alongside the

Dualist system. Vienna and Budapest could not agree as to whether they should be assigned to the Austrian or Hungarian half of the Empire, since their allocation would not only alter the power-relationship but also the ethnic balance. Instead therefore, they were administered separately, as they had been since 1878, by the Common Finance Ministry.

Place-names in this book are generally given according to current usage. The exception is when there is an accepted English term (thus, Cracow rather than Kraków, Lvov rather than L'viv or Lemberg, Ljubljana rather than Laibach).

1

Introduction

Mark Cornwall

As the Habsburg Monarchy entered the twentieth century on 1
January 1901, one of its most important regional newspapers, the
Reichenberger Zeitung, wrote that it was doing so under the 'most
unfavourable auspices'. According to this north Bohemian journal,
the Empire was falling behind economically, unable to rise from its
lethargy to compete with surrounding states. Added to this was the
political and national confusion which had lately engulfed it, making
it the laughing stock of all Europe. The conflict among the nationalities had done more damage to the Monarchy than the most
unfortunate war of the past century; and, perhaps worst of all, the
Germans of Austria were divided amongst themselves and seemed
bent on self-destruction. With signs everywhere of stagnation and
decline, the newspaper concluded that 'the peoples of the old
imperial state await with justifiable pessimism' the fatherland's future
development.[1]

This was of course only one 'establishment' viewpoint, chiefly that
of a threatened German-Austrian Liberal caste which had crucial
economic interests to maintain. It was a view perhaps mirrored in the
celebrated decadence of *fin-de-siècle* culture, notably in Vienna. But
in the next decade the Monarchy would be considered by some
contemporaries to have proved resilient in the face of internal and
external challenges. The British journalist, Henry Wickham Steed,
for example, could write in 1913 that 'its internal crises are often
crises of growth rather than of decay'.[2] Even so, the fatalistic stance
set out by the *Reichenberger Zeitung* also continued to ring true for
many in the remaining years left to the Habsburg Empire. In the
words of an associate of the psychiatrist Sigmund Freud, alongside
the blossoming economic and cultural life 'there was much pessimism
and resignation with regard to the long-term future'.[3]

In October 1918, the negative prophecies suddenly became horribly
realistic: after a four-year struggle against a host of foreign and

domestic enemies, Austria-Hungary disintegrated into 'national' components. These final two decades of Austria-Hungary's existence left a dramatic mark upon both older and younger generations who experienced them. Amongst the older generation, some like Josef Redlich felt that they had lived through the death of a tremendous 'ideal'—'a great piece of our own spiritual existence' had died.[4] Others, such as T.G. Masaryk, the president of the new Czechoslovak state, had crossed the Rubicon from belief in the Habsburg state to belief in an independent democratic Czechoslovakia which would rise from its ashes; his vision undoubtedly carried many (but certainly not all) older Czechs and Slovaks with him.

Amongst the younger generation, especially those born in the 1890s, many were decisively affected, first, by the tense ethnic strife at an imperial and grassroots level before 1914; and second, by the trauma of surviving a World War which not only destroyed the Monarchy but polarized further the peoples who had lived in it. There were of course, from these two decades, a multitude of youthful memories which cannot be neatly categorized. But in the 'successor states' of the inter-war period, a good number of this younger generation were encouraged to interpret the Monarchy's final years in an exaggeratedly nationalistic manner in order to make sense of the new world around them. For young Czechs or Slovenes, the last years had been a prelude to their deliverance from 'foreign oppression', and they had played their part in creating the new utopias of Czechoslovakia or Yugoslavia. For young Hungarians and especially young Germans, the last years had meant a betrayal of their kingdom or empire (respectively) by people with whom they had cohabited for centuries. Their own sacrifice in the war had gener-ally been for nothing in view of the truncated states in which they were now forced to live. Not surprisingly, many were pushed in a radically nationalistic and militaristic direction in the 1920s.

In the inter-war period, this splintered memory on the ruins of the Habsburg Empire was naturally reflected in the first works which sought to interpret the Monarchy's collapse. In each of the 'successor states' nationalist historians—for example, the Czech, Jan Opočenský —explained the collapse in terms of newly vibrant national missions which had fought free of an oppressive Habsburg yoke. Dozens of memoirs from politicians and military veterans gave weight to this version of the past.[5] Alternatively, it was usually in the 'rump' Austria or Hungary that old Habsburg officials, officers and diplo-mats sat down to record their 'loyalist' version of events against the treacherous forces which had engulfed the Monarchy. Out of Vienna came the Austro-Hungarian documents which sought to justify imperial foreign policy before 1914; while by 1938, a team of ex-Habsburg officers had completed a seven-volume official history of *Austria-Hungary's Last War 1914–1918*.[6] Only a few scholars attempted a deeper theoretical analysis. Notable was Oszkár Jászi's sociological study of the Monarchy's centripetal and centrifugal dynamics.[7] Most impressive was Josef Redlich's grand work on the 'Austrian imperial idea' which reached back to the early nineteenth century to explain the clash between the Habsburg dynastic concept and the rise of popular sovereignty.[8] Usually, however, authors were too close to events to evaluate the Empire with such coolness or detachment.

Surprisingly perhaps, the 'nationalist-loyalist' divide of interpretations did not disappear even in the decades after the Second World War. One example from Austria would be the historian Hans Übersberger's Serbophobe work on Habsburg foreign policy,[9] although by the 1960s, a new generation of Austrians, including Fritz Fellner and Helmut Rumpler, were approaching old Vienna's mindset with a more critical eye.[10] Meanwhile, after 1950 in the communist 'successor states', Marxist historiography simply added a new social-ist veneer to the previous negative approach to the Habsburg state; thus, Hungarian historians in the 1960s pressed the point that Hungary had been economically exploited under the dualist system. But perhaps the best work from the region on the subject came from the 1970s onwards, in the more relaxed academic climate of Hungary and Yugoslavia. There emerged, for example, out of the federal structure of Tito's Yugoslavia, imaginative interpretations both of how Yugoslavia had been created and of late Habsburg develop-ments specific to Croatia, Slovenia or one of the other constituent Yugoslav regions.[11]

For a broader, detached approach to the Monarchy as a whole, one had to turn particularly to those American and British-based historians who took up the baton, most notably Robert A. Kann, Arthur J. May and C.A. Macartney.[12] From the 1960s, the new American 'Habsburg scholars' were often of east-central European extraction themselves, sometimes with an unconsciously pro-Habsburg agenda, since they had witnessed how the Monarchy's demise paved the way for oppressive regimes in the region, first Nazi Germany and then the Soviet Union. But generally, from the basic western historiographical base provided by Kann and Macartney,

Map 1. The Habsburg Empire in the Twentieth Century.

innovative approaches to the later Habsburg Empire have flourished in the past thirty years. They have supplied key interpretations for the diplomatic, economic, social and cultural history of the Monarchy's final decades.[13] The number of regional and grassroots studies are also now burgeoning, as the bibliography to this volume attests.

Since Austria-Hungary's demise, therefore, it can be said that 'the Habsburg experiment' has regularly been reassessed by historians, particularly because of the memories and other legacies which its ruin left scattered across twentieth-century Europe. Most recently, from the early 1990s, an upsurge in interest came because of the collapse of communist Eastern Europe, the Soviet Empire and the multi-national states of Czechoslovakia and Yugoslavia. The disintegration of the Habsburg system or Empire suddenly appeared relevant and perhaps even instructive. At the same time, in tune as we have seen with new lines of approach, historians in the past decade have been researching a very varied picture of the late Habsburg years. But a fundamental issue lurking behind most studies is still the extent to which Austria-Hungary was a vibrant or moribund entity in the early twentieth century and the factors, long-term and short-term, which caused its collapse in 1918.

Most historians have continued to divide, rather like their late Habsburg contemporaries, in their pessimism or optimism about the Monarchy's fate. Sometimes their perspective is tied to their own political views—in short, conservative or liberal transforming, respectively, into a positive or negative appraisal of the Empire. Often however it stems from their predominant historical approach, whether economic, diplomatic, social or even cultural. The example of two American historians is here instructive. On the one hand, Solomon Wank has suggested that pessimism was indeed justified. He argues that the Habsburg imperial structure was in a long-term crisis, for it could not adapt to the new nationalist forces without at the same time delegitimizing its own imperial ideology. Thus the Empire's dissolution was virtually inevitable, and simply postponed until the First World War because of an indulgent international states system.[14] An alternative path for late Habsburg research has recently been advocated by Gary Cohen. He stresses that too much emphasis has long been given to the Monarchy's domestic conflicts and its final demise. Instead, we need more research on the stability and adaptability of political culture in these final decades, more attention to the periphery rather than the centre, in order to show how society and government were successfully interacting. If this might be termed the 'constructive' approach, rooted in new facets of historical investigation, it also contributes vitally to our understanding of the Monarchy's essence and the perennial issue of why it did not survive. As Cohen himself has admitted, 'how to explain the dissolution of the Habsburg Monarchy certainly remains a proper subject for research'.[15] Indeed, we can go further and say that it hovers over these diverse historical approaches which do not exclude but complement each other.

The seven essays in this volume reflect this diversity of treatment. Each author has taken a separate theme, but contributes overall to our evaluation of the Habsburg Empire in its last years and the short-term reasons for its collapse. The range of perceptions—the mixture of 'realities'—for those who lived through this period, has already been highlighted. It makes such a collection of essays a pertinent form with which to explore the whole subject. In turn, the angles chosen do not claim to be comprehensive; a number of aspects (economic stability, the Polish or Romanian questions) are touched on by various contributors and can be pursued further from these openings through extensive bibliographies. Most of the chapters appeared in some form in an earlier edition of this book (1990). All have now been enlarged and substantially revised, while Catherine Albrecht's essay supplies us with a valuable new synthesis of the national struggle in Bohemia.

Two major threads run through the book. First, it is clear that Austria-Hungary by the early twentieth century faced a mass of new challenges provoked by the forces of European modernity: both to its international position and in its domestic political and social structures. Second, it is unquestionable that the war, which the Habsburg elite consciously entered in 1914 to scotch the 'Serbian challenge' once and for all, was a watershed, disastrous for the Monarchy's potential survival.

Both threads stand out in Roy Bridge's fresh analysis of Austria-Hungary's foreign policy. He shows how, already by 1900, the flexible options that had functioned well in the past to preserve the Monarchy's Great Power position in the Balkans were ceasing to operate. Partly this was due to a modernizing Balkan peninsula which could not be kept eternally 'on ice', the only way perhaps to guarantee a cooperative relationship between Austria-Hungary and its Russian rival. Partly, however, it was the Ballhausplatz's (the foreign ministry's) actual strength of confidence which rebounded upon it, notably in the Bosnian crisis of 1908–9. The Monarchy fatally alienated Russia and was increasingly forced back upon a single option, Germany: an ally with whom it entered the World War despite having few vital interests in common. Through war, Austria-Hungary lost any further flexibility of manoeuvre on the international scene. Instead, each of the Great Powers in their own way threatened the Empire's future existence, whether it won or lost the fight.

In the pre-war domestic scene too, the Monarchy's dualist structure and its Liberal establishment faced growing threats from the 1890s. Lothar Höbelt details the rising political, social and ethnic challenges in Austria, accelerated all the more by the introduction of universal male suffrage to the Reichsrat in 1906. However, Höbelt—to some extent like Bridge's interpretation of the pre-war international scene—senses a healthy flexibility in the Austrian political system, which continued to function through a series of shifting checks and balances. He notes agreement between Poles and Ruthenes in Galicia, hints at a pending Czech-German compromise in Bohemia, and gives a revisionist twist to the government of Count Karl Stürgkh. Only with the war, he suggests, was the fluidity of this system stopped.

Less optimistic is Tibor Zsuppán's assessment of the Hungarian half of the Monarchy. Having celebrated its 'millennium' in 1896, Hungary lurched a few years' later into a constitutional crisis with the Habsburg crown which led to the latter imposing authoritarian rule in 1905. Zsuppán notes that the challenge by a vociferous Magyar opposition to the dualist system was just one of the irreconcilable pressures which beset the Liberal establishment in Budapest. The threat to the Magyar social elite by disenfranchized social and non-Magyar groupings also remained unsolved in the pre-war period, even if the elite under István Tisza readily took up the struggle from 1910. As in Austria, the war years made these competing mindsets more rigid, but Zsuppán is more pessimistic than Höbelt about the chances of peaceful reform in Hungary if the war had not intervened.

Two contributors examine the dangers posed to the Monarchy's survival by the Bohemian and South Slav questions respectively. Catherine Albrecht seeks to explain the complexity of the Czech-German struggle in Bohemia. She shows that it was a conflict which evolved not only politically but also at a grassroots non-political level, creating an intense 'small national war' in the localities. She identifies the Badeni crisis of 1897 as a crucial milestone in the conflict's escalation, derailing common Czech-German social and economic interests. And, in contrast to Lothar Höbelt, she judges that the mounting radical action and rhetoric seriously damaged the evolution of Austrian parliamentary government and strengthened the bureaucratic state. The Czech–German relationship became a 'zero-sum game', which by the last years of the war each side hoped to win by forcefully imposing its own national solution in the territory of Bohemia.

The impact of the Badeni crisis on national perceptions is also highlighted by Janko Pleterski, in his chapter on the South Slav question. Pleterski details the myriad perceptions of what consti- tuted the pre-war 'Yugoslav problem'; and perhaps most interest- ingly from a Slovene perspective, sets a lesser-known 'Adriatic' dimension alongside the Serbian–Bosnian relationship. He paints a picture of a region where the Yugoslav question shifted constantly after 1900, caught in a vice of external influences and dangers (Serbia, Italy, the Germans, the Magyars), and where new alliances by a new generation of 'angry young men' were developing across the Monarchy's internal borders.[16] There was no agreed solution to the South Slav question. Indeed, the Habsburg authorities could only view it as an illegitimate issue that had to be crushed by force. After July 1914, as before (but now with more rigid agendas by competing camps at home and abroad), the South Slav question continued to change shape depending on external and domestic circumstances. Only war made an independent Yugoslav outcome thinkable or possible. Here Pleterski (like Cornwall later) stresses the domestic Yugoslav popular mobilization from 1917 as crucial to our understanding of how Yugoslavia was created while the Dual Monarchy collapsed.

If before the First World War the Austro-Hungarian Empire was perceived by many of its inhabitants to be suffering from a number of 'illnesses', few believed that these were terminal. Few conceived of a world where the Monarchy would not exist. The Monarchy at war altered many of these perceptions and is the subject of the final two chapters of the book. Rudolf Jeřábek, in his unravelling of the struggle on the Eastern front, underlines the misplaced confidence which had led Austria-Hungary to assert itself as a Great Power in 1914. He complements Bridge's essay by demonstrating how, in the military sphere, the Monarchy's Great Power façade was quickly exposed in all its fragility. The Eastern front proved a fatal drain on resources with no rewards: it exemplifies how one aspect of the war could have wide repercussions for the Empire's sustainability.

Mark Cornwall takes this theme further in his essay, weighing up the factors that produced the final disintegration of Austria-Hungary and highlighting some critical 'staging posts' in that process. The chapter proposes that dissolution occurred not simply, as Alan Sked has reiterated, because the Habsburg Monarchy lost a war upon which it had staked its *raison d'être* as a Great Power.[17] This cannot be divorced from the way the war acted as a fatal catalyst upon a range of unresolved national and structural tensions from the pre-war period. For many inhabitants, the harsh regimes imposed early in the war seriously weakened the Monarchy's legitimacy; and their commitment was further shaken during the reign of Emperor Karl. Karl is judged more critically than usual in this essay: his notions of reform were rarely divorced from Dualism and a 'German course' for Austria. As a result, while his 'new regime' permitted a shift of power from the centre to the periphery, it also accelerated national polarization and non-Habsburg popular mobilization at a time of economic crisis. The chapter acknowledges the catalytic role of external forces in this process. But, overall, in contrast to Bridge, it gives 'primacy' to domestic circumstances in understanding Austria-Hungary's disintegration.

An appendix to this volume presents, for the first time in English, the minutes of the final meetings of the Monarchy's Common Ministerial Council. They are a useful reminder of the need to examine a full range of mentalities and perceptions when evaluating the last years of Austria-Hungary. Historians may seek to redress an overly fatalistic view of the Empire, or even bemoan its demise in view of what succeeded it.[18] But there is a danger of anachronism if we stray too far from how contemporaries perceived their Empire. In July 1914, the decision-makers in Vienna judged (rightly or wrongly) that the Monarchy was in crisis; in October 1918, national leaders in Prague or Zagreb judged (rightly or wrongly) that their people would not be secure in a future Monarchy. Both groups took fatal decisions on the basis of these perceptions. Many were shocked at what happened in 1918: the German–Moravian writer Richard Schaukal was one, exclaiming in his poem *Schönbrunn* that the '[Habsburg] dream was over, a bleak day dawns'.[19] But many others had in the previous decade lost any dual allegiance which they may have felt to both Empire and 'nation', in favour of the latter. They were indifferent, or even rejoiced that they no longer lived in the Habsburg Empire. In the words of one Czech nationalist siren, Viktor Dyk, 'We are free we are free! And our liberty heals at last the wounds of a bitter era.'[20]

NOTES

1. 'Oesterreich an der Wende des Jahrhunderts', *Reichenberger Zeitung*, Nr 1, 1 January 1901.
2. Henry Wickham Steed, *The Hapsburg Monarchy* (3rd ed., London, 1914) p. xiii.
3. Robert Waelder, quoted in William Johnston, *The Austrian Mind. An Intellectual and Social History 1848–1958* (Berkeley, 1972) p. 31.
4. Josef Redlich, *Das österreichische Staats- und Reichsproblem*, 2 vols (Leipzig, 1920–6) I, p. vi.
5. See Jan Opočenský, *Konec monarchie Rakousko-Uherské* (Prague, 1928); and for example the Czech memoirs collected together in Alois Žipek (ed.), *Domov za války. Svědectví účastníku*, 5 vols (Prague, 1931). This is not to suggest that some historical works about the 'national struggle' were not of a high quality. See for example those by the Czech historian Milada Paulová, about the Yugoslav émigrés: *Jugoslavenski Odbor* (Zagreb, 1925); and about the Czech resistance: *Dějiny Maffie. Odboj čechů a jihoslavanů za světové války 1914–1918* (Prague, 1937).
6. Ludwig Bittner and Hans Übersberger (eds), *Österreich-Ungarns Aussenpolitik 1908–1914*, 8 vols (Vienna, 1930); Edmund Glaise-Horstenau et al (ed.), *Österreich-Ungarns letzter Krieg*, 7 vols (Vienna, 1930–8). See also another notable work from this period, Edmund von Glaise-Horstenau, *The Collapse of the Austro-Hungarian Empire* (London and Toronto, 1930) which presents an imperial perspective but manages to maintain a certain detachment.
7. Oscar Jászi, *The Dissolution of the Habsburg Monarchy* (Chicago, 1929).
8. Redlich, *Das österreichische Staats- und Reichsproblem*, 2 vols (Leipzig, 1920–6).
9. Hans Übersberger, *Österreich zwischen Russland und Serbien. Zur südslawischen Frage und der Entstehung des Ersten Weltkrieges* (Cologne, 1958).
10. See Fritz Fellner's perspective from the late 1960s: 'The Dissolution of the Habsburg Monarchy and its Significance for the New Order in Central Europe', *Austrian History Yearbook*, vols. 4–5 (1968–9) pp. 3–27. Since the 1970s admittedly, the Austrian Academy of Sciences has taken a lead with its formidable encyclopaedic work in (so far) seven volumes: Adam Wandruszka, Helmut Rumpler and Peter Urbanitsch (eds), *Die Habsburger Monarchie 1848–1918*, 7 vols (Vienna, 1973–2000).
11. See for example the works of Mirjana Gross, Dragovan Šepić, Bogdan Krizman and Janko Pleterski in former Yugoslavia; and Péter Hanák in Hungary.
12. Robert A. Kann, *The Multinational Empire. Nationalism and National Reform in the Habsburg Monarchy 1848–1918*, 2 vols (New York,

1950); Arthur J. May, *The Hapsburg Monarchy 1867–1914* (Cambridge, Mass., 1960); May, *The Passing of the Hapsburg Monarchy 1914–1918*, 2 vols (Philadelphia, 1966); C.A. Macartney, *The Habsburg Empire 1790–1918* (London, 1968). Helmut Rumpler recently admitted that the re-evaluation of the Habsburg Monarchy came largely from the West, while Austrian historiography played no leading role in the process: see Helmut Rumpler, *Österreichische Geschichte 1804–1914. Eine Chance für Mitteleuropa* (Vienna, 1997) pp. 13–14.

13. See for example, F.R. Bridge, *The Habsburg Monarchy among the Great Powers 1815–1918* (Oxford, 1990); David F. Good, *The Economic Rise of the Habsburg Empire 1750–1914* (Berkeley, 1984); István Deák, *Beyond Nationalism. A Social and Political History of the Habsburg Officer Corps 1848–1918* (Oxford, 1992); Carl Schorske, *Fin-de-siècle Vienna* (New York, 1980).

14. Solomon Wank, 'Some Reflections on the Habsburg Empire and its Legacy in the Nationalities Question', *Austrian History Yearbook*, 28 (1997) pp. 131–46; and Wank, 'The Habsburg Empire' in Karen Barkey and Mark von Hagen (eds), *After Empire. Multiethnic Societies and Nation-Building* (Boulder and Oxford, 1997) pp. 45–57.

15. Gary B. Cohen, 'Neither Absolutism nor Anarchy: New Narratives on Society and Government in Late Imperial Austria', *Austrian History Yearbook*, 29 (1998) part I, pp. 37–61; quote on p. 38.

16. As one example of this phenomenon, see the recent study on Croatia by Mark Biondich, *Stjepan Radić, the Croat Peasant Party, and the Politics of Mass Mobilization, 1904–1928* (Toronto, 2000) pp. 42ff.

17. Alan Sked, *The Decline and Fall of the Habsburg Empire 1815–1918* (2nd ed., London, 2001) p. 301. In his new chapter for this second edition, Sked gives no space to the final dissolution except for a rather opaque comment: 'both military defeats and the politics of wartime meant that the internal and external circumstances of the Monarchy made its dissolution unavoidable'.

18. See István Deák, 'The Fall of Austria-Hungary: Peace, Stability and Legitimacy', in Geir Lundestad (ed.), *The Fall of the Great Powers* (Oxford, 1994) pp. 82–102; Jean Bérenger, *A History of the Habsburg Empire 1780–1918* (London, 1997); and, for an extreme example, François Fejtö, *Requiem pour un Empire défunt* (Paris, 1988).

19. Dominik Pietzcker, *Richard von Schaukal. Ein österreichischer Dichter der Jahrhundertwende* (Würzburg, 1997) pp. 228ff. In February 1917, Schaukal had been asked by the Austrian Ministry of Interior to work on a revised version of the Austrian national anthem.

20. Quoted from Dyk's poem *8 November 1918*, in Jaroslav Med, *Viktor Dyk* (Prague, 1988) p. 214.

2

The Foreign Policy
of the Monarchy

F.R. Bridge

Within months of the celebration of Franz Joseph's diamond jubilee in December 1908 the Bosnian annexation crisis ended with a triumph that seemed to demonstrate beyond question the Dual Monarchy's ability to maintain its position in the ranks of the Great Powers. If, in the early decades of his reign the Emperor had seemed destined only to lose territories, he had finally succeeded in adding to his dominions, and his Foreign Minister, Alois Lexa von Aehrenthal (now raised to the rank of Count) spoke elatedly of the final incorporation of the occupied provinces as a 'text-book example' of the efficacy of a diplomacy backed by determination and military power. To contemporary observers the Monarchy seemed indeed to have emerged at last from a dispiriting decade in which its very future as a Great Power had been called into question. In 1899 the French and Russians, impressed by the turbulence of the Badeni era, had thought it politic to modify the terms of their alliance to guard against a German attempt to expand towards the Adriatic if the Dual Monarchy should break up. And there was evidence of an equally sceptical view of the Monarchy's future in Berlin, where, at the height of the Hungarian crisis in 1905–6, Chancellor Bülow saw fit to circulate secretly to all Germany's missions abroad an explicit disavowal of any such expansionist ambitions in the event of the dissolution of the Monarchy. By contrast, in 1910 a British newspaper was proclaiming that the past decade of upheaval had proved to be the harbinger of 'a lusty rebirth'.[1] With the benefit of hindsight it may be said, however, that the victory achieved in the annexation crisis proved to be a Pyrrhic one. It had certainly not solved the long-term problem of upholding the Monarchy's existence as an independent Great Power within the European states system.

This problem was a long-standing one, and the form it assumed in 1908 was only a variation on one that had faced Habsburg policy-makers for a century: the problem of overstretch. Austrian control of Germany and Italy established at the Congress of Vienna had been the linchpin of the Central European order that emerged after the defeat of Napoleon, just as Austrian support for Ottoman control of the Balkans helped to stabilize a potentially explosive situation in the Near East. The fact remained, however, that the Monarchy, a weak agrarian power that lacked both the economic resources of the Western powers and the manpower with which Russia compensated for its backwardness, simply lacked the military strength to fulfil unaided the responsibilities thrust on it by the coalition that had established the 1815 order. Hence, Metternich's untiring efforts to enlist the support of one (or ideally both) of the 'real' Great Powers, Great Britain and Russia, for the maintenance of the status quo; and to establish the states system on a principled basis of legitimacy and respect for the sanctity of treaties, as opposed to the realist tenets of *Machtpolitik*. The fact that the Monarchy could continue to rely on these supports even after Metternich's fall from power enabled it to survive intact the upheavals of 1848–9. By the same token, however, in the decade after the Crimean War the Monarchy's inability to count on either Great Britain, retreating into isolation, or Russia, now openly revisionist, left it to face unaided the challenge from Piedmontese nationalism backed by Napoleon III in 1859 and allied to Bismarckian *Realpolitik* in the 1860s. By 1866, the Monarchy had been expelled by brute force from its 1815 position in both Italy and Germany.

The experiences of these disastrous decades cast a long shadow over Franz Joseph's reign, and gave birth to precepts that were to become fundamental themes of the foreign policy of the Dual Monarchy. In the first place, the Emperor emerged more than ever convinced of the importance of upholding the Monarchy's legitimate treaty rights. If this was, for Franz Joseph, primarily a matter of honour, it was also sound common sense. Indeed, it would have been suicidal to have attempted to base his position on anything else. As his Foreign Minister explained on the eve of war in 1866:

> The result of war might be that Austria would be dismembered, perhaps destroyed, but she must defend herself and her rights or fail in the attempt to do so; and she was resolved not to acknowledge the principle of nationalities, which was now put forward as an argument to induce

her to give up Venetia. What was the Austrian Monarchy? It was an Empire of nationalities. If she gave up Venetia today to please King Victor Emmanuel . . . where would his ambition lead him? . . . The Prince of Servia [sic] might also claim the Serbs in Austria and demand that they should be annexed to his principality; in fact . . . we are determined to take our position in defence of our principles and our rights, which are based on treaties, and if war should be the consequence we shall do our best to protect the various possessions and interests of which the Empire is composed.[2]

It was this principled attitude that led Franz Joseph to take up the sword both in 1859 and in 1866; and in 1914 he was to do so again: 'if the Monarchy goes to ruin, it should at least do so with honour.'[3] At the same time, however, the experiences of the wars of 1859 and 1866 had done lasting damage to Franz Joseph's confidence in the military capacity of both himself and the Monarchy. If one striking feature of Habsburg policy after 1866 was its stubbornly principled character, this was counterbalanced—perhaps even more strikingly— by a deep reluctance to resort to the military option so long as honour of the dynasty could be upheld by other means.

The success of Habsburg statesmen in avoiding a recourse to arms for half a century after 1866 is a tribute to their skill and adaptability in exploiting the possibilities offered by what remained, until 1912 or so, a fairly fluid states system to safeguard the Monarchy's interests by peaceful means. The chief threat to those interests, once the Monarchy had abandoned its Italian and German missions in the 1860s, lay in the south. Already in the 1860s there were politicians in Belgrade and Bucharest who sought to emulate Cavour and liberate their fellow-countrymen in the Serbian- and Romanian-inhabited territories of the Monarchy; but the Imperial and Royal Army could cope with any threat from the small states on its southern borders. It would be another matter, however, if the Monarchy's irredentist neighbours should gain the support of a Great Power, after the manner of 1859–66. This would portend, at best, a paralysing encirclement of the Monarchy by Russia and her satellites, at worst, a conflict ending with its actual dismemberment. To ward off or counter such a threat, Habsburg diplomacy could have recourse to any one, or a combination of three remedies short of war. First, it could seek to draw into its orbit the rulers of the Balkan states, bribing them to abandon their designs on the Habsburg or Ottoman Empires in exchange for economic and political rewards.

Second, it could enlist the support of other Great Powers with a similar interest in restraining the Balkan states and halting the advance of Russian influence in the Near East. Third, it could seek to establish a working relationship with Russia itself, putting the emphasis on common, rather than conflicting, interests in the Near East and on cooperation to oppose revolutionary Balkan nationalism in the cause of monarchical solidarity. None of these 'pacific' remedies was to prove a panacea, as will be seen. But for more than four decades Habsburg decision-makers were to manoeuvre between them with agility and, for the most part, with some degree of success.

As regards the first—control of the Balkan states—it must be said that Habsburg diplomacy achieved only a limited success. True, in the 1880s, Russia's efforts at San Stefano on behalf of 'Big Bulgaria' had inspired such terror in the other Balkan states as to drive almost all of them into the arms of Vienna. The Austrians made good use of this to secure secret alliances with the Austrophile ruler in Serbia (1881) and with the Hohenzollern king of Romania (1883) although only the first contained a formal commitment to clamp down on irredentism. When, in the later 1880s the Austrians managed, with British and Italian assistance, to capitalize on nationalist resentment of Russian control in Sofia the whole Balkans seemed to have passed into the Austro-Hungarian camp. This situation was too good to last. By the mid-1890s the Bulgarians had returned to their preferred policy of balancing between Vienna and St Petersburg. As for the Monarchy's relations with Romania, they were plagued by a tariff war, the result of Hungarian insistence (to the despair of the Foreign Ministry) on protection against agrarian exports from Romania; and Magyarization policies in Transylvania served to provoke even more indignation in Bucharest. With Serbia too, after the expiry of the alliance in 1895 and the installation, in a bloody *coup d'état* of June 1903, of a new dynasty dependent on recklessly nationalist elements in the army, relations went from bad to worse. An Austrian attempt to call Serbia to order by economic coercion—the closing of the frontier to Serbian exports in the so-called 'Pig War' of 1906–11—proved entirely counterproductive: Serbia found other trading partners and the annexation of Bosnia raised Serbian hatred of the Monarchy to fever heat. After this, even Aehrenthal's attempts at economic concessions and conciliation brought no improvement. By 1913, his successor, Leopold Count Berchtold, was questioning their usefulness in any case. As he sternly reminded the Germans, no compromise was possible between Austria-Hungary's determination to defend her integrity and Serbian national aspirations. If the Serbs persisted in the latter the result could only be war.

If this bleak diagnosis was unimaginative, it was perhaps realistic. It is true that, as a remedy for South Slav discontent inside the Monarchy, the rigid adherence to Dualism favoured by most decision-makers was hardly very constructive. On the other hand, the problem was also an external one, and this aspect of it was hardly amenable to treatment by domestic reforms. (Indeed, the elimination of Archduke Franz Ferdinand came as a relief to elements in Serbia who had feared that he might some day attempt to resolve the Monarchy's South Slav problem by a structural reform.) It must also be emphasized that in the context of the *mentalités* prevailing among ruling elites in all the European Great Powers in this period, attitudes adopted by Vienna and Budapest that might seem high-handed today were only what was normal in the heyday of the European empires— witness the attitudes of the European Great Powers towards lesser peoples in 'decaying empires' such as Morocco, Persia or Egypt, or even towards other Great Powers outside the European Concert, such as Turkey or Japan. If the Austrians were all too ready to employ schoolmasterly language in calling the governments of the Balkan states to order, their contemporaries in London and St Petersburg were not one whit different. At least one British ambassador in Vienna sympathized with the Austrian point of view:

> I cannot tell you how exasperated people are getting here at the con-
> tinual worry which that little country [Serbia] causes to Austria under
> the encouragement from Russia. It may be compared . . . to the trouble
> we had to suffer through the hostile attitude formerly assumed against
> us by the Transvaal Republic under the guiding hand of Germany.[4]

Such *mentalités*, and the resentment they inspired among aggrieved states that were not part of the Great Power Concert, exacerbated an inherently intractable problem; and were a contributory factor to the Monarchy's failure in the long run to save itself by winning friends and influencing people in the Balkans. Indeed, by 1914 Vienna was haunted by the prospect of a new Balkan league, this time aiming at the destruction of the Monarchy. In default of an awesome military success, such as the crushing of Serbia, the remedy of security through control of the Balkan states seemed about to disappear.

Perhaps more rewarding, and certainly more congenial, were Austrian hopes of enlisting support of other Great Powers that might share their apprehensions about the growth of Russian power. The British, for example, had rendered invaluable assistance in restraining the Russians in the aftermath of both the Congress of Vienna and the Congress of Berlin; and for a decade after 1887 the Mediterranean Agreements between Austria-Hungary, Great Britain and Italy had seen Russian influence virtually expelled from the Balkans altogether. One problem with Great Britain, however, was that, as an essentially naval Power, she could do little to help the Monarchy directly in a clash with Russia; and ever since the Crimean War voices had been raised in Vienna that warned against the danger of being used as a British battering ram. Another difficulty was that the vicissitudes of the parliamentary system meant that British support was always liable to be withdrawn at short notice—for example, when in 1880 the Liberals under Gladstone switched to a policy of harassing Turkey and seeking an accommodation with Russia. Even Lord Salisbury, the architect of the Mediterranean Agreements, steadfastly refused to transform them into an actual alliance that would firmly commit Great Britain to fight to keep the Russians out of Constantinople—although the tradition persisted in the Foreign Office that 'on the whole, we lean rather towards Austria than to Russia'.[5] By 1907, this was ceasing to be the case: the Anglo-Russian Convention of 31 August 1907 at last gave the British security in India; and although Aehrenthal was right to regard it as essentially an Asian agreement, he failed at first to discern its implications for Austria-Hungary and the Near East. True, some Foreign Office observers were looking rather far ahead when they concluded in February 1908 that the indignant reaction of the Russian press to Aehrenthal's Sandžak railway project indicated that 'the struggle between Austria and Russia in the Balkans is evidently now beginning, and we shall not be bothered by Russia in Asia';[6] and that 'this marks a very important development of the Anglo-French and Anglo-Russian agreement policy. Russia is now asking for our cooperation in the Near East' and her overtures were 'welcome on every ground'.[7] The fact remained, nevertheless, that given the ranking of the security of India and the alignments of the Balkan states in Britain's order of priorities, reliance on the support of Great Britain was ceasing to be an available option for the Dual Monarchy.

Cooperation with Italy was problematical in a different way. If the British were sometimes rather too detached from Balkan affairs, the Italians all too often took a disconcertingly active interest in them. For the Austrians they were indeed useful as partners in the

Mediterranean Agreements. As late as 1912 they rendered sterling service in joining with Austria-Hungary to establish an Albanian state that kept Serbia (and her Russian protectors) away from the Adriatic. In general terms too, the Triple Alliance of 1882 was useful insofar as it relieved the Austrians of the fear of an attack from the south-west and enhanced their freedom of manoeuvre, both in the Balkans and in their dealings with Russia and Germany. It was this last consideration, particularly, that made Aehrenthal so anxious to cultivate Rome throughout his term of office. On the other hand, Italy's growing interest in establishing her own influence on the other shore of the Adriatic made her an uncomfortable partner. When the Alliance was renewed in 1902 Vienna turned down an Italian offer of more extensive support against Russia precisely because this might enhance Italy's claims to a role in Balkan affairs.[8] The famous Article I of the Triple Alliance, that obliged the two Powers to consult each other about possible changes in the Near East (in the event of which each might claim compensation from the other), made it plain that the Alliance was essentially one of mutual restraint, in which each partner was primarily concerned to keep an eye on the other. The tension between them was exacerbated after the turn of the century, as Italian irredentism spread from the parties of the Left to the nationalist Right, and as a naval race developed between the two allies in the Adriatic. Although the alarms occasioned by the Tripoli War and the Balkan Wars seemed to bring Italy back into the bosom of the Alliance, the struggle that developed in 1914 between the two allies for control over their Albanian protégé made it unlikely that the Monarchy would receive any effective help from Italy in a major confrontation with other Great Powers.

At first sight, a policy of enlisting German support seemed a better proposition: after all, the Austro-German Alliance of 1879 envisaged a war in which the two allies would fight together against Russia. For Bismarck, however, the alliance was always primarily a strictly defensive device for use in the event of a Russian attack. It offered the Austrians no assistance in day-to-day diplomacy: as Bismarck brutally informed them at the start, it was not designed to support any particular policy in the Balkans whatever.[9] For decades, the Austrians could only watch in helpless frustration as Bismarck strove to restrain Vienna and mollify St Petersburg by such devices as the Three Emperors' Alliance; and even after Bismarck's fall, people in Berlin were struck by his son's continuing 'fanatical hatred of Austria'.[10] True, there were brief periods when the Germans were

LIBRARY

4005527

unnerved by the prospect of isolation within the states system as a whole—after the abandonment in 1890 of the Reinsurance Treaty with Russia, in the years between the Algeciras Conference and the Bosnian crisis, and again in the summer of 1914; at such times they were willing to offer Vienna diplomatic and military support beyond the terms of the Alliance. However, whenever the Germans felt they had some freedom of manoeuvre—in the era of the *Freie Hand* after 1895, or as late as the Russo-German meeting at Potsdam in 1910—they refused to jeopardize their relations with other Powers for the sake of Austria-Hungary's Balkan concerns. Indeed, as they began to develop their own economic interests in the Balkans and the Ottoman Empire, they proved all too willing to shoulder their allies out of the way: by 1913, according to the Austro-Hungarian Chief of Staff, Germany was seeking to 'annihilate us' in the Balkans. In fact, even if the Austrians managed to activate their partnership with Germany, there was always the risk—and this was to become a serious problem after 1914—that, as the weaker partner, they would find their interests sacrificed to those of the stronger.

If attempts to influence Balkan governments or to enlist the support of other Great Powers against Russia often ended in disappointment, there remained a third option to secure the Monarchy's interests short of war: a *modus vivendi* with Russia herself. This option, exemplified in the Three Emperors' League of 1873–8, the Three Emperors' Alliance of 1881–7 and the Austro-Russian Entente of 1897–1908, was in terms of day-to-day diplomacy the most rewarding—witness the fact that it was in this option that the policy-makers in Vienna had put their trust for about half of the period between the wars of 1866 and 1914. Such an entente presupposed, of course, that the two empires would give priority above all to their common interest in monarchical solidarity and the avoidance of war. Nor were these mere phrases: as the Austro-Hungarian ambassador at St Petersburg warned in 1885, 'there is in Europe a great revolutionary subversive party, just waiting for the crash, and for the great conservative Powers to weaken and exhaust each other in conflict, and then the radical reform can begin'.[11] In the troubled years around the turn of the century in particular, the governments in Vienna and St Petersburg, the former at loggerheads with Czech and Hungarian nationalists, the latter increasingly preoccupied with Far Eastern affairs, were more than usually prepared to defuse any crisis that might blow up in the Near East. Hence their agreement in 1897 to keep the Balkans 'on ice'. By 1903, the two Powers were jointly directing the Concert in implementing a programme of reforms designed to stave off a threatening rebellion in the Ottoman province of Macedonia; they were referred to jointly as 'the Entente Powers' in the diplomatic parlance of the time. Their neutrality treaty of October 1904, binding them to neutrality if either should be at war with a third, not only marked the apogee of their Entente but cast a curious light on their longer-standing alliance commitments to other members of the European states system.

The problem with any Austro-Russian entente, however, centred on the difficulty of coping with changes in the status quo. Although both empires could live comfortably enough with the existing order in the Near East, the prospect of alterations to it all too easily awakened the suspicions of each that the other was about to gain an unacceptable advantage. For example, the collapse of the Three Emperors' League in 1878 had been precipitated by a foolhardy Russian bid for control of the Balkans. The Three Emperors' Alliance of 1881 had marked an advance in cooperation, insofar as it included specific provisions designed to reconcile Austro-Russian interests in the event of changes in Bosnia and Bulgaria. But even here, recriminations had arisen that had destroyed the Alliance by 1887. That the Entente of 1897 proved the longest lasting of these arrangements perhaps owed something to the simple fact that it was so limited and negative: the two Powers concentrated their efforts on the maintenance of the status quo, and fought shy of attempting to implement their agreement in principle to define future frontiers in the Balkans. Significantly, it was their attempt in the summer of 1908 to extend the Entente to provide for changes in Bosnia and at the Straits (at Constantinople) that precipitated its collapse.

Already, in fact, the Entente had been undermined by internal developments in Russia that were quite beyond the control of the two foreign offices. Defeat in the Far East and revolution at home saw the establishment in 1905 of a semi-parliamentary regime under which foreign policy became a matter for lively debate in the Duma and the press. The effect of this was to enhance the influence of nationalist, pro-Slav pressure groups at the expense of the advocates of monarchical solidarity associated with the defeated autocracy. From the spring of 1906 a public outcry against Austria-Hungary's bullying of Serbia in the 'Pig War' was followed by a sustained press campaign against Russia's cooperation with Austria-Hungary over Macedonian reforms. In February 1908, Aehrenthal's Balkan railway projects were excoriated in the Russian press as an unwarrantable extension of Austro-Hungarian influence in the Near East. The Russian Foreign Minister, Alexander Izvolsky, notoriously vain and sensitive to public criticism, bowed before the storm; by the time of the Reval meeting between Nicholas II and Edward VII in June 1908, he had decided to substitute an Anglo-Russian for the Austro-Russian partnership in Macedonia. It was significant, however, that almost simultaneously he was making an even more far-reaching approach to Vienna. This was his famous offer of 2 July of a deal in which Russia would connive at an Austrian annexation of Bosnia-Hercegovina and the Sandžak in return for Austrian acquiescence in the opening to Russian warships of the internationally controlled Black Sea Straits.[12] Far from abandoning the Far East in order to launch, under pressure of public opinion, a challenge to Austria-Hungary in the Balkans, Izvolsky was convinced that Russia, in her convalescent state, was in no position to challenge anybody: the more ententes she could establish, the better. In this context, the future of the Austro-Russian Entente appeared more promising than ever in the summer of 1908.

The view from Vienna was somewhat less rosy. The hopes that Aehrenthal had cherished on taking office in October 1906 of reviving the Three Emperors' Alliance, both to bolster monarchical elements in Russia and to render the Monarchy less dependent on Italy and Germany, had been dashed by Izvolsky's sensitivity to nationalist criticism of the Austro-Russian Entente; and Aehrenthal's initial reaction to the Russian feeler of 2 July 1908 had been distinctly wary. It was only the revolution at Constantinople in mid-July, raising the prospect of chaos in Turkey, or even of a Young Turkish bid to recover control of Bosnia-Hercegovina that caused him to think again. In mid-August the Council of Ministers in Vienna endorsed his plans to put an end to the ambiguous status of the occupied provinces by incorporating them into the Monarchy in full sovereignty—a move that was also designed to demonstrate the futility of Serbian nationalist hopes of some day acquiring them. It must be emphasized that the annexation, coupled as it was with the renunciation of Austria-Hungary's garrison rights in the Sandžak of Novibazar to the south, was essentially a move to consolidate, rather than to extend, the Monarchy's position in the Near East. It was in no sense intended as a challenge to Russia or a deviation from the Entente. On the contrary, the latter seemed set fair to develop further when Aehrenthal decided to take up the Russian offer of 2 July and met Izvolsky at Buchlau, in Moravia, on 16 September. There,

Izvolsky agreed, in exchange for Austria-Hungary's renunciation of the Sandžak and a promise of support for Russia's desiderata at the Straits, to adopt a 'benevolent attitude' towards an annexation of Bosnia, accepting Aehrenthal's dismissal of any claims that Serbia might put forward to territorial compensation. It seemed that the Entente had successfully negotiated the hazard—the problem of changes to the status quo—that had so often proved fatal to Austro-Russian cooperation in the past; and that a piece of chancellery diplomacy in the style of the nineteenth century had been able to cope with the forces of nationalism surging up in the twentieth.

This soon proved disastrously unrealistic. It was not simply that the Buchlau agreement itself was dangerously flawed: as the Russian archives show, Izvolsky was planning all along, unbeknown to Aehrenthal, to enhance Russia's influence both in Turkey and the Balkan states by promoting a conference in which Austria-Hungary would be arraigned before Europe for violating the Treaty of Berlin. What finally destroyed the Entente was the explosion of popular indignation that the annexation provoked in Russia. It drove the Tsar and Izvolsky to go back on the Buchlau agreement and pledge their support, not only to the protests of Turkey but also to Serbian demands for territorial compensation. In the face of these elemental forces the diplomatic devices of a tiny decision-making elite that had contained Austro-Russian differences over the Eastern Question for the past century were swept away. With them disappeared, most ominously, the Entente that had been one of the most productive options open to Austro-Hungarian decision-makers for the past decade.

The upshot was a six-month diplomatic crisis, one of the most disturbing features of which were the mobilization measures ordered by Belgrade, to which the Austrians responded by troop concentrations in Bosnia and a threatened military chastisement of Serbia. The outcome of the crisis was in fact a foregone conclusion as Austria-Hungary's diplomatic position was extraordinarily strong: the loss of the Russian entente had been more than made good—at least temporarily—by far-reaching pledges of diplomatic, and even military, support from Berlin, where Izvolsky's conference proposals evoked painful memories of Germany's diplomatic defeat at the Algeciras Conference of 1906. The Russians, by contrast, were all too conscious of the limited nature of British and French diplomatic support, and of their own inability to back up their diplomacy by a threat to resort to force—as, indeed, Izvolsky himself confessed to the

THE LAST YEARS OF AUSTRIA-HUNGARY

Austro-Hungarian ambassador. In this situation, Aehrenthal could afford to stand firm, demanding that Russia should not only recognize the annexation but persuade her Great Power partners and her Serbian protégé to do so.

Obviously, given the prevailing imbalance of military forces between the contending groups of Powers, there was never any danger that the annexation crisis would end in war between the Great Powers. Rather, the threat hanging over Izvolsky—apart from the revelation of his activities at Buchlau—was the threat of an Austro-Hungarian punitive expedition against Serbia and the blow that this would deal, by exposing Russia's impotence to prevent it, to her standing as a Great Power, both in the Balkan capitals and in Europe generally. It was this consideration that brought St Petersburg to submit to Germany's diplomatic 'ultimatum' of 23 March 1909, paving the way for the recognition of the annexation by Serbia and the other Powers that ended the crisis. Aehrenthal, for his part, while he wondered at one point whether a peaceful settlement based on Serbian promises of good behaviour was worth having[13] (a doubt that was later to be more than justified by events), in the end shrank from the expense of a military operation and settled for a diplomatic solution. There was perhaps, after all, nothing more an invasion could have achieved, given the opposition inside the Monarchy, particularly from the Magyars, to the annexation of Serbian territory. But he was in effect gambling on the possibility of achieving a *modus vivendi* with the Monarchy's obstreperous neighbour.

As it turned out, of course, Austro-Serbian relations went from bad to worse. Aehrenthal's characterization of the annexation as a 'text-book example' of successful diplomacy was questionable on other grounds too, above all in terms of the effect of the crisis on the functioning of the states system and on the international atmosphere generally. It was not so much that it set a precedent for the breakdown of 1914—the military balance in 1908–9 had been such as to preclude a military outcome. The militarization during the crisis of at least Serbian and Austro-Hungarian diplomacy was, however, a new and striking development, and one that was indeed ominous for the future. As for the other Powers, the lesson of Austria-Hungary's successful application of the principle of negotiation from strength, backed up by an awesome demonstration of Austro-German solidarity, was not lost on any of them. It did not need the British to remind the Russians that if they had an eye to the future 'they will lose no time . . . in preparing for the conflict which must inevitably follow if Germany intends to pursue the policy of domination in Europe'.[14] The Russians themselves were determined at all costs that the humiliation of 1909 must never be repeated, and set about increasing their armaments on land and sea. One of the most important results of the crisis, therefore, was an intensification of the armaments race that opened the door to further militarization of diplomacy in future crises.

On the diplomatic front, Aehrenthal's high-handed methods had been ill-received in the Western capitals. The British had been drawn into the role of Russia's chief supporters, and into encouraging Russian efforts to establish a league of Balkan states that would 'spell checkmate to Aehrenthal's policy of obtaining Austrian supremacy in the Balkans',[15] adding a new 'European'—and anti-Austrian—aspect to the Anglo-Russian Entente. Worst of all, perhaps, the Austro-Russian Entente, for so long an important weapon in the Habsburg diplomatic armoury, had been lost, as it turned out, for ever. Although the Russians now prudently sought to repair the wire to Berlin, if only to guard against a repetition of 1909, they showed no interest in repairing the wire to Vienna. The Germans for their part hoped to use an accommodation with Russia to dislocate the Triple Entente; and as they admitted in their talks with the Russians at Potsdam in 1910, they had no desire to see the Austrians advance any further in the Near East. As a result, with the British and Russian options both closed to them, the Austrians risked falling into an uncomfortable dependence on distrustful Italian and self-seeking German allies.

Of this danger Aehrenthal, of all Franz Joseph's foreign ministers the most obsessively sensitive to the charge of enslavement to Berlin, was acutely aware. The fear that any new crisis in the Near East must inevitably drive the Monarchy into an unhealthy dependence on its northern ally was certainly one element in that desperate concern to uphold the status quo that characterized his policy from the end of the annexation crisis until his death in office in February 1912. For much the same reasons he worked steadily, and with a degree of success, to improve the Monarchy's relations with Italy, restraining the demands of his military and naval colleagues that were fuelling an Austro-Italian armaments race. He even secured the removal of the Italophobe Conrad von Hötzendorf from the post of Chief of Staff in December 1911. In the Western capitals at least, his efforts were appreciated, and the Monarchy's relations with France and Great Britain gradually recovered from the shock of the Bosnian crisis—

although not to the extent that an Anglo-Austrian entente to oppose Russia would ever again be an option available to policy-makers in Vienna.

In the Balkans, however, Aehrenthal's efforts were less successful, if not even counterproductive. Balkan governments, determined on expansion at the expense of the Ottoman Empire, were anything but impressed by Aehrenthal's incessant adjurations to respect the status quo. Russia, by contrast, offered them more palatable advice and by the time of Aehrenthal's death a league of Balkan states was in process of formation under Russian patronage. In less than a year it would result in the expulsion of the Ottoman Empire from Europe and a shift in the balance of power in the Near East to the Monarchy's grave disadvantage. In any case, even in Aehrenthal's lifetime, disruptive developments were occurring further afield, in Morocco, Tripoli and the Eastern Mediterranean, that reflected the emergence of new currents in world affairs that were quite beyond the control of the almost 'Balkan' Monarchy, even under a minister of Aehrenthal's strength of mind and determination.

His successor, Leopold Count Berchtold, was a man of very different stamp. Aehrenthal had always kept the reins firmly in his hands; he was, according to a British ambassador 'so very "authoritaire"', not permitting any of his underlings to 'express any political view to foreign heads of mission during his absence from Vienna'.[16] Under the diffident, pliable Berchtold by contrast, many voices were heard in the making of policy, not only those of Italophobes such as Archduke Franz Ferdinand and Conrad (restored in December 1912 to the post of Chief of Staff), but of a cohort of younger officials in the Ballhausplatz.[17] These were men such as Hoyos, Forgách and Szápary, trained in Aehrenthal's school and imbued with his high notions of the Monarchy's future as a Great Power, but lacking that steadying self-assurance that had given their mentor the confidence to eschew desperate military gambles. This group, like Conrad, viewed the Monarchy's relations with its Balkan neighbours in Social Darwinist terms and became increasingly inclined, especially as the Monarchy's international predicament deepened after 1912–13, to seek salvation in a resort to arms.

In fact, in his first six months of office, Berchtold managed to impose his own imprint on policy. His painful experiences as ambassador in St Petersburg during the Bosnian crisis had convinced him that Aehrenthal's forceful, high-handed approach was mistaken, and that the Monarchy's interests would be better safeguarded by renouncing single-handed action in favour of cooperation with the other Powers, even taking the lead in restoring the Concert of Europe. In July 1912, he even attempted to bring the British option back into play, with a proposal to London for joint action to limit the repercussions of Italy's war with Turkey in the Mediterranean and the Aegean. In August, as war threatened in the Balkans, he attempted to rally the Concert behind a proposal to defuse the Macedonian crisis by administrative reforms; and in October readily joined with the Russians as joint spokesmen of the Concert to warn the Balkan states against resorting to arms. Admittedly, the results of his efforts were disappointing: the British showed no interest in his proposed Mediterranean entente; no other Power was prepared to follow his lead in Macedonia; and the joint Austro-Russian démarche in the Balkan capitals failed to prevent, if it did not actually precipitate, the headlong rush of the Balkan states to put an end to the Ottoman Empire in Europe once and for all. In sum, Berchtold found, as so many of his predecessors had found, that a weak Power could only succeed in leading the Concert if the other Powers were prepared voluntarily to follow. In the summer of 1912 this was all too patently not the case. Even so, at the end of the year, as the upheaval in the Balkans intensified, Berchtold was still trying to reduce the risk of a clash between the Great Powers. He went to some trouble to circulate to them in good time a statement of Austro-Hungarian interests that would have to be safeguarded in any new settlement of south-east Europe, and agreed to entrust the negotiation of such a settlement to the concerted action of the Powers in the London ambassadors' conference of December 1912 to August 1913.

As it turned out, the experience of trying to activate the Concert during the Balkan Wars wrought a sea-change in Berchtold's attitudes. In the first place, the Austrians discovered to their discomfort—as France had discovered in the era of the Congress system, Russia at the Congress of Berlin, and Germany at Algeciras—that the decisions of the Concert were all too often merely a reflection of the relative strengths of the power-groupings within it. In the second place, even when the Austrians managed to secure majority support for their plans, translating this into effective action was a very different matter. True, Berchtold's hopes were initially justified when in December 1912 the London Conference endorsed Austro-Italian demands for the creation of an Albanian state barring Serbia from the Adriatic. This reflected the fact that Germany had openly declared her support (armed if necessary) for her allies, whereas Great Britain and France were unwilling to take an equally firm stand in support of Russia's claims on behalf of her Serbian protégé. When in early 1913 the Concert came to determine the inland frontiers of Albania, however, the position was reversed. The Monarchy found itself isolated in resisting Serbian and Montenegrin claims in north Albania, as Italy confined her efforts to resisting Greek claims in the south, while the German Emperor made clear to Vienna his aversion to risking a European war for the sake of 'the grazing lands of the goats of Scutari'.[18] As a result, Berchtold had to accept defeat over a whole series of disputed towns, of which he managed to save only Scutari for Albania. His faith in the Concert was gravely undermined, therefore, when in this last instance Montenegro proceeded to occupy the town, in defiance of the pronouncements of the Concert backed up by a naval demonstration—from which Russia, significantly, held aloof. When, in May, however, the Austrians lost patience and threatened direct military action, the Montenegrins immediately came to heel. The 'Scutari crisis' of mid-1913 served both to confirm Vienna's growing scepticism about the effectiveness of the Concert and to strengthen the hands of those groups who were urging Berchtold to seek salvation in unilateral threats of force.

Admittedly, these groups could still be restrained by a delicate international constellation and the frowns of Berlin and Rome. When Serbia and her allies shifted the Balkan balance radically in their favour at the expense of Bulgaria in the Second Balkan War, Austria-Hungary was confined to the role of helpless spectator—all the more so as Franz Joseph and Franz Ferdinand refused to contemplate intervention once their sole remaining Balkan ally, Romania, had joined forces with Serbia and Greece. In the 'October crisis' of 1913 by contrast, an Austro-Hungarian ultimatum, dispatched with German approval and Italian acquiescence, forced Serbian forces to withdraw from territory assigned to Albania by the London Conference. Although here the Austrians had acted to enforce a decision of the Concert, they acted without the consent of the Triple Entente Powers. Once again the dangerous lesson had been drawn by decision-makers in Vienna (and now even by the cautious Hungarian premier István Tisza) that the Great Powers had failed 'all along the line in respect of everything that is pronounced in the name of Europe. If, however, one Power says that it will not shrink from war, that makes a visible impression.'[19] This disturbing tendency to resort to militarized diplomacy was confirmed by two further ultimata, dispatched jointly by Austria-Hungary and Italy to Athens in October 1913 and March 1914, ordering the Greeks to withdraw from territory about which the Concert had not even reached a final decision.

Even more ominously, these trends must be seen in the context of an increasing militarization of diplomacy generally in the years leading up to 1914. If the Balkan Wars and Italy's attack on Turkey in 1911 provide the most obvious examples, it was significant that, during the crisis over Serbian access to the Adriatic at the end of 1912, the Russians had backed up their diplomacy by a trial mobilization and by temporarily increasing the size of their army by one-third by retaining with the colours the contingent of recruits due for release in October 1912. The Austrians similarly had increased the size of the Common Army and concentrated their forces, not only against Serbia, as in 1908–9, but against Russia in Galicia. These extraordinary military measures helped to keep tension high well into the spring of 1913; the Russians were already planning to repeat the exercise of retaining the senior contingent in October 1913, and a law of June 1914 made it a permanent feature of Russian military planning. Moreover, the expansion of the Balkan states suggested that in any future war the Monarchy would have to look to the defence of its southern frontiers. The likely impact of this on its efforts on the Polish front was certainly a factor in Berlin's decision to expand the German army in 1913. To this, the French in turn responded with the Three Year Service Law and the Russians with the Great Plan, the combination of which threatened by 1917 to do more than make up for the latest efforts of the Central Powers. The military imbalance that had helped to maintain the peace in 1909, even in 1913, was ceasing to operate. The armaments of the Power blocs were reaching a dangerous state of equipoise, in which the Central Powers might be tempted to make use of the military superiority that still remained to them to resolve their problems by force, while the French and Russians, although not seeking an armed confrontation, would no longer feel constrained to shrink from one at the price of a diminution of their Great Power status as they had done in 1909.[20]

By 1914, as far as the external security of the Monarchy was concerned, the main threat that had developed from the transformation of the balance of power in the Near East took the form of a possible reconstitution of the Balkan League. If the Balkan states could ever resolve their differences—for example, by a repartition of territories in Macedonia and Albania—they would constitute in effect a seventh Great Power, with a combined force of well over 30 divisions (as opposed to the Monarchy's 48); and any future expansion would have to be at the expense, not of Turkey, but of the Monarchy itself. Given, on the one hand, the inability of the Austro-Hungarian authorities to satisfy the demands of their South Slav and Romanian subjects, and, on the other, the inexorable growth of irredentism in both Serbia and Romania, a revived Balkan league would be, as the *Neue Freie Presse* warned its readers in February 1914, 'a dagger in the hand of Russia pointed straight at the heart of Austria'.[21] To make matters worse, the chances that the Monarchy might be able to count on German and Italian support in re-establishing its authority over the Balkan states were beginning to appear disconcertingly slim. In March, the German Emperor dismissed as 'crazy' Austrian talk of preventing by force a union of Serbia and Montenegro that would give the former access to the Adriatic. Whereas this had been a key point of Triple Alliance policy a year previously, Wilhelm II now declared that a war over such an issue would leave Germany 'completely cold'.[22] Similarly, whereas Vienna and Rome had been able to work together to establish an Albanian state, the rivalry between them for the control of their new creation was by June 1914 leading the German ambassador in Vienna to fear for the very future of the Triple Alliance.[23]

Meanwhile, Germany's Balkan policy, which concentrated on culti-vating Romania and Greece (and even their Serbian ally) was not only completely at cross purposes with Berchtold's attempts to reconcile Romania with Bulgaria so as to hold Serbia in check, but seemed actually to be furthering the efforts of France and Russia to create a new Balkan league. The Tsar's state visit to Romania in June 1914 was regarded in Berlin with perfect aplomb, while Germany's repeated advice to the Austrians to win over Serbia by commercial concessions was greeted in Vienna with utter incomprehension and dismay. Berchtold's remedy, however, was still not to resort to force. Great Britain, although not actively ill-disposed towards the Monarchy, might be useless; Russia and her French financial backers were positively dangerous; but it might yet be possible, if Berchtold could persuade the Germans to join in a coordinated diplomatic campaign, to re-establish the Monarchy's diplomatic position in the Balkans by bringing together Romania, Bulgaria and Turkey under the auspices of the Central Powers. Serbia, even if hopelessly hostile, would thereby be rendered innocuous, and, even more important, the nightmare of a revived Balkan league would be dispelled. This, at any rate, was the gist of a policy document—the so-called Matscheko Memorandum—that lay on Berchtold's writing table waiting his final signature prior to dispatch to Berlin, when on 28 June 1914 Archduke Franz Ferdinand and his wife arrived in Sarajevo.

The Sarajevo assassinations transformed the situation, posing a direct challenge to the Habsburgs as lords of Bosnia, and indeed, so it seemed to Vienna, to Austria-Hungary's continued existence in the ranks of the Great Powers. In the Ballhausplatz there was unanimity that if the Monarchy failed to respond with vigour, this would serve notice abroad that the Monarchy lacked even the will to defend its vital interests. In these circumstances, a low-key diplomatic campaign as envisaged in the Matscheko Memorandum would have not the slightest chance of success, and the formation of a predatory Balkan league would proceed apace. On the other hand, Austro-Hungarian military success, particularly if Russia could be obliged to acquiesce in it, would restore the position of the Central Powers in the Near East at one stroke. As Berchtold coolly admitted, it would imply 'the complete renunciation by Russia of all influence in the Balkans'.[24] By the same token, however, St Petersburg might well consider this incompatible with Russia's honour, and with her continuing existence as a Great Power. Russia was no longer, as in 1909, simply unable to consider resorting to military action. In the circumstances, therefore, the actions of the Sarajevo assassins had confronted the decision-makers in Vienna and St Petersburg with a situation that hardly admitted of a diplomatic solution. Berchtold therefore revised the Matscheko Memorandum, turning it into an appeal to the Germans to endorse a military action to 'eliminate Serbia as a power-factor in the Balkans'. As Franz Joseph explained to Wilhelm II, it was essential 'to tear apart the web' that the Monarchy's enemies were spinning over its head. Obviously, given the clear danger of an Austro-Russian war, Vienna would have to secure a promise of German support before taking action; and it was by no means certain, in view of recent pronouncements from Berlin, that this could be taken for granted.

In the event, the Germans issued the famous 'blank cheque', promising full diplomatic and, if necessary, military support. In one sense, this was simply another instance, like those of 1890 and 1909, of Austria-Hungary's success in exploiting Germany's anxieties about the general international situation in order to seize the lead in the Dual Alliance. The Germans were afraid that if they refused their support, Austria-Hungary might lapse into apathy and cease to function as a Great Power, or, even worse, might actually seek an accommodation with Russia, leaving Germany to face the appalling diplomatic and military consequences of isolation. On the other hand, the Germans had good positive reasons of their own for endorsing, indeed encouraging, their ally to act against Serbia. They calculated, like the Austrians, that a successful military coup and the diplomatic defeat of Russia would ensure the Central Powers' domination of the Near East (and of Germany's causeway to Asia Minor). More than this, if it precipitated the collapse of the Triple Entente and the return of Russia to a 'Three Emperors' Alliance', it would give Germany diplomatic mastery of the continent. If the diplomatic gamble on localization should fail and Russia committed herself to Serbia, then again the Germans had good reasons of their own for trying to impose their will through a continental war before the military balance shifted irrevocably against them. It was also clear that while the Germans were offering the Monarchy their full support, they were at the same time hoping to influence its decisions. Their preferred option was still a diplomatic victory—hence their advice to Vienna to act quickly while the shock of the Sarajevo assassinations might yet influence the Russians to stand aside.

What was still not clear was which of the Dual Alliance partners was actually in control of its policy. The Austrians, while they welcomed the assurance of German support and became absolutely set on military action against Serbia, paid no attention at all to German advice to act quickly. Their preparations proceeded at a leisurely pace—the harvest was not yet in, the army could not be ready for action for six weeks, and the Ballhausplatz was meticulously compiling a dossier on Serbian misdeeds that it hoped would influence European public opinion.[25] Once the ultimatum was presented on 23 July and the danger appeared that Sir Edward Grey might try to mobilize the Concert to devise another fudged diplomatic solution—and even Wilhelm II declared that Serbia had accepted so many of the Austrian demands that 'all danger of war has now disappeared'—the Austrians acted with great speed and determination in declaring war on Serbia. They were equally single-minded when they started their military operations: Conrad, deeply suspicious of German ambitions in the Balkans and determined to establish Austro-Hungarian control over Serbia once and for all, sent the main body of the Monarchy's forces against Serbia, regardless of the growing Russian menace in the north and the Monarchy's commitments to Germany. It was only now that the furious row that erupted between the allies at last made it clear that the leadership of the alliance lay not with Vienna but Berlin. An even more flagrant breach of faith by Germany—who refused to undertake any offensive at all from East Prussia—forced Conrad into a belated and disastrous attempt to counteract the vast Russian force in Poland by transferring troops from the Balkan front to Galicia. The result was the disastrous battle of Lvov (Lemberg), which destroyed the Austro-Hungarian army as a first-class fighting force. As Norman Stone observes, the Germans 'had won this competition in *deutsche Treue* and Austria-Hungary bled to death in order to defend Berlin'.[26]

It was not that the Austrians had been unaware of the wider consequences of their actions. Franz Joseph himself had remarked, *à propos* the ultimatum to Serbia, that 'Russia cannot possibly swallow this'.[27] Yet in the critical Council of Ministers of 19 July the question of war with Russia had not been seriously addressed. The determination to settle the Serbian question once and for all had simply overridden all other considerations. Even so, in deciding to stake everything on a joint military enterprise with Germany the statesmen of the Monarchy were embarking on a fearful gamble: and for their narrow, almost obsessive, concentration on the threat from Serbia and the Monarchy's position in the Near East to the exclusion of the wider, European issue, they were to pay a fearful price. Moreover, as the Balkan war expanded into a world war, it became increasingly clear that among the chief threats to the Great Power status of the Monarchy was that same German ally to which it had turned for salvation.

In some respects, the very geographical and economic situation in which it found itself made any decision to fight a great risk for a weak Great Power like the Monarchy. This had, after all, been one of the major arguments against resorting to war for the past half-century. From the first weeks of the war, it appeared that the Monarchy faced severe problems of overstretch, when the need to divide its forces between the northern and southern theatres was to deny it success in either. Added to this, the Monarchy's lack of the resources to sustain a conflict on a European scale brought it inexorably into economic dependence on Germany; while its continued military failures made the Germans increasingly disinclined to show any consideration for the interests of the 'weak brother' when they conflicted with their own.

To make matters worse, by choosing the military option in 1914 and involving itself in a life-and-death struggle on a European scale, the Monarchy had closed off those diplomatic alternatives to the Dual Alliance by which it had manoeuvred to maintain its independence within the states system over the past hundred years. True, the Balkan option was still theoretically on offer; but the waiting attitude of the Balkan states coupled with the Monarchy's military failures made it distinctly problematical. The Russian and British options, by contrast, increasingly unrealistic though they had lately come to appear, were now lost beyond recall. Both Powers had now become open enemies. True, only the Russians from the start inscribed actual destruction of the Monarchy on their banners; the British, as will be seen, were prepared as late as 1917–18 to find some role for it in a revised European order. Even so, in the contest to enlist allies in the European struggle even the British were prepared to support the irredentist claims of states such as Italy and Romania, to a degree that seemed to Vienna incompatible with the Monarchy's fundamental war aim, the maintenance of its Great Power status. Nor was it just in the Entente camp that perspectives changed with the expansion of the war. To German minds, victory was now the overriding war aim; and if the Monarchy could contribute to this by buying off potential opponents with cessions of territory, this was only reasonable. Austrian minds, however, were still focused on the integrity and Great Power status of the Monarchy, and Berchtold could only retort, equally reasonably, that if the Monarchy was to be dismembered anyway, there was no point in fighting at all. These differences of perspective lay at the root of the struggle that was to dominate the Monarchy's relations with Berlin throughout the last four decisive years of its existence.

For Vienna throughout the July crisis, the elimination of the Serbian threat had been the primary objective. Any risks to European peace had been very much secondary considerations. But it soon appeared, as mobilizations and declarations of war in the next few days transformed the Austro-Serbian conflict into a world war, that the 'real' Great Powers, on whom the fate of the Monarchy would now depend, had a very different order of priorities. However decisive Vienna's role might have been in events up to 1 August, once world war broke out (1–4 August) the Monarchy immediately fell into the background. It was significant that not until 6 August did the Monarchy declare war on Russia, whereas the Western Powers did not declare war on the Monarchy for nearly a fortnight (12

August).[28] For Austria-Hungary, war was primarily a war in defence of the integrity and Great Power status of the Monarchy; for the other Great Powers this was very much a subordinate element in the first general conflict for a century, in which far bigger interests of their own were at stake. For them, the Monarchy was only important insofar as it affected those bigger interests. Even as late as January 1918 the Entente Powers were prepared to accommodate the Monarchy if it in turn could show itself flexible and adaptable enough to accommodate their broader interests. As it turned out, Vienna preferred to repeat, for even higher stakes than in 1914, the gamble on a German victory, with even more disastrous results. Even the gamble of 1914, however, involved risks greater than any taken for the past hundred years.

For over a century the Monarchy had managed to survive by astute manoeuvring between friends and potential foes. Even in the last general war (1813–14) it had enjoyed important advantages: it had been part of a large, victorious coalition in which stronger potential rivals had supported it as a factor in the balance against France or between themselves. The fact that it was never committed to the total victory of one side or the other had left it with a measure of freedom of manoeuvre, of which it made the most in influencing the final peace settlement. In July 1914 things were very different: two fairly evenly matched groups of Powers were engaged in a *guerre à outrance*, with aims that could be achieved only by the total defeat of their opponents. The Monarchy had made its own contribution to the impasse: the annihilation of Serbia was now only a means to what Berchtold termed 'our chief aim . . . the permanent weakening of Russia'[29]—an objective which, so long as Russia counted for anything, itself ruled out any possibility of compromise, not only with Russia but with her western allies. This very circumstance meant that the Monarchy had lost that freedom of manoeuvre within a constellation of five or six Great Powers that had served it so well for the past century. The result was a dangerous dependence on the German ally, a dependence that increased steadily as the Monarchy suffered military defeats and as the strains of a prolonged war—to which even Germany in the end succumbed—took their toll on the militarily, economically and technologically more backward 'weak brother'. By gambling on European war to defend its integrity and independence as a Great Power, the Monarchy in fact risked seeing those same interests imperilled by the very ally in whose hands its fate now came to lie.

There were serious differences between the allies from the very start. Conrad had long felt that Germany was seeking to 'annihilate' Austria-Hungary commercially in the Balkans; and his disastrous decision to concentrate his forces against Serbia rather than against Russia (contributing to the loss of Galicia in the autumn), was motivated by a determination to secure exclusive control of Serbia for Austria-Hungary. The Austrian perspective was in a sense narrower than the German: Vienna had no interest in the fate of Alsace-Lorraine, nor in German plans to direct Turkish activity towards Egypt, rather than the Black Sea or the Balkans. But in another sense, the Austrians were more farsighted, feeling that their prime objective, the independence and integrity of the Empire, could be secured only by a strong position and a lasting peace in the Near East. For Germany, the aim was the destruction of all three Entente Empires and victory at any cost—especially if the cost would be borne by an Austro-Hungarian ally.

The disappointments of the first six months of the war brought these differences to a head, as the Germans, increasingly desperate, considered buying a separate peace from Russia at the expense of the cession of Austrian Galicia. Similarly, they pressed the Austrians to make generous concessions of territory to Italy and Romania—Transylvania was, in Kaiser Wilhelm's view, 'a crumb'. The Germans offered Bulgaria a wide measure of influence in the western Balkans; and the second Turkish alliance in January 1915 undertook an extraordinarily onerous commitment to defend Turkey against any Balkan state for twenty years after the final peace. None of this was to the taste of the Austrians; and although they found themselves dragged into Turkish and Bulgarian diplomatic entanglements willy-nilly, they drew the line at cessions of territory. The Emperor felt equally strongly about Italy, and when Berchtold began to toy with the idea of concessions to Rome, replaced him in January 1915 by Count Burián. Such offers of territory as were subsequently made to Italy were too patently insincere to allow the neutralist party in Rome to stave off the declaration of war on the Monarchy in May. But the military successes of the Central Powers in the summer of 1915 brought Bulgaria into the war on their side and seemed to justify Germany's reckless diplomacy. The prospect of victory, however, only brought the Monarchy problems from another quarter.

The future of the Russian kingdom of Poland had been the subject of desultory debate between the allies since the beginning of the war. Whereas the Austrians felt that feeling amongst the Galician Poles—

after all, one of the 'ruling races' in Cisleithania—would necessitate the attachment of the kingdom to the Monarchy, the Germans found this 'totally unacceptable', but did not press what was as yet a hypothetical issue. With the fall of Warsaw to the Germans in August 1915 allied disagreements could no longer be concealed. The Austrians worked out a plan for 'sub-Dualism', with the Poles assuming in Cisleithania a position similar to that of Croatia in Transleithania. The Germans, however, made their consent to this conditional not only on the cession of a hefty strip of Polish territory to Germany, but on the Monarchy's accepting an 'indissoluble connection' with Germany, even 'giving up its sovereignty as far as necessary'.[30] These conditions, reminiscent of those imposed on the defeated German states in 1866, the Austrians refused point-blank to accept in their hour of victory. Indeed, as the Germans continued to be hard pressed on the Western front, and as the war in the south continued to go well, with the fall of Serbia by the end of the year, the Austrians began to display still more independence. They stubbornly refused to put their forces under a joint allied command. Early in 1916 they pressed on to conquer Montenegro and Albania, and to plan a campaign against Italy instead of turning to the north as the Germans were urging. All this only convinced Berlin that to yield control of Poland to a Monarchy so greatly aggrandized in the south would leave the latter too powerful altogether. They therefore withdrew their consent to the 'Austro-Polish' solution and simply proposed the establishment of an autonomous kingdom, perhaps with an archduke on the throne, but essentially under German control. When the Austrians in turn refused to agree to this it seemed that, although deadlock had now been reached between the allies on several fronts, the Austrians were still managing to stand up for their own interests.

All this was changed by the catastrophic turn of events in the second half of 1916. The disaster was, at least in part, brought upon the Austrians by themselves, the consequences of the ill-considered use they made of the freedom of action that remained to them. Conrad's stubborn concentration on Italy certainly contributed to the great Russian breakthrough in Galicia in July; and this in turn, rather than Austrian resistance to territorial concessions, led to the entry of Romania into the war and the invasion of Transylvania. Although Germany came to the rescue, and Mackensen was in Bucharest by Christmas, the whole position of the Monarchy had been irretrievably weakened not so much against the enemy, as against its own ally. Internally, the temporary loss of Transylvania had dealt a shattering blow to Tisza's authority in Hungary, where the old cry was again raised that Hungarian interests had been sacrificed to Vienna's western preoccupations. Most importantly, although the Monarchy was still determined to hold on to its gains in the south even against Germany, it was, in its weakened state at the end of 1916, in no position to argue about much else with Berlin. The Austrian defeats, the German Foreign Minister observed with satisfaction, 'speak the plainest language'.[31]

The new relationship between the allies was demonstrated most immediately in the military field—when a joint command under Hindenburg was instituted in September—and in the Polish question, when the Austrians had to agree to the proclamation of an autonomous Poland under joint Austro-German control in November. On broader issues too, such as the general definition of war aims, the Germans increasingly called the tune. It should be said that the ideas of the Ballhausplatz under Burián as to what constituted a peace 'on the basis of reason'—the abandonment by the Entente of Belgium, Poland and the whole of the Balkans—bore little more relation to the realities of the military situation than the even more extreme demands of the Germans. But it was an indication of Berlin's new confidence and ruthlessness that the Germans simply did not bother to consult Vienna when they formulated their reply to President Woodrow Wilson's peace feeler and took the fateful decision to embark on unrestricted submarine warfare at the beginning of 1917. Although the Monarchy was only a helpless spectator of these events, the very fact that the United States entered the war against Germany in April only intensified the fears for the future that preoccupied Karl (Emperor since November 1916) and his new Foreign Minister, Count Czernin.

Despite the restoration of the military position by the beginning of 1917, the new Emperor was alarmed by the evidence of war-weariness and political dissent at home, which was orchestrated rather than appeased by the resuscitation of the Austrian Reichsrat in May. The February revolution in Petrograd had not only dashed Karl's faint hopes of a monarchical peace and a revival of the Three Emperors' Alliance of the previous century; it had tightened the links between Russia and the West and raised the spectre of revolutionary republicanism. All this worried the Emperor, who admonished his German allies in April: 'We are fighting against a new enemy, more dangerous than the Entente: against international revolution, which finds its strongest ally in the food shortages.' Czernin added his own warning: 'if the monarchs of the Central Powers are not able to conclude peace *in the next few months*, the people will do so over their heads, and the waves of revolution will sweep away everything' that the allies had been fighting for.[32]

Even leaving aside the weakened position of the Monarchy within the alliance, however, the Emperor lacked the authority, and his minister the will, to impose their views. What even the venerable Franz Joseph had failed to hold, the untried young Emperor with his Italian wife would never retrieve. Wilhelm II's views were clear enough: 'the ultra-bigoted House of Parma, in league with its fanatical father-confessors, hates the Protestant House of Hohenzollern. Under Vienna's leadership they are aiming at an alliance ... Italy, France, Poland, Lithuania, *to the sea*!'[33] If the dynasty's supranational connections undermined its credibility, Czernin's failing lay in the opposite direction. Very much the representative of the German ruling elite and of the 1867 system at home, he clung desperately to the German alliance abroad. However much he might indulge his hopes of influencing and moderating the policy of Berlin, he was always prepared in the last resort to fall in line. In this situation the futile efforts of monarch and minister to defend the interests of the Monarchy, against friend and foe, in the next eighteen months served only to demonstrate the Monarchy's increasingly helpless dependence on its powerful ally.

Not that the Germans were responsible for the failure of Karl's proposals for a general compromise peace, made to France in the spring of 1917 through his brother-in-law, Prince Sixtus of Bourbon-Parma. The Germans in fact knew little about the negotiations although their reaction would have been predictable enough had they discovered that Karl was offering what he incautiously described in writing as the '*justes révendications*' of France in Alsace-Lorraine. The move came to nothing. The Entente wanted not a general peace but a separate peace with Austria-Hungary which would leave them free to concentrate on crushing Germany; they also demanded concessions of Austrian territory to Italy. Both of these demands Karl rejected as dishonourable and incompatible with the Monarchy's interests—as any of his predecessors would have done.

Czernin's peace efforts did not get further than a series of rather unsatisfactory negotiations with Germany. His plans to persuade Berlin to settle for a moderate peace in the west by conceding to Germany full control of Poland—the Monarchy settling for control of the Balkans—seemed to win German acceptance at an allied conference at Kreuznach in May 1917. Czernin had his doubts about the extravagance of German ambitions in Russia; and he still had to accept a measure of German involvement in the Balkans—a naval base in Albania, and control of the oil and railways of Romania— that would have horrified his pre-war predecessors. But the failure of the plan was testimony not to any inherent flaws in it, but to the difficulty of reconciling the defence of the Monarchy's interests through diplomatic schemes with the realities of German *Weltpolitik* and the complicated domestic situation in the Monarchy. In the first place, it soon transpired that Germany was not in the least interested in a compromise peace with the Western Powers; in the second, the Austrian Poles—on whom the government relied for its majority in the Reichsrat—expressed their opposition in no uncertain terms.

In September 1917 therefore, Czernin went back to the Germans with a proposal to 'turn Kreuznach on its head', offering them full control of Romania in return for a personal union between the Monarchy and Russian Poland (apart from a narrow frontier strip). Again, the Germans demanded a high price: both Poland and Austria-Hungary would have to 'join up with [*sich anzuschliessen*] the Empire in both military and financial-political terms'.[34] Despite Tisza's warnings against making the Monarchy a simple satellite of Germany, Czernin was at first prepared to accept these demands in the 'non-binding principles' of 22 October. He clung to the hope that the Monarchy, strengthened by the addition of Poland, would be able to hold its own against a Germany which would, after all, be the most hated nation in the world after the war and would need the Monarchy's support. But even Czernin rebelled when he learned the details of Germany's economic, and even territorial, ambitions on Poland, and discussions were suspended. The whole experience had been eloquent of the dangers implicit in Czernin's policy of cooperating with the Germans in the hope of controlling them— dangers which were to be demonstrated with even more disastrous consequences in the peace negotiations with the Bolsheviks that were about to start at Brest-Litovsk.

The negotiations were conducted against a background of deepening war-weariness inside the Monarchy, of which the Emperor was fully aware: 'if peace does not come at Brest', he told Czernin, 'then the Revolution will come here, no matter how much there is to eat.' A negotiated peace with Russia was rendered impossible, however, by the doctrine, advanced by the Germans and wholeheartedly endorsed by Czernin, of 'self-determination of governments' (rather than 'self-determination of peoples' as propounded by the Bolsheviks). This was an attempt to allow the Central Powers to retain control of the Russian borderlands, where they had established puppet governments, while conceding nothing to the minority races within the Central Empires. The result was the breakdown of the negotiations at Brest and the further alienation of the nationalities of the Dual Monarchy from the regime. This latter problem was exacerbated by the one negotiated peace Czernin did achieve: the 'bread peace' concluded with Ukraine in February 1918. The territorial and political concessions made to the Ukrainians convinced both the Poles of the Monarchy and those of the Polish kingdom that they had nothing to hope for from the House of Habsburg. As for influencing the Germans, the latter remained supremely indifferent to all Czernin's pleas for moderation—even when he backed them up with a threat to abandon the Alliance—and felt themselves justified when he meekly appended his signature to the draconic *Diktat* they imposed on the Bolsheviks in March. In the *Diktat* imposed on Romania at Bucharest in May, the Austrians were able to salvage for themselves a little more influence in Romania than the German military had originally been prepared to concede. But the latter retaliated by declaring that this must entail a reopening of the Polish question. Altogether, in terms of the internal coherence of the Monarchy and its standing as an independent Great Power, the peace treaties of the spring of 1918 were little short of disastrous, alien-ating the minorities at home and demonstrating the Monarchy's almost total inability to control the actions of its ally abroad.

Even more disastrous for the Monarchy were the effects of the treaties on the general international situation. This was improving at the beginning of 1918 when the collapse of Russia and the Austro-Hungarian victory over Italy at Caporetto had encouraged the idea in Entente circles that the preservation of the Monarchy as a factor in the post-war balance of power might be both desirable and feasible. In January, both Wilson and Lloyd George made it clear that the destruction of the Monarchy was no part of the Entente programme, provided of course that it could demonstrate its ability to shake off German control and play an independent role—for example, by reforming its domestic structure so as to give more weight to the various nationalities. It seemed for a moment that the Monarchy might recover that alternative 'western' option that had been closed to it since the outbreak of the war.

But this was not to be. For Czernin and the ruling elite the preservation of the 1867 system at home was a *noli me tangere*; and if this involved a simple gamble on a German victory abroad, so be it. In an utterly uncompromising speech on 2 April Czernin announced the Monarchy's full support for all Germany's war aims. The immediate result was the so-called Sixtus Affair: the French Prime Minister Clemenceau's publication of Karl's offers of the previous year, which Czernin forced the Emperor to disavow. Although the Emperor now, in turn, dismissed Czernin, the damage had been done. Taken together with the Monarchy's complicity in the Treaty of Brest-Litovsk, the affair demonstrated that the die-hard German-Magyar elite, not the Emperor, determined Austro-Hungarian policy. In Entente circles, notions of preserving the Monarchy as a useful element in the balance of power gave way to the idea of promoting the independence of the nationalities as a barrier to German domination of central Europe. For the Monarchy there now remained only the desperate gamble on a German military victory.

The danger that reliance on a powerful ally to defend the Monarchy's position as an independent Great Power might lead to the undermining of that position by the ally itself had been apparent ever since 1914, and was by the spring of 1918 more threatening than ever. The Germans were determined to make all the capital they could out of the Sixtus Affair, even 'to control the economy of Austria-Hungary, like those of Poland and Russia'.[35] They summoned Karl and his new Foreign Minister Burián to Spa and there forced them to accept in principle the so-called *Mitteleuropa* treaties, committing them to a political alliance, a military convention, and a commercial union; and not even offering any concessions in Poland in return. True, the Austrians kicked against the pricks, declaring the whole arrangement dependent on a satisfactory solution of the Polish question. In the last months of the war they made further defiant gestures, refusing to support German operations in the Transcaucasus, and persisting with the requisitioning of grain in Ukraine, despite German complaints that this was alienating a useful satellite. But these were mere gestures in peripheral areas. On important issues the Germans took the decisions. Despite defeats in the west after July, they remained completely indifferent to Karl's pleas for peace—'we are absolutely finished'—and on 24 September rejected out of hand the most detailed Polish proposals the Ballhausplatz ever devised: for Germany, Poland was the 'cornerstone of our policy in the south-east'.[36] Clearly, in the event of a

German victory the survival of Austria-Hungary as an independent Great Power would be problematical.

By the autumn of 1918, however, the Monarchy was not facing problems of victory, but those of defeat. The immediate causes of this defeat—the disintegration of the army and the outbreak of revolution at home—cannot be elaborated here. But the Ballhausplatz too had made its contribution, insofar as since the spring of 1918 it had helped to convince the Entente that the Monarchy was hopelessly enslaved to Germany, and that support for the liberation of the nationalities must go hand in hand with the destruction of German power. Things might perhaps have turned out differently had the decision-makers in Vienna and Budapest responded to Entente pressure at the beginning of the year and given an entirely new direction to the Monarchy's foreign and domestic policy. But such a revolution was unthinkable for most of the ruling German-Magyar elite, for whom the maintenance of the 1867 system was just as important as, if not inseparable from, the maintenance of the Monarchy's position as a Great Power. The dynasty might be able to take a supranational, open-minded view. But the elite that controlled the machinery of state had by 1918 become just as infected with the virus of nationalism, and just as narrowly inflexible, as the subject nationalities. Whatever faint possibilities might have existed for a fresh approach before the war, it was clearly impossible for a young and inexperienced Emperor to prevail in giving a new direction to foreign and domestic policy against the vast majority of that ruling elite and in the middle of a great war. As in Russia two years before, albeit for somewhat different reasons, the dynasty and the elite that controlled the machinery of the Empire had become mutually estranged. The catastrophe of 1918, at once cause and symptom of their estrangement, brought them both to destruction.

NOTES

1. F.R. Bridge, *Great Britain and Austria-Hungary 1906–1914. A Diplomatic History* (London, 1972) p. 36.
2. F.R. Bridge, *The Habsburg Monarchy among the Great Powers, 1815–1918* (Oxford, 1990) p. 81.
3. David Stevenson, *Armaments and the Coming of War. Europe 1904–1914* (Oxford, 1996) p. 398.
4. Cartwright to Nicolson, private, 31 January 1913, in G.P. Gooch and H.W.V. Temperley (eds), *British Documents on the Origins of the War*, 11 vols (London, 1926–38) vol. IX part 2, no 582.

5. C.H.D. Howard (ed.), *The Diary of Edward Goschen, 1900–1914*, Camden 4th ser., 25 (London, 1980) p. 18.
6. Bridge, *Great Britain and Austria-Hungary*, p. 81.
7. Ibid, pp. 83–4.
8. F. Fellner, 'Der Dreibund: Europäische Diplomatie vor dem ersten Weltkrieg', in Heidrun Maschl and Brigitte Mazohl-Wallnig (eds), *Von Dreibund zum Völkerbund. Studien zur Geschichte der internationalen Beziehungen 1882–1919* (Munich, 1994) p. 55.
9. Bridge, *The Habsburg Monarchy*, p. 139.
10. Ralf Forsbach, *Alfred von Kiderlen-Wächter (1852–1912). Ein Diplomatleben im Kaiserreich*, 2 vols (Göttingen, 1997) I, p. 87.
11. Bridge, *The Habsburg Monarchy*, p. 170.
12. On the ensuing negotiations and their significance see the correspondence published by I.V. Bestuzhev in 'Borba v pravyaschikh krugakh Rossii po voprosam vneshnei politiki vo vremya bosniikigo krizisa', in *lstoricheskii Arkhiv*, 5 (Moscow, 1962), and [in translation] by F.R. Bridge in the appendix to 'Izvolsky, Aehrenthal, and the End of the Austro-Russian Entente, 1906–8', in *Mitteilungen des österreichischen Staatsarchivs*, 29 (1976) pp. 315–62
13. Forsbach, *Alfred von Kiderlen-Wächter*, I, p. 300.
14. Bridge, *Great Britain and Austria-Hungary*, p. 137.
15. Ibid, p. 125.
16. Ibid, p. 21.
17. John Leslie, 'The Antecedents of Austria-Hungary's War Aims: Policies and Policy-Makers in Vienna and Budapest before and during 1914', *Archiv und Forschung. Wiener Beiträge zur Geschichte der Neuzeit*, 20 (Vienna, 1993) pp. 377–79.
18. Robert Kann, *Erzherzog Franz Ferdinand Studien* (Vienna, 1967) p. 77.
19. Ministerratsprotokoll, 3 October 1913, in Ludwig Bittner and Hans Übersberger (eds), *Österreich-Ungarns Aussenpolitik, 1908–1914*, 8 vols (Vienna, 1930) VII, no. 8779.
20. Stevenson, *Armaments and the Coming of War*, pp. 417ff.
21. Bridge, *The Habsburg Monarchy*, p. 333.
22. J. Lepsius, A. Mendelssohn-Bartholdy and F. Thimme (eds), *Die Große Politik der europäischen Kabinette 1871–1914*, 40 vols (Berlin, 1922–7) vol. XXXVIII, no. 15539.
23. Ibid, no. 14520.
24. Bridge, *The Habsburg Monarchy*, p. 336; Hugo Hantsch, *Leopold Graf Berchtold*, 2 vols (Graz, 1963) II, p. 664.
25. F.R. Bridge, 'The British Declaration of War on Austria-Hungary in 1914', *The Slavonic and East European Review*, 47 (1969) p. 410.
26. Norman Stone, 'Moltke-Conrad: Relations between the Austro-Hungarian and German General Staffs, 1909–1914', *The Historical Journal*, 9 (1966) p. 202.

27. Bridge, *The Habsburg Monarchy*, p. 341.
28. Italy declared war on Austria-Hungary in May 1915, but not on Germany until August 1916. The United States declared war on Germany in April 1917, but not on Austria-Hungary until December.
29. Fritz Fischer, *Griff nach der Weltmacht* (Düsseldorf, 1964) p. 157.
30. Joachim Lilla, 'Innen- und aussenpolitische Aspekte der austro-polnischen Lösung, 1914–1916', *Mitteilungen des österreichischen Staatsarchiv*, 30 (1977) p. 233.
31. Fischer, *Griff nach der Weltmacht*, p. 302.
32. Ibid, p. 460.
33. Ibid, p. 568.
34. Ibid, p. 574.
35. Ibid, p. 704.
36. Ibid, pp. 853, 857.

3

'Well-tempered Discontent'
Austrian Domestic Politics

Lothar Höbelt

Old Austria was not a parliamentary monarchy. The Habsburg Emperors, in Walter Bagehot's famous phrase, were not content 'to be consulted, to encourage and to warn'. They guarded their prerogatives jealously and certainly still saw themselves as chief executives, not just heads of state. In foreign affairs and army matters Franz Joseph retained a more or less free hand. (The so-called Delegations that vetted the army budget were little more than a rubber stamp, even if the number of recruits to be conscripted had to be negotiated with both the Austrian and Hungarian parliaments.) The same could not be said for domestic politics, taxes, schools, railways and other matters that belonged to the staple diet of the two parliaments. Laws could only be passed with the consent of parliament. Even if the appointment of government ministers in Austria was reserved for the crown, the same was the case in Britain—and in Hungary too. The degree to which the Reichsrat in Vienna was able to assert itself depended on its composition. The decisive factor was the fragmentation of representation. In that respect there was a marked difference between Austria and Hungary. If elections produced a clear-cut overall majority (as they almost always did in Budapest) the monarch's choice was clearly limited as the victorious party would be able to insist on its choice of prime minister. On the other hand, if—as in Austria—the Lower House consisted of no less than eight nationalities, each equipped with several rival political camps, that situation inevitably resulted in a 'hung parliament' which gave a lot of leeway to the Emperor even at the best of times. The only Austrian ministry which Franz Joseph had ever had to accept against his wishes was the *Bürgerministerium*, the Liberal government which had taken over after the defeat of Königgrätz in 1866. But those days were long past.

After 1879, there was no coherent or cohesive parliamentary majority. Count Taaffe, descendant of a family of Irish 'wild geese', substituted a coalition government, the 'Iron Ring'. It was he who coined the phrase that the art of governing Austria consisted in keeping all its nationalities in a state of 'well-tempered discontent'. When that got out of hand in the 1890s, chaos reared its head, or so it seemed. National minorities—in a state that knew no majority— resorted to obstruction in parliament. The all-too liberal standing orders dating from the 1870s made that fairly easy. It was not necessary to brandish pocket-knives or bring musical instruments into the chamber; and even classic filibuster speeches (the record stood at sixteen hours) were an extravaganza. 'Technical' obstruction could be practised simply by any group of more than fifty MPs insisting on endless roll-calls or listing countless interpellations.

Obstruction was first extensively practised by the Germans after 1897, but the custom spread. Whenever that happened, the government would prorogue parliament and continue to govern by emergency decree—the famous 'paragraph 14' of the 1867 constitution. Admittedly, weighty issues such as raising the number of recruits that were drafted annually could not be effected by emergency decree, but a routine administration would carry on. Budgets were almost never passed on time. But life went on by means of continuing resolutions: the previous year's budget figures, for example, were simply repeated unchanged. Since far-reaching reforms could not be pushed through in this system, the antics of the disruptive radicals actually played into the hands of conservatives with a small 'c'.[1]

Yet the salient fact was that even these spells of authoritarian government were not supposed to last too long. In later life Franz Joseph no longer wanted to overturn the constitution even if he was content to fiddle with the small print. Any prime minister that failed to overcome obstruction in the medium term was bound to raise questions about his business acumen. In the short term, however, the twin brothers of obstruction and rule by decree might offer a way out of a political impasse: parliamentarians could safely oppose un- palatable but necessary measures, in the certain knowledge that these would be imposed anyway, with no blame at all attached to them. If party leaders could not enjoy the perks of government office, why incur the wrath of their constituents?

Obstruction, of course, never reared its head in the Upper House of the Reichsrat—the House of Lords—whose assent was essential for bills to be passed into law. By 1908, two-thirds of the Lords consisted of life peers, many of them of aristocratic descent too. To nobody's surprise the government could almost always rely on a safe majority in the Upper House. At times, however, it might even be convenient for the government to have bills which it disliked defeated there rather than have them vetoed by the Emperor.[2]

It is a truism that politics in the Habsburg Monarchy was almost always tied up with the nationality question in one way or another. A matter like the language of instruction in a small town grammar school could make or break cabinets. It was also no accident that in an Empire where the executive wielded comparatively greater power than in other constitutionally governed countries, civil service job prospects were a matter of prime political importance. Apart from the ethnic composition of the civil service proper, the founding and funding of schools and universities was a perennial bone of contention between rival ethnic groups. A second Czech university (to be founded in Moravia) was high up on the agenda, as was an Italian law faculty, which everyone agreed should be established but no one could say where. Governmental efforts were supplemented on all sides by the subscriptions of private associations, such as the *Deutsche Schulverein* or the Czech *Ústřední Matice Školská*, which built schools in mixed-language areas but often tried to get them 'nationalized' after a time so as to shift their funding onto the tax-payer.

If higher education in particular was a topic that intensified rather than lessened national strife, economic development and investment in the material infrastructure were often thought to provide an antidote. Economic lobbies conformed to regional, rather than ethnic patterns. Silesians of all possible ethnic backgrounds might be expected to welcome a canal link between the Oder and the Danube, just as Styrians or Tyroleans of all persuasions might be sceptical of pouring hundreds of millions into far-away projects from which they would stand to benefit little. More than any other head of government, Ernst von Koerber (1900–4) had used this ploy to overcome obstruction. However, the political success of his infrastructure projects—no matter what their economic merits might be—was subject to the law of diminishing returns.[3] Moreover, sources of investment dried up as the balance of payments dipped into the red after 1909, and budget figures got worse because of increased army spending in the pre-war years, with one mobilization following another during the Balkan crises. In 1910, the government got into a row with the Poles—usually among its more reliable supporters—for calling a halt to canal construction in Galicia, admittedly rather a wild-eyed scheme from the start. Concern with economic issues like these certainly contributed to the growing force of regionalism in Austria, over and above the loyalties of nationalism. It also served to increase the truculence of agrarian interest groups, the most powerful of all economic lobbies, who were clamouring for higher tariffs. Protective tariffs, however, spelt higher food prices that were unpopular with urban consumers. That was the reason why middle-class politicians, who felt the Social Democrats breathing down their necks in defence of consumer interests, had to think twice before agreeing to them. In September 1911, there were riots in Vienna because of sky-rocketing meat prices. When consumers agitated for food imports, however, they usually ran up against the veto of the Hungarians: the Monarchy after all was a customs union.

By 1908, Austria had already survived the worst. From 1897 to 1899 the Empire had gone through the throes of the Badeni crisis, when the German parties had first pioneered obstruction and parliamentary government had come to a standstill. After the government had finally given in, it was the turn of the Czechs to prove that they could behave equally well (or badly). These years served to convince the Emperor and the ruling elite that they had little to lose by electoral reform, even if reform would do away with the most reliable pillars of the throne, the eighty-odd seats in the Lower House reserved for the great landowners. In 1906 universal male suffrage was introduced. It was not quite a 'leap into the dark', for the newly enfranchised electorate had been tested in an experimental fifth curia established ten years before.[4] It has even been suggested that Franz Joseph himself had come to appreciate the 'internationalist' and thus potentially unifying tendencies of the Social Democrats. This is highly unlikely. Universal suffrage was punishment inflicted upon the middle-class parties for their irresponsible behaviour in the decade before 1907. It played upon the self-interest of the middle classes— its voters, if not its politicians. Under the new set-up they would have to do better or risk electoral defeat at the hands of the Social Democrats. Most of all, reform did away with the urban bias of the old parliament: agrarian parties of all stripes were to be its main beneficiaries.[5]

The ethnic balance of power was hardly touched by the reform of 1907. The Ruthenes (or Ukrainians) of eastern Galicia were for the first time assured of a foothold in parliament, while the 'ruling races', the Germans and Poles, lost some influence. What did change was the internal composition of the ethnic blocs. The National Liberals, who had dominated the old parliament on both the German and Czech side, were cut down to size and reduced to about a third of their former glory. These parties, the Young Czechs on the one hand, the different brands of '*Deutschfreiheitliche*' on the other, were anti-clerical, distinctly middle-class parties, run by the archetypal 'men of property and education'. These Liberals, or rather 'libertarians' in the American sense of the word, would be considered right-wing today, but were perceived as being on the Left then because their sometimes strident nationalism made them sceptical of the power of the crown and the church.

In the German case, the *Deutschfreiheitliche* parties provide a good example of how the shock of electoral reform served to concentrate minds wonderfully.[6] Without ever stopping their infighting completely, their different parties retained their separate organizations at a provincial level, but at least succeeded in forming a united front in parliament after 1910. The next year, by clever management, they even staged an electoral comeback which made them the biggest bloc in the Reichsrat. The *Nationalverband* [National Union], as their umbrella organization was called, was famous for its jealousies and internal wrangles, but still managed to hang together. Something like *Sammlungspolitik*—the rallying of establishment forces in support of the government, to use the Reich German term—was certainly possible to achieve.

The *Nationalverband* was dominated by Germans from the Bohemian lands. The term 'Sudeten German' was coined for them around that time because the Sudeten range of mountains was the nodal point where Bohemia, Moravia and Silesia met. Politics in Bohemia was based on class and ethnicity. Here the traditional cleavage of clerical versus anti-clerical had ceased to matter. As stalwart supporters of Sudeten German interests, the German Radicals under the flamboyant leadership of Karl Hermann Wolf had after the turn of the century taken over from the elitist leadership of the smart set in Prague. The German Agrarians also had their stronghold in Bohemia, with clear material interests to take care of, but no very distinct ideological profile. Old-style Liberal politics by business leaders and establishment figures continued to thrive only in the German diaspora of Moravia and Silesia, where the Germans, almost by definition, formed the upper crust of society. But they were captains without an army. Gustav Gross, a bulky giant of a university professor with a Santa Claus-like white beard who became leader of the *Nationalverband* after 1911, was one of these establishment figures. During his tenure he tried to reach out to the Radicals and sometimes even danced to their tune.

In the Czech case too, the once all powerful Young Czech Party had started to look old by 1900. Instead of one united catch-all party, the Czechs developed a five-party system (the *Pětka*) after the turn of the century. Numerically, the two strongest forces on the Czech scene were the Social Democrats who scored a higher percentage of votes in Bohemia than anywhere else, and the Agrarian Party who came first in terms of seats, if not in votes. The Agrarians had taken over many of the Young Czech strongholds such as the prosperous sugar beet-growers in the central parts of Bohemia. In Moravia, it was the Catholic People's Party that made inroads among the smallholders even though it was somewhat ostracized on account of its strongly dynastic leanings. In urban areas, the Young Czechs now also had to compete with a motley collection of smaller parties to the left of them, centred around the Czech National Socialists, who appealed to workers and lower middle-class elements, combining strident nationalism with professed pacifist leanings. (This was where Tomáš Masaryk and his small band of 'Realists' including the young Edvard Beneš belonged). Indeed, from being a quasi-revolutionary party of national unity, the Young Czechs had in the course of a few years seen their position transformed into that of the most conservative of Czech political groups, a fate ominously reminiscent of the Old Czechs whom they themselves had seen off a dozen years earlier. Young Czech leaders like Karel Kramář still cut a grand figure on the Austrian stage because of their experience and their contacts, but their position at home had become precarious after 1907.[7]

Theoretically, at least, most Czech parties clung to the concept of Bohemian state right, which meant insisting on the indivisibility not only of Bohemia, but of all the Czech lands, including Moravia and Silesia. As a maximum goal, the state right programme aimed at a 'trialist' solution, with the 'crown of St Wenceslas' on a par with the Hungarian crown of St Stephen. As a minimum, this meant advocating some sort of devolution or 'home rule' for Bohemia. In practice, Kramář probably realized that fighting the bureaucratic structure of the Empire was a futile effort; what was needed was to break the link between these structures and the Sudeten Germans. If the Czechs were to rule in Prague, they had to take the commanding heights in Vienna and turn their guns on the Germans. If the Austrian constitution was to be changed, and Dualism to be replaced with something more to the liking of the Slavs, it would have to be a revolution from above.

On neither the German nor the Czech side was there a real Tory party. Apart from the Polish *szlachta*, there was no powerful landed gentry in Austria or anything like a solid class of Prussian Junkers which might form the backbone of an upper-class conservative party. Instead, the so-called 'Conservatives' were a clerical party with a peasant and smallholder following. If the Church of England has been called the Tory party at prayer, the Austrian 'Conservatives' were the Catholic Church in politics. It is true that the more prosperous farmers tended to be less church-bound. But peasant parties of a strongly Catholic hue topped the polls in most rural districts, except in the case of the Czechs where the Catholics were a force to be reckoned with only in Moravia. In Bohemia the Agrarian Party was much closer in ideology to the Young Czechs, but no less bitter rivals for that.

In the German parts of Austria, the old-style 'Conservatives' with their Alpine strongholds in Tyrol and Upper Austria acquired an urban following after their merger with Karl Lueger's Christian Socials in 1907. Lueger's party was in many ways a uniquely Viennese phenomenon. He started out as a populist maverick Liberal propounding 'gas and water socialism' and ended up as a pillar of the establishment and a respected imperial statesman. His achievement was to weld together all the disparate forces fighting the (supposedly Jewish) upper middle-class oligarchy of Vienna's nineteenth century Liberals. Though always said to rely most strongly on the proverbial small shop-keepers, the Christian Socials for a time managed to reach into all strata of society except for the very highest and the very lowest. Less elitist and more democratically minded than the Liberals, they were pioneers of 'machine-politics' and 'gas and water social- ism' in Austria. As time went by, they increasingly stressed their loyalty to the Catholic Church. In 1907, Lueger joined forces with the rural Conservatives despite some private misgivings. Ultimately, this merger (strongly supported by Lueger's deputy, Albert Gessmann) led to an agrarian and clerical preponderance within the ranks of the Christian Socials that cost the party a lot of support among urban voters—for example in the 1911 elections. However, they managed to hold on to the Vienna city council until 1918.[8]

What the Christian Socials shared with a good number of their anti-clerical *Deutschfreiheitliche* opponents outside Vienna was their emphasis on *Mittelstandspolitik*. That term did not serve just as a euphemism to describe the non-working-class part of the population, but was elevated to an almost ideological pitch directed as much against 'capitalism' as against 'socialism'. Rather like American Populists and Progressives, denunciations of 'big business' belonged to the staple diet of aspiring middle-class politicians, perhaps even more so than of the Marxists who were supposed to take a more fatalistic view of economic development. *Mittelstand* as it was generally understood included the mill-owner as well as the petty civil servant, but definitely excluded both the manual worker and the robber baron dabbling on the stock exchange. Both migrant labour and mobile capital fitted uneasily into the concept of staid middle-class values. Yet, admirable as it was in creating a certain kind of cohesiveness and communitarian feeling among the middle classes, both old and new, that kind of thinking more often than not was heavily tinged with anti-Semitism.

During the hey-day of Liberalism there had been a certain trade-off between anti-clericalism and anti-Semitism. (After all, why would you object to a non-Catholic if you were anti-clerical yourself?) Starting in the 1880s, however, Georg von Schönerer and others pioneered a racialist brand of anti-Semitism, claiming that the Jews were biologically unfit to be proper Germans. It is ironic, incidentally, that the sort of reverse discrimination against the Jews advocated by German rabble-rousers exactly mirrored the sort of resentment directed against the Germans by most other ethnic groups who felt crowded out of plum jobs. Whereas Schönerer or Lueger complained that Jews made up a disproportionate number of students or the professional classes for instance, Czech or Slovene politicians might add that the same held true for the Germans as a whole.[9]

Yet in the end Lueger's nemesis proved to be not the 'Jewish Liberals' but the Social Democrats. The Social Democrats came a strong second in 1907, even if the French-style voting system meant that their candidates were often defeated in the run-off elections. Even so, they managed to win a quarter of German, Czech and Italian seats, and a tenth of those further east. Their internationalist outlook, underpinned by Marxism, did not prevent them from falling prey to national rivalries. Their central tenet ever since the Congress of Hainfeld in 1889 had been the concept of the unity of the working classes. This led them—and even more so, the trade union movement—to rely on a highly centralized structure. However, many of their leaders like Viktor Adler and Engelbert Pernerstorfer had gone through their political apprenticeship on the German nationalist Left and to some extent shared its belief in the leading role of the Germans even if they interpreted it differently.[10] Among Czech Social Democrats there was, consequently, ill-feeling about German hegemony and in 1911 they separated and set up their own 'autonomist' socialist party. During the First World War, Polish Socialists followed suit.

Ideologically, the Social Democrats as a whole tended to pay lip-service to Marxist doctrine but their revolutionary rhetoric sat uneasily with their essential pragmatism. The older generation of their leaders perhaps still owed more to Ferdinand Lassalle and his ideas of state intervention than to Marx. Increasingly, the Social Democrats also took over from the old-style Liberals as the standard-bearers of anti-clericalism; in Vienna in particular, they became bitter rivals with the Christian Socials. Among some parts of the electorate, notably among transport workers like railway employees or in mixed-language areas where ethnic tension was rife, they also faced competition from more nationalist-minded surrogates such as the small German Workers Party or the Czech Radicals. Both these parties finally started to call themselves National Socialists; the German one would ultimately be taken over by Hitler in the inter-war period while the Czech one would be patronized by Edvard Beneš.[11]

So, as a result of electoral reform, the Austrian parliament was even more fragmented than before. Ethnic cleavages were still dominant, but party competition within each ethnic group had increased. This was nowhere more noticeable than in the case of the Poles. In the nineteenth century, Galician politics had been monopolized by the Polish Conservatives. In Austria they were the nearest equivalent to a real Conservative party solidly based on a land-owning gentry (*szlachta*) with a particularly die-hard wing from Podolia, the eastern part of Galicia where the Polish minority lorded it over their Ruthene peasantry in time-honoured fashion rather like the Anglo-Irish absentee landlords. No matter what their internal disagreements might be, towards Vienna they followed a policy of 'not in front of the children!' Governments could side with the Czechs or the Germans, but they would always pander to the Poles. Galicia did not enjoy any special constitutional privileges, but had any number of administrative ones. Every governor of Galicia after 1868 reflected main-stream Polish opinion; Polish was the language of administration; every cabinet included a Galician *Landsmannminister* as an institutionalized lobbyist for Polish interests in Vienna. For a few years the same arrangement—of having a national trustee take part in cabinet meetings as a sort of ombudsman—was also offered to Czechs and even Germans, but the practice was discontinued after 1910.

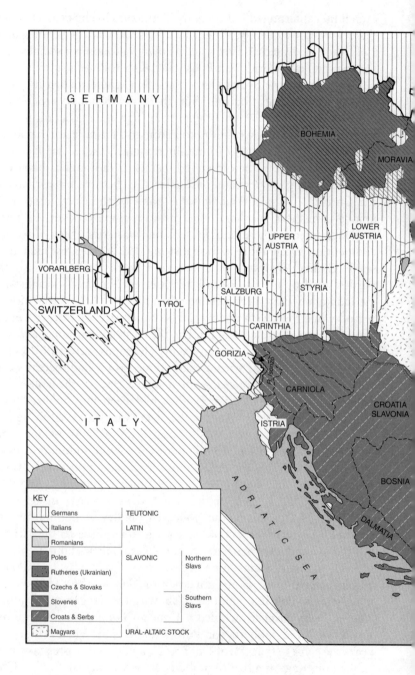

GERMANY

BOHEMIA

MORAVIA

LOWER
AUSTRIA

UPPER
AUSTRIA

VORARLBERG

SALZBURG

STYRIA

SWITZERLAND

TYROL

CARINTHIA

GORIZIA

R. Isonzo

CARNIOLA

CROATIA
SLAVONIA

ISTRIA

ITALY

BOSNIA

DALMATIA

ADRIATIC SEA

KEY

▥ Germans	TEUTONIC	
▨ Italians	LATIN	
Romanians		
Poles	SLAVONIC	Northern Slavs
Ruthenes (Ukrainian)		
Czechs & Slovaks		
Slovenes		Southern Slavs
Croats & Serbs		
Magyars	URAL-ALTAIC STOCK	

Map 2. The Nationalities of Austria–Hungary.

Table 1. The Composition of the Lower House of the Austrian Reichsrat.

Parties	Seats held			Votes (in 1,000s)	
	1906	1907	1911	1907	1911
Germans	205	232	232		
Liberals & Nationalists	142*	86	112	510	553
Christian Socials	55	96	76	720	618
Social Democrats	8	50	44	513	542
Czechs	87	108	108		
Agrarians	9	28	37	207	253
Social Democrats	2	24	26	400	373
Young Czechs	46	21	19	117	96
Clericals	3	17	7	182	208
National Socialists	8	6	13	75	74
Others	19	12	6	70	56
Poles	72	79	83		
Peasant Parties	8	30	25	270	188
National Democrats	–	14	10	106	111
Democrats	–	12	15	46	78
Social Democrats	2	6	8	66	65
Conservatives	62**	15	17	132	169
Others	–	2	8	19	66
Ruthenes	10	32	31		
Young Ukrainians	9	25	28	407	376
Old Ruthenes (Russophile)	1	5	2	163	124
Social Democrats	–	2	1	26	20
Slovenes	15	24	24		
Clericals	11	18	20	97	95
Liberals	4	6	4	51	51
Italians	18	19	19		
Clericals	4	10	10	60	41
Liberals	14	4	6	40	59
Social Democrats	–	5	3	20	23
Croats	10	11	11		
Main Stream	9	9	7	39	44
Pure Party of Right	1	2	4	16	31
Romanians	5	5	5	51	55
Serbs	2	2	2	12	11
Zionists	1	4	1	32	32
Total	425	516	516	4,617	4,537
(Social Democrat total	12	87	82	1,041	1,039)

*Includes 33 great landowners.
**Includes all other Polish deputies who were not members of the peasant or social democrat parties.

The advent of universal suffrage by 1907 produced a successful revolt against the Polish Conservatives by urban 'Democrats'. In the long run, however, Polish politics were to follow a regional, not social or ideological pattern. Anti-clerical sentiment never figured prominently in Polish politics and the old elites proved quite adept at infiltrating the popular parties. Leon Biliński, the wily leader of the Cracow conservatives (the Stańczyks) was probably the only party leader who was thought of as a possible prime minister. After the shock of 1907 he teamed up with the Peasant Party to defeat the Endecja (the National Democrats); in return the Endecja formed an alliance with the Podolian conservatives and the bishops. Biliński represented the classical line of regarding Russia as the chief enemy of the Poles; for that reason he was content to tolerate the Ruthenes as soon as they distanced themselves from their old-style Russophile leadership. For his rivals in Lvov and further east, however, the chief threat was no longer the Tsar but the rising tide of Ukrainian nationalism. Party competition meant that Poles no longer spoke with a united voice. Governments could now transfer their time-worn 'divide and rule' strategy to Galicia.[12]

Meanwhile in the south, suffrage reform clearly benefited the Slovenes who were manoeuvring to bolster their bargaining power in the Austrian system by teaming up with the Croats of Dalmatia. Here they faced the dilemma of either following their strongly Catholic orientation, or taking a non-sectarian stance by embracing a Yugoslav course which would include the Orthodox Serbs.[13] In turn, their Adriatic rivals, the Italians, had discovered their shared Latin roots with the handful of Romanian politicians from the opposite end of the Empire. (In the Bukovina, Romanians, Ruthenes and Germans had established a comparatively harmonious relationship.)[14] Yet on their own, the half-dozen smaller ethnic groups could do little to influence events. The Ruthenes and Italians had traditionally looked to the Germans, the South Slavs to the Czechs for guidance and support. But even these alliances could not be taken for granted. Ethnic rivalries had a way of sometimes coming up with politically counter-productive quarrels, such as that over the location of an Italian law faculty which served to drive Italians and Germans apart.

Towards the end of 1909, a provisional reform in the Reichsrat served to take the sting out of obstruction, to some extent at least. The Speaker was now empowered to re-arrange the agenda and postpone calls for emergency debates. Strictly speaking, the expedient was of dubious legality but it was annually renewed and made technical obstruction in the House almost impossible. It did not stop the practice of filibustering which might be effective at the committee stage of a bill. Smaller parties still used it enthusiastically to score propaganda victories or put pressure on the larger groups by ambushing their pet projects. Yet none of the leading players resorted to obstruction again until the early weeks of 1914.

Even when parliament operated smoothly, true coalition government, with party leaders taking over departments of state, was a rarity. The last one was Beck's from 1906 to 1908. However, the circumstances under which he operated were exceptional. Once it became clear that the Emperor was set on electoral reform, a bandwagon effect was started. Beck's cabinet was to all intents and purposes almost an all-party government. No party wanted to be left out of the bargaining over skillfully gerrymandered seats; and hardly any group wanted to be made responsible for sabotaging universal suffrage, lest it be punished for it by the electorate later on. Beck topped up his success when in late 1907 he managed to sell the renewal of the Trade and Customs Agreement with Hungary to the newly elected House. The agreement was set for another ten years under terms comparatively favourable to Austria, in exchange for largely symbolic gains on the part of the Magyars. These concessions to the Magyar national spirit, however, finally earned the Prime Minister the enmity of the heir apparent, Archduke Franz Ferdinand, who was widely held responsible for Beck's downfall in the autumn of 1908.[15]

Indeed, the existence of a rival court centred around Franz Ferdinand at the Belvedere palace added another complication to the Austrian machinery of government. Given the extreme old age of the monarch who had celebrated the diamond jubilee of his reign in 1908, it was perhaps only natural that most leading statesmen, politicians as well as bureaucrats, should every now and then anxiously look over their shoulder to make sure that Franz Ferdinand approved of them. To make matters worse, Franz Joseph and his nephew were ill-suited in temperament. The Emperor was determined to let sleeping dogs lie. A believer in short-term solutions and a master of bureaucratic detail, he never cared for large-scale reform initiatives. Franz Ferdinand, on the other hand, while clearly a conservative or even a reactionary, gave every sign of being forceful and reform-minded, albeit with strong prejudices. His anti-Magyar antics in particular have given rise to the legend that he actively advocated a 'trialist' solution for the Monarchy. But this is a misreading of his intentions which were sternly centralist. His head of cabinet probably summed up the views of his master correctly: 'This slogan of Trialism is all right to scare the Magyars but it must not seriously lead to anything more.'[16] The heir apparent surrounded himself with conservative aristocrats from Bohemia such as Counts Clam and Czernin: for his wife, Sophie, was a Czech countess. But these families had ceased to believe in historic state right and despaired of their nineteenth-century alliance with the Czech people; indeed, any reform initiative which they championed was unlikely to please advocates of a decentralized or democratic Monarchy. Anyway, for the time being, the uncertainties and rumours surrounding the intentions of the future Emperor certainly did not make the task of pleasing two masters at the same time any easier for Austrian statesmen.

After Beck's resignation the top job was handed on amongst the upper echelon of the Austrian bureaucracy. First in line was Baron Richard Bienerth (grandson of Austria's first constitutional prime minister in the 1860s, Anton Schmerling). Bienerth proved adept at a feat that had eluded Beck by retaining the support of both the Emperor and the heir apparent. But in parliament, his approach was less inclusive than Beck's. Originally, he was supposed to continue an all-party government revolving around an axis of the two big winners of the 1907 elections, the German Christian Socials and the Czech Agrarians, both populist but basically conservative. When this fell through, he rallied a fairly close but coherent working majority behind his government that included the German middle-class parties, the Poles and the Italians. He was given high marks by the Germans for refusing to compromise the integrity of the civil service in the interest of buying off opposition groups; never in the pre-war period did the German nationalists act and feel more like a committed government party than during Bienerth's tenure in 1909 and 1910. The drawback was that a fairly coherent working majority also meant a fairly homogeneous opposition that might find it easy, and be tempted at any moment, to cross the threshold into obstruction. It was no coincidence that during Bienerth's period in office Czechs, Slovenes and Russophile Ruthenes teamed up to form a Slavic Union. In 1909—prior to the amendment of the standing orders—Bienerth twice had to give in and close the parliamentary session in the face of their obstruction. (Ironically the amendment itself was actually part of a manouevre by the Slavic Union to split the Germans and become the dominant partners in a new coalition government.) In the end, however, it was the withdrawal of support by the Poles (the Endecja in particular) that made Bienerth face the voters two years earlier than planned, in 1911.

The elections of June 1911 resulted in a government victory. In Galicia, Biliński staged a triumphal come-back and almost annihilated the Endecja; in Bohemia, the Social Democrats lost a dozen seats. Only Vienna proved to be the exception. In the capital, German Radicals, the rump of the Liberals and the Social Democrats all teamed up to roundly defeat the Christian Socials, still weakened by internal upheavals after Lueger's death the year before. Lueger's heirs felt cheated, blamed Bienerth for their misfortune and withdrew their support from his government. After a brief trial balloon by Baron Paul Gautsch, who unsuccessfully tried to include the Czech parties in his government, Count Karl Stürgkh took over in November 1911. Stürgkh, who had been a parliamentarian (for the great landowners) as well as a civil servant, was close to former Prime Minister Koerber. In both Bienerth's and Stürgkh's cabinet, ministries were headed by senior civil servants rather than politicians (except for the Poles). One or two of those ministers might be of Czech descent, but the particularly sensitive, so-called 'political departments' —Justice, Education and Interior—remained in German hands. In parliament, Stürgkh worked with a more subtle combination of parties drawn from almost all the different nationalities. Rather than relying on a given working majority, he tried to manipulate party competition within ethnic groups to his best advantage. Ideally, this left the opposition too fragmented to make much of an impact. One could also advance the argument that these cross-cutting cleavages relieved overall political tension. But to manoeuvre successfully required Stürgkh to display a talent for duplicity that became almost legendary, promising all things to all people and still being believed.

Stürgkh's biggest parliamentary victory was to pilot a new army bill through the House in both 1912 and 1913 which massively increased the intake of recruits. Foreign policy crises both served to demonstrate the need for rearmament and put opposition parties in a difficult position lest they appear unpatriotic. Despite having to spend most of 1912 in a darkened room because of chronic eye trouble, and a constant chorus of carping criticism by all the great and good who resented his manipulative ways, the myopic Styrian Count was riding high in the Emperor's favour.[17] Stürgkh added another feather to his cap when he won his battle for a Galician Compromise in late 1913 which for the first time gave Ruthenes a say in provincial government. The way that this came about was an impressive demonstration of how Austrian politics could be manipulated. Biliński and his comparatively mild brand of Cracow conservatives favoured electoral reform for the Galician diet (the Sejm) for reasons of their own, because it spelt gains for their allies, the Polish Peasant Party, at the expense of their Podolian rivals and the Endecja. Stürgkh realized that in order to win the necessary two-thirds majority in the Sejm for a Polish-Ruthene Compromise he had to offer the opponents of reform a political carrot. To succeed, the Compromise had to be enacted by its enemies, not by its supporters. Accordingly, in 1913 he appointed a new governor of Galicia, wrested patronage from Biliński, and went on to break his hold over the Peasant Party. In return for not obstructing the concessions to the Ruthenes, Biliński's enemies among the die-hard Podolians were offered a chance to shore up their position within the Polish spectrum. This sudden change of tack left most participants bemused, but Stürgkh pressed his advantage. In February 1914 the Galician Reform Bill sailed through the Sejm against only scattered and token resistance. For Stürgkh it held the fringe benefit of outwitting his closest rival Biliński who was prevented from counter-attacking openly because he did not want to be seen sabotaging the reform which his allies relied on.[18]

In the long run, however, discontent in Prague counted for more than goodwill in Lvov. Over the course of the years the Bohemian problem had reached an unenviable degree of complexity. It was also made more difficult by the memory of broken promises on both sides—in 1871 when Franz Joseph had not followed up his offer of a settlement, and after 1890 when the Czechs had reneged on their deal with the Bohemian Germans.[19] On the face of it, the Bohemian problem bore some resemblance to Britain's Irish problem. Roughly two-thirds of its population were Czech. Granting a sort of 'home rule' to Bohemia on, for example, the Galician model was something which the vocal and influential German minority would never consent to. On the other hand, the Czechs fiercely resisted all moves towards a peaceful partitioning of Bohemia. As a second-best solution, Czechs insisted on full equality of their language with German, traditionally the language of administration in Imperial Austria. The Germans worked towards a sort of informal autonomy of their home districts. Even without official sanction, this was what eventually came to pass. Czech civil servants could not be prevented from communicating in Czech even when they should have been talking in German; Germans in turn refused to offer Czech-language facilities in parts of Bohemia where no or few Czechs were resident. Koerber summed up the dilemma: 'If the Germans want to feel entirely secure in their linguistic areas, they have to grant full freedom of action to the Czechs in their territory.'[20]

Since 1908 the Germans had again used obstruction in the Bohemian diet in Prague, thus effectively starving the provincial authorities of funds. This was a double-edged strategy as it also affected parts of the German community such as teachers who were denied a pay-rise. The Czechs in turn might be tempted to retaliate by obstruction in the Reichsrat. This was why the so-called 'Bohemian Compromise' loomed large on every prime minister's agenda. If passions in Prague became too inflamed, Vienna might be made to feel the consequences. On the other hand, few any longer hoped to achieve a breakthrough in the endless negotiations conducted in the palaces of Prague. The outline of a solution was certainly within sight; yet there were few politicians willing to gamble their reputations on selling it to the voters. The government was content with stopping things going from bad to worse. As Bienerth once confessed: 'Primarily I am interested in the talks not breaking down. Whether they achieve anything is less important.'[21]

In July 1912, however, the talks did in fact grind to a halt. Part of the reason for this was that Franz Ferdinand made it known that he would not accept any strings attached to his future authority. For the Bohemian Compromise was a three-cornered affair. It involved not just Czechs and Germans, but also the central administration. Even though the position of the Vienna government was usually closer to that of the Germans, their interests were by no means identical. To some extent, raising the banner of national autonomy meant carving up the Empire among its constituent nations. Czechs and Germans might even arrive at a compromise at Vienna's expense. As one of Franz Ferdinand's followers put it: 'If the Czechs and Germans ever really bury the hatchet, they will start treating the Emperor the way the Hungarians do!'[22] The aristocratic great landowners too, were not at all keen on a reform which might do away with their privileged position in the Bohemian diet. Cosmopolitan bureaucrats and businessmen, or members of endangered minorities (like Jews in Prague), might also be wary of a compromise that offered them little protection. Rather paradoxically, it was the supposedly 'moderate' elements closest to the 'supranational' ideal of the Monarchy who thus stood to lose out, both politically and in terms of their clientele, if the Compromise actually came to pass.

With matters in Bohemia slowly drifting towards a crisis, financially at least, Stürgkh finally stepped in on 26 July 1913, dissolving the provincial administration and appointing a caretaker committee that promptly raised taxes by decree. This was an expedient of doubtful legality (as most expedients were). Representatives of both nationalities attacked it: the Germans because it deprived them of their stranglehold on the diet; the Czechs because it went against their state right convictions. Privately, however, a number of leading politicians from both sides reassured the Prime Minister that their fury was mainly for public consumption and that they were quite relieved not to be burdened with the blame for making hard choices themselves.

While defending Stürgkh, Karel Kramář, the Young Czech leader, hoped to take advantage of the situation by finally driving a wedge between the Sudeten Germans and the Vienna government. He reasoned that once the Germans broke with the government, the bargaining position of the Czechs would improve dramatically. For that to happen, the Germans must be made to bear the blame for any breakdown of negotiations. The Bohemian governor, Prince Franz Thun, a former and perhaps future prime minister, seemed to be sympathetic to this strategy. But Kramář's master plan was undermined by an enemy within. The Czech Agrarians under the leadership of a socially conservative, but fairly nationalistic group that later on became known as the 'ur-oxen' were not content to wait for the success of Kramář's high level intrigues. Instead, in early 1914, they threw their considerable weight behind obstruction in the Reichsrat. If they did not want to lose face completely, the Young Czechs therefore had to follow suit and abandon their hopes of being offered a share of power in Vienna.[23] Without going to any great trouble to sort out matters, Stürgkh accepted the challenge and prorogued parliament on 16 March 1914. There are some indications that this was more than just a stop-gap solution to provide for a cooling-off period. Stürgkh may have intended to return to quasi-absolutist rule for a slightly longer period than in the past, even if war had not intervened.

The First World War changed the practice of Austrian domestic politics in more ways than one. As the supposedly quick campaign degenerated into the bloody stalemate of trench warfare, it turned the authoritarian expedient of spring 1914 into a permanent fixture. Before the war, the socialist Karl Renner had quipped: 'Austria is a tyranny tempered by sloth.' But incompetence took on a less benign aspect as the government tried and failed to manage a wartime economy. Austria experienced its taste of what can only be described as 'socialism from above': raw materials were rationed, savings eaten up by inflation and war bonds. Food had to be sold at maximum prices. Agricultural production predictably plummeted, the black market soared. Corruption and influence-peddling were rampant. Wartime losses and hardship exacerbated political strains and tensions. One of the lasting legacies of the war years was a system of rent-control that was not relaxed in Vienna until the 1980s.

In John Boyer's words, 'the war reprivatised politics'.[24] With parliament closed and censorship imposed, politics was lacking a public forum. War also led to a blurring of lines between existing parties. Like all the other Powers, Austria-Hungary experienced a debate on war aims. The blueprints that created most excitement, however, were concerned less with territorial aggrandizement than with gains at the expense of domestic enemies. The German parties put their hopes on the creation of a Polish state, to be ruled by the Habsburgs but separate from Austria. With Galicia subtracted, the Germans would once again be assured of an overall majority in any Austrian parliament. Moreover, the close wartime collaboration with Germany ought to be made permanent within a Central European military and economic union (*Mitteleuropa*). In this way Austrian Germans would get rid of Galicia as a potential trouble-spot, while acquiring extra safeguards for their position in the rest of the Empire.

In the face of these high hopes Stürgkh did his best to continue with business as usual. It is a tribute to his talent for dissimulation that he still managed to keep on the right side of both parties in every ethnic dispute. Yet the war clearly exposed the limit of his powers. Increasingly, the Army High Command, even though far from victorious at the front, was determining policy. Kramář was sentenced for high treason despite Stürgkh's defence of him; Polish, Ruthene, Czech, Slovene and Italian politicians were interned for suspected enemy sympathies;[25] Galicia was placed under military control. The high-handed behaviour of military authorities sometimes had a way of turning even the most loyal areas into hotbeds of republicanism. Stürgkh, therefore, was not at all averse to Hindenburg and Ludendorff curbing some of the pretensions of the Austrian generals in 1916. On the other hand, there was a new-found solidarity between authoritarian 'Habsburg' officers and formerly rebellious German nationalist activists who indulged in a big show of wartime patriotic fervour. In return, Czechs, Italians—and sooner or later the

Poles as well—began to have second thoughts about the viability or desirability of the Monarchy if the Central Powers lost the war. Irredentism ceased to be a pipe-dream, as its fulfilment might be just around the corner. Most Czech parties developed a sort of dual leadership: one that kept in touch with the underground and abroad through the so-called 'Mafie'; another that continued to work within the system. Even in Galicia, after 1917 at least, both Left (the Socialists) and Right (the Endecja) distanced themselves from the Monarchy. The German Social Democrats, on the other hand, were quite cooperative but might be forgiven for suspecting that defeat could yet prove them victorious.[26]

Stürgkh had reasons of his own for not re-opening the Reichsrat. He wanted to postpone the day when all the cheques he had signed would be presented. With discontent mounting, for economic reasons apart from everything else, he found it increasingly difficult to hold the line. In late 1915 even the leaders of the docile Upper House presented him with an informal motion of no confidence. The Emperor, however, was even less willing than before to permit changes: he clung to his trusted advisers. It was only in October 1916 that the bullets of Friedrich Adler, son of the veteran Socialist leader, Viktor Adler, put an end to this most consummate of political conjurers: Adler assassinated Stürgkh over lunch at the Hotel Meisl & Schadn.

A few weeks later, Franz Joseph who had been born in an age of cavalry charges, died in an era of poison gas and submarine warfare. His passing opened a new—and as it turned out—last chapter. His great-nephew Karl I, well intentioned but indecisive, was often said to be under the thumb of his strong-willed wife Zita. Yet at the beginning, he relied heavily on aristocrats drawn from the circle of advisers around the late Franz Ferdinand. Karl wanted to re-open parliament as a conciliatory gesture—and would finally do so in May 1917. However, his first prime minister Count Heinrich Clam-Martinic promised to meet the conditions of the German parties first. As a minimum, these included a down-payment on autonomy for the Germans of Bohemia. In itself, this was fair enough, but doing so without any compensating concessions to the Czechs meant alienating them for good. War-time exigencies and military objections ruled out any chance of relaxing the central government's grip on the Czech regions. In the end, therefore, Clam's government thought twice about it and reneged on its promises to the Germans. The Germans had to realize that their overblown expectations were not going to be fulfilled.

What was worse, the same held true for the Poles. The independent Poland which they had been promised existed only in name. In the meantime, all they got was a regime of occupation, just when the Russian Revolution seemed to be opening more alluring possibilities. Thus, by the spring of 1917 the Austrian government, apart from the smouldering resentment of the 'ethnic underdogs' who saw no point in fighting on, also faced a wave of discontent on the part of the traditional 'ruling races'. As a result, both the German *Nationalverband* and the Polish Club (*Koło Polskie*) showed serious signs of disintegration. In May 1917, the Polish Club finally toppled Biliński who had clawed his way back to its leadership and passed an internal vote of no confidence in the Clam government.[27] It is true that for the time being, the Poles could still be persuaded to work with Clam's successor, Ernst von Seidler (June 1917 to July 1918). But the signing of a peace treaty with Ukraine in February 1918 proved to be the last straw. A domestic re-alignment seemed to be under way: the Poles were furious at concessions to Ukrainian nationalism; while in the Reichsrat it was Ruthenes and German Social Democrats who helped Seidler's regime by passing the budget. The Social Democratic leadership also proved quite cooperative in dampening the wild strikes that erupted in January. Such cosiness between the government and the war-weary Left was reversed however when the scandal over the Emperor's secret negotiations with France, the so-called Sixtus Affair, broke in April. The government's priority shifted to appeasing the suspicious German Radicals. Even in circles far removed from the quixotic irredentism of Schönerer's Pan-Germans there was now a widespread feeling that Austria could only pull through under Germany's political tutelage and with its economic assistance, even if that meant a certain loss of independence. As a conservative Count predicted with exasperation: 'In the end, Ludendorff will come and clear up.'[28] Thus, banking on military victory seemed the best, because it was the only hope that the Habsburg Monarchy could survive in its traditional form.

In the last few months of the Monarchy, the moves for Sudeten German autonomy that had been part and parcel of a Bohemian Compromise solution mooted as long ago as 1890 were finally enacted. There was little consistency in these last-minute efforts to muddle through in time-honoured fashion. In July 1918 a new prime minister, Baron Max von Hussarek, promised the Germans that Bohemia might yet be partitioned, and the Poles that Galicia would certainly not be. With only a smattering of German and Polish hard-core nationalists withdrawing their support, Hussarek managed to survive by a fairly narrow margin in the Reichsrat. In a way it was ironic that an Empire that had so often been ruled by decree fought so hard for every parliamentary vote during the last few months of its life.

But the real decisions were already being taken elsewhere. When Karl ascended the throne, the war had hung in the balance. During 1917 it had appeared to swing in the Central Powers' favour, a fact that explained German ebullience.[29] In the spring of 1918 as the *Kaiserschlacht* ground to a halt a few miles from the English Channel, the tide turned irreversibly. While the Germans were still busy creating statelets out of the corpse of the Tsarist Empire, the Entente Powers were already settling down to do the same to Germany's Habsburg ally. All the Emperor could do was to channel these developments into evolutionary channels. His so-called 'People's Manifesto' of 16 October 1918 managed to do just that. Wilson's promise of national self-determination became the catchword of the day. The Lower House of parliament segregated into National Councils that set up shop as the 'founding fathers' of independent nation-states. However, to put self-determination into practice was easier said than done. For many mixed-language areas the end of the Monarchy spelt a switch of rulers, a 'world turned upside down' rather than a peaceful parting of the ways. Most of the Empire's 'successor states' would continue to be plagued by ethnic strife.[30]

Old Austria was the paradox of being a liberal Empire, not thanks to the tolerant spirit of its operators or to a scrupulous regard for legality, but because of a unique system of checks and balances that consisted of a finely tuned stand-off between an authoritarian bureaucracy, elitist liberals and anti-liberal mass-movements.[31] The forces of patriotism and nationalism, that unleashed a dangerously totalitarian potential when combined, in fact neutralized each other in Austria, at least in the pre-war period. The war changed all that: state activity expanded and assumed undreamt-of proportions. The bureaucracy no longer acted as a distant arbiter but decisively affected the lives of all its subjects. War also created a centralizing dynamic that was inevitably charged with ethnic implications in a multi-national Empire.

In 1914, there was no inkling of a revolutionary situation in Austria-Hungary. The Monarchy did not represent an Empire on the verge of dissolution. It is a moot point to try to pinpoint the juncture when its constituent nations and their political elites actually despaired of the Austro-Hungarian Empire. There was no clear-cut distinction between irredentists and loyalists. Politics is the art of the possible. It was practical constraints, not abstract ideals, that shaped political actions. Since the days of Metternich, however, Austria had lived through a period of relative decline, and the strain of holding on to its position as a Great Power was only too apparent. What set Austria-Hungary apart from all the other Great Powers was that it simply could not afford to lose another major war. The nationality problem would not tear the Monarchy apart on its own but it made sure that it would not survive a revolution. Germany and Russia could survive catastrophic defeats and live to fight another day; the Habsburg Empire could not. Foreign policy for Vienna was not a matter of gains or losses but of life and death. They all knew it, but that knowledge did little to improve their performance or steady their nerves.[32]

NOTES

1. Gernot Hasiba, *Das Notverordnungsrecht in Österreich (1848–1917). Notwendigkeit und Mißbrauch eines 'staatserhaltenden Instrumentes'* (Vienna, 1985). I have elaborated these points a little further in: Lothar Höbelt, *Parliamentary Politics in a Multinational Setting: Late Imperial Austria* [Working Papers in Austrian Studies 92–6] (Minneapolis, 1992).

2. Paradoxically, its position was to be strengthened with the advent of universal suffrage for the Lower House. In return for not blocking the Reform Bill, the Upper House was given guarantees against any sudden mass creation of peers by the crown.

3. Alexander Gerschenkron, in *An Economic Spurt that Failed* (Princeton, 1977), has provided us with a one-sided, but informative polemic in favour of Koerber's strategy. For economic trends in general see David Good, *The Economic Rise of the Habsburg Monarchy 1750–1914* (Berkeley, 1984); for the war years in particular: Eduard März, *Austrian Banking and Financial Policy. Creditanstalt at a Turning Point 1913–1923* (London, 1984).

4. Under the curial system of voting, parliament had been divided into four different categories of reserved seats: for great landowners, the chambers of commerce, and tax-payers in boroughs and in the countryside. The fifth curia (whose voters included all men over 24 who were literate and had lived in a constituency for six months) had been added by Badeni in 1896.

5. William A. Jenks, *The Austrian Electoral Reform of 1907* (New York, 1950), covers the parliamentary debates on the subject.

6. Lothar Höbelt, *Kornblume und Kaiseradler. Die deutschfreiheitlichen Parteien Altösterreichs 1882–1918* (Vienna, 1993) pp. 256–90.

7. Bruce Garver, *The Young Czech Party 1874–1901 and the Emergence of a Multi-Party System* (Yale University Press, 1978) includes a final chapter on the 'successor parties'; Andrew P. Kubricht, *The Czech Agrarian Party 1899–1914* (Ph.D. Ohio State University, 1974), is stronger on the pre-1907 period. See also the final chapters of Otto Urban's magisterial *Česka společnost* (Prague, 1982) now translated into German: *Die tschechische Gesellschaft 1848 bis 1914* (Vienna, 1994). For Moravia: Jiří Malíř, *Od spolku moderním politickým stranam* (Brno, 1996) is the standard work.

8. See John Boyer's masterful account: *Culture and Political Crisis in Vienna. Christian Socialism in Power, 1897–1918* (Chicago, 1995).

9. Probably the most balanced account of that story is Bruce Pauley, *From Prejudice to Persecution. A History of Austrian Anti-Semitism* (Chapel Hill, 1991).

10. Gerhard Ardelt, *Vom Klassenkampf zum Burgfrieden. Studien zur Geschichte der österreichischen Sozialdemokratie 1888 bis 1914* (Vienna, 1994) is a collection of essays on the dilemmas of the workers' movement. Mark E. Blum, *The Austro-Marxists 1890–1918. A Psycho-biographical Study* (University of Kentucky Press, 1985) provides sketches of socialist leaders. See also: Trevor Thomas, 'Bohumil Šmeral and the Czech Question, 1904–14', *Journal of Contemporary History*, 11 (1976) pp. 79–98.

11. See Raimund Löw, *Der Zerfall der 'Kleinen Internationale'* (Vienna, 1984); and Andrew G. Whiteside, *Austrian National Socialism before 1918* (The Hague, 1962).

12. Galician conservatives, unfortunately, have yet to find their Macaulay. For those with a smattering of Polish, Biliński's memoirs should make interesting reading (*Wspomnienia i dokumenty*, 2 vols, Warsaw 1924–5); they might also profit from: Janusz Gruchala, *Rząd austriacki i polskie stronnictwa polityczne w Galicji wobec kwestii ukraińskiej 1890–1914* (Katowice, 1988). The rest of us have to make do with bits and pieces gleaned from books like A. Markovits and F. Sysyn (eds), *Nationbuilding and the Politics of Nationalism. Essays on Austrian Galicia* (Cambridge, Mass., 1982). See also Paul R. Magocsi, *Galicia. A Historical Survey and Bibliographic Guide* (Toronto, 1983).

13. Carole Rogel, *The Slovenes and Yugoslavism 1890–1914* (New York, 1977); Feliks Bister, *'Majestät, es ist zu spät. . .'. Anton Korošec und die slowenische Politik im Wiener Reichsrat bis 1918* (Vienna, 1995).

14. Umberto Corsini, 'Deputati delle terre italiane ai parlamenti Viennesi', *Archivio Veneto*, Quinta Seria, 97 (1972) pp. 151–226; John Leslie, 'Der Ausgleich in der Bukowina 1910', in Emil Brix and Josef

Leidenfrost (eds), *Geschichte zwischen Freiheit und Ordnung* (Graz, 1991) pp. 113–44.

15. See Johann Christoph Allmayer-Beck, *Ministerpräsident Baron Beck* (Vienna, 1956), a biography both scholarly and readable by his great-nephew.

16. Haus-, Hof- und Staatsarchiv, Nachlass Franz Ferdinand, Box 11, no. 124, letter from Colonel Brosch, 17 June 1910. The most scholarly study of the heir apparent is still Robert A. Kann, *Franz Ferdinand Studien* (Vienna, 1976). The relevant essay on Bohemia has been translated: R.A. Kann, *Dynasty, Politics and Culture: Selected Essays,* ed. Stanley B. Winters (New York, 1991) pp. 151–89. Steven Beller, *Francis Joseph* (London, 1996), provides an entertaining and thought-provoking introduction to the career of his uncle; and see also Samuel R. Williamson, 'Influence, Power and the Policy Process: the Case of Franz Ferdinand, 1906–1914', *The Historical Journal,* 17 (1974), pp. 417–34.

17. Frank E. Norgate, *The Internal Policies of the Stürgkh Government November 1911 to March 1914: A Study in a Holding Action* (Ph.D. New York, 1978) is a useful survey. For an analysis that combines domestic and foreign policy aspects see John Leslie, 'The Antecedents of Austria-Hungary's War Aims: Policies and Policy-Makers in Vienna and Budapest before and during 1914', in Elisabeth Springer and Ludwig Kammerhofer (eds), *Archiv und Forschung* (Vienna, 1993) pp. 307–94.

18. Österreichisches Staatsarchiv, AVA, Ministerratspräsidium, Box 241 contains the correspondence between Stürgkh and the Galician governors. Olga Narkiewicz, *The Green Flag. Polish Populist Politics 1867–1970* (London, 1976) chapter 5, provides the best account of the fall-out for the Peasant Party that split into a 'Left wing' under Stąpiński and a 'Piast party' under the future Polish Prime Minister Witos. However, her characterization of that result (p. 143) as a collapse of the 'undercover intrigues' of the Austrian government probably underestimates Stürgkh's potential for mischief. With hindsight, weakening Biliński's bloc may have been a mistake, but in 1913 Stürgkh was quite content to see his rival's wings clipped.

19. On the Bohemian problem see the two biographies by Harald Bachmann: *Adolf Bachmann* (Munich, 1962) and: *Joseph Maria Baernreither* (Neustadt a.d. Aisch, 1977). The Czech view is best represented by Karel Kazbunda's study, *Otázka česko-německá v předvečer velké války,* ed. Zdeněk Kárník (Prague, 1995).

20. Franz Adlgasser and Margret Friedrich (eds), *Heinrich Friedjung, Geschichte in Gesprächen. Aufzeichnungen 1898–1919,* 2 vols (Vienna, 1997) II, p. 255: quoting Koerber, October 1909.

21. Haus-, Hof- und Staatsarchiv Vienna, Nachlass Baernreither, Box 5, vol. 9, p. 80: diary, November 1910.

22. Ibid., vol. 10, p. 6: diary, 18 November 1911, quoting Count Galen, the father confessor of the heir apparent's wife. For the social background see Gary Cohen, *The Politics of Ethnic Survival. Germans in Prague 1861–1918* (Princeton, 1981).
23. See the correspondence between Stürgkh and Thun in Österreichisches Staatsarchiv, AVA, Ministerratspräsidium, Boxes 350, 351, 355. Within the Czech Agrarians, it seems, the party's leader (and smallholder champion) Antonín Švehla advised caution, but former Minister Karel Prašek and the Moravian estate-owner František Staněk, the leader on the Vienna stage, charged ahead. The Young Czechs retaliated for their dashed hopes by 'outing' Karel Šviha, the parliamentary leader of the National Socialists, who had supported obstruction, as a police spy—a charge that certainly throws an interesting light on late Habsburg 'political culture'. As always, I have to thank Robert Luft for his illuminating insights into the Bohemian political scene.
24. Boyer, *Culture and Crisis*, p. 448. See also Richard Kapp, 'Divided Loyalties: The German Reich and Austria–Hungary in Austro–German Discussions of War Aims, 1914–1916', *Central European History*, 17 (1984) pp. 120–39; John Leslie, *Austria–Hungary's Eastern Policy in the First World War* (Ph.D. Cambridge, 1975); and to follow up the story: the penultimate chapter of Piotr Wandycz, *The Lands of Partitioned Poland, 1795–1918* (Seattle, 1974).
25. One Polish MP, Thaddeus Tertil, formerly of the Endecja and mayor of Tarnów, got into trouble merely for not being arrested by the Russians when they occupied his home-town.
26. See H. Louis Rees, *The Czechs during World War I* (New York, 1992); Victor Mamatey, 'The Union of the Czech Political Parties in the Reichsrat, 1916–18', in *The Habsburg Empire in World War I* (New York, 1977), pp. 3–28. For the position of the trade unions: Margarethe Grandner, *Kooperative Gewerkschaftspolitik in der Kriegswirtschaft* (Vienna, 1992).
27. For a more detailed account see Lothar Höbelt, 'Late Imperial Paradoxes: Old Austria's Last Parliament 1917–18', *Parliament, Estates and Representation*, 16 (1996) pp. 207–16; Felix Höglinger, *Ministerpräsident Heinrich Graf Clam-Martinic* (Vienna, 1964).
28. Nachlass Baernreither, Box 7, vol. 19, p. 26; quoting Count Larisch during the Sixtus Affair. For the foreign policy background to these crises see Oleh Fedyshyn, *Germany's Drive to the East and the Ukrainian Revolution, 1917–18* (New Brunswick, 1971); Tamara Grieser-Pecar, *Die Mission Sixtus* (Vienna, 1988).
29. Carvel de Bussy (ed.), *The Memoirs of Alexander Spitzmüller (1862–1953)* (New York, 1987) p. 164 provides us with an Austrian Minister of Finance who in early 1917 still wondered whether Austria-Hungary would not be paid a war indemnity.

30. See Helmut Rumpler's two studies: *Max Hussarek. Nationalitäten und Nationalitätenpolitik in Österreich im Sommer des Jahres 1918* (Graz, 1965); and *Das Völkermanifest vom 16. Oktober 1918* (Vienna, 1966).
31. Or, in the words of John Boyer (*Culture and Crisis*, p. 330): 'The administrative state still controlled, in the sense of setting the permissible context of meaning and action, the limits of popular aggression.'
32. I fully agree with the criticism of my earlier writings by Alan Sked, *The Decline and Fall of the Habsburg Empire 1815–1918* (London, 1989) pp. 264–69.

4

The Bohemian Question

Catherine Albrecht

The conflict that broke out in Bohemia following the publication of the Badeni language ordinances in April 1897 was preceded by a long history of growing tension between Czech and German political leaders. Public awareness of the cultural differences between Czechs and Germans in Bohemia predated the revolution of 1848. A common Bohemian identity among inhabitants of the province gradually eroded; by the late 1860s Czechs and Germans were divided into two political camps. Mutual social and cultural contacts were undermined during the 1880s, when Czechs and Germans engaged in sharp competition for control of provincial institutions. Many of the remaining ties between the two national communities were decisively broken by the intense conflict provoked by the Badeni language laws of 1897. The period between 1897 and the end of the Habsburg Monarchy is often characterized as one dominated by intense hostility and competition, increasingly strident demands, and harsh, unyielding rhetoric on both sides of the national divide in Bohemia. At the same time, however, strongly worded demands for national 'rights' often masked quiet co-operation between Czechs and Germans on issues of common concern.

The Bohemian crisis of the late nineteenth and early twentieth centuries has therefore elicited broad debate over its depth, causes and potential solutions. Although the growing radicalism of both Czech and German nationalism has been explored in recent literature, many questions remain unresolved. Why, for example, did national demands continue to dominate over social and economic concerns, even after the expansion of the franchise in 1897 and 1907? Were there real opportunities (whether seized or missed) for collaboration and co-operation across national lines? Have historians exaggerated or misunderstood the extent of national conflict in the early twentieth century? And finally, to what extent did the conflict between Germans and Czechs in Bohemia undermine the stability of the Habsburg Monarchy as a whole?

This chapter will outline briefly the background of Czech–Germans relations before 1897 and then explore in greater depth the issues that contributed to the intense national hostility in Bohemia in the last two decades of the Habsburg Monarchy.

National Movements before 1897

The cultural and linguistic renaissance of the Czechs began in the 1780s among a small group of scholars and publicists. By the 1830s, this renaissance had developed into a small national movement, still focused primarily on cultural expression in literature and the arts. Strict limits on political activity in the Habsburg Monarchy confined national expression to privately organized balls, literary salons and informal meetings in cafes. In the face of a common threat from the absolutist government, German- and Czech-speaking Bohemians retained a common identity and social and cultural contacts in such fora as the provincial Museum or the Royal Scientific Society.

The decade of the 1840s saw incipient political awakening and growing, if still muted, demands for political and economic change. German and Czech Liberals cooperated in their common aim to gain increased civil and political rights. Personal friendships, such as that between the budding Czech national leader, František Ladislav Rieger and German-Bohemian publicist Anton Springer, were strengthened by shared political goals. Utraquist organizations, such as the Union for the Promotion of Industry, founded in 1844, promoted common economic interests.

The revolution of 1848, however, cracked the façade of common interests. United in their opposition to the authoritarian rule of Clemens von Metternich and Habsburg absolutism, Czechs and Germans soon found themselves at odds over the principles on which a revolutionary government should be based. Should the political power to reform the Austrian state be centred in Vienna, as Germans sought, or devolve to the crownlands, as Czech leaders demanded? Should the autonomy, self-governance, and linguistic and cultural rights of the Czechs and other ethnic minorities be strengthened, and if, so, by what means? And finally, what role, if any, should Austria play in the unified German state proposed by the Frankfurt parliament? František Palacký's famous refusal to attend the Frankfurt parliament, in which he asserted his identity as 'a Bohemian of the Slav race' and declared that 'if Austria did not exist, we should have to create her', shocked his German Bohemian compatriots and thrilled his Czech followers.

The reactionary policies of the Bach era of the 1850s temporarily suppressed the political claims of Germans and Czechs and brought them together in common opposition to neo-absolutism. At the same time, the Austrian government in the 1850s created the structures of municipal self-government, and established chambers of commerce, savings banks, and other institutions designed to promote economic development. The re-establishment of parliamentary government in the 1860s provided a new forum for the articulation of national and political goals. The issues that had emerged in 1848—federalism versus centralism, historic state right and the unity of the Bohemian crownlands, protection of the linguistic and cultural rights of ethnic groups, the extension of the franchise, cooperation among the Slavs of the empire, and Austria's relationship with Germany—remained prominent and potentially divisive.

In the 1860s and 1870s, both Czechs and Germans followed liberal political leadership. The Czech National Party under the leadership of František Palacký and his son-in-law F.L. Rieger was based on a combination of liberal demands, a strategic alliance with the Bohemian 'feudal' aristocracy, and staunch support for the concept of historic state right and the unity of the crownlands of Bohemia, Moravia and Silesia. German Liberals dominated the parliament of the Austrian half of the monarchy from the *Ausgleich* of 1867 until the advent of Prime Minister Eduard Taaffe in 1879. Czech National Party leaders —known as Old Czechs—were now challenged by more radical Young Czechs under the leadership of Karel Sladkovský, who sought a broad extension of the franchise, condemned the compromises made to achieve an alliance with the nobility, and advocated an active policy of engagement in political affairs rather than the passive resistance practised by the Old Czechs after 1867. In 1871, Prime Minister Hohenwart brokered a compromise that would have acknowledged the historic rights of Bohemia. When this was rejected by German Bohemians, the Young Czechs broke with the Old Czechs, formed their own National Liberal Party, and in 1874 entered political life.

Competition between Germans and Czechs intensified in the 1880s. Taaffe's government forced the German Liberals into a minority position in the Reichsrat and offered significant concessions to the Czechs in exchange for their support. Among the concessions were the division of the university in Prague into autonomous Czech and German sections, the broadening of the franchise to include voters who paid at least five gulden in direct taxes, and the Stremayr language ordinances of 1880 that permitted Czech to be used in communications between bureaucratic officials and the public. These concessions altered the character and focus of national competition within Bohemia. Instead of differing on fundamental political goals while cooperating in daily life, Germans and Czechs began to compete fiercely for the control of public institutions, ranging from chambers of commerce (three of which came under the influence of Czech small business in the early 1880s) to the organs of municipal self-government. German Bohemians responded to the threat of Czech control of the structures of government by boycotting the Bohemian diet in Prague and demanding the administrative division of the province. In 1883, after the Czechs gained a majority in the diet, the German Liberal leader Franz Schmeykal demanded that Bohemia be divided into German and Czech areas, each of which would be represented in a separate curia in the provincial diet.[1] This demand remained a staple of German Bohemian political platforms from the 1880s onwards. Czech political leaders opposed it on the grounds that it would undermine the historic unity of the province, whose role and autonomy they sought to strengthen.

The results of the census of 1880, the first to use the 'language of daily life' as the basis on which to determine nationality, demonstrated strong growth in the Czech-speaking population of Bohemia, especially in the industrializing border regions.[2] German Bohemians responded by organizing national defence associations, like the *Deutsche Schulverein*, founded in 1880 to support German minority schools and counter the educational activities of the Czech Central School Society (*Ústřední Matice Školská*).[3] On their side, the Czechs began to devote more attention and resources to supporting the linguistic identity and educational rights of Czech workers, small shopkeepers, and officials along the nationality frontier. The skirmishes had begun in a 'small national war' that was to break out in full force in the 1890s.[4]

The changes in the balance of demographic, economic and political power between the two nationalities in Bohemia were mirrored by significant changes within each national political camp. The Linz programme of 1882 outlined an extensive platform of German national and social demands and led to the emergence of more radical German-national parties.[5] Among the Czechs, the Young Czech National Liberals grew increasingly dissatisfied with the political and social conservatism of the Old Czech leaders who cooperated with the Taaffe government. Competition for new voters from among the five-gulden men encouraged political leaders to embrace radical programmes of national self-protection that were often directed as much against Jews as against the opposing nationality. The new voters were interested less in traditional liberalism under an elite leadership than in protection of their economic interests and social position. Thus, suffrage reforms that extended the franchise to the lower middle class created conditions under which increasingly extreme national demands and tactics were used to attract new voters. New, more radical and nationalistic political parties were particularly successful in exploiting crises to gain electoral support.

The Badeni Crisis

Liberal political parties began to lose influence in the early 1890s, as is illustrated by the failure of the *Punktace* or compromise of 1890. The compromise, described by Lothar Höbelt as the final trump card of the Liberals, was negotiated secretly between leaders of the Old Czech and German liberal parties.[6] It aimed to bring Germans, who had boycotted the Bohemian diet since 1886, back into political engagement. The proposed compromise would have divided the administrative apparatus of Bohemia, creating separate school and agricultural councils, and establishing separate national curias for voting. The Young Czech political leadership (and the Czech voting public) saw the compromise as a concession to German demands to divide the province and reduce Czech self-governance. Their attack on the Bohemian compromise led to a decisive Young Czech victory in parliamentary elections in 1891. The failure of the compromise also discredited Prague's German leaders who had negotiated it and lent greater authority to those in the borderlands who had opposed it.

The Young Czech Party in the early 1890s had the character of an umbrella coalition encompassing moderates like Josef Kaizl and Karel Kramář, radicals like Eduard Grégr and Jan Vašatý, and agrarian leaders like Antonín Švehla. It was in opposition from 1893, when the German Liberals formed their last government, until 1895, when Count Casimir Badeni was appointed Prime Minister. Badeni's tasks were two-fold: to extend the franchise (the issue on which Taaffe's government had fallen in 1893) and to reach a compromise with the Czechs. The franchise was extended in 1896 to include a new fifth curia of voters, and parliamentary elections in February 1897 resulted in greater representation for more radical nationalist

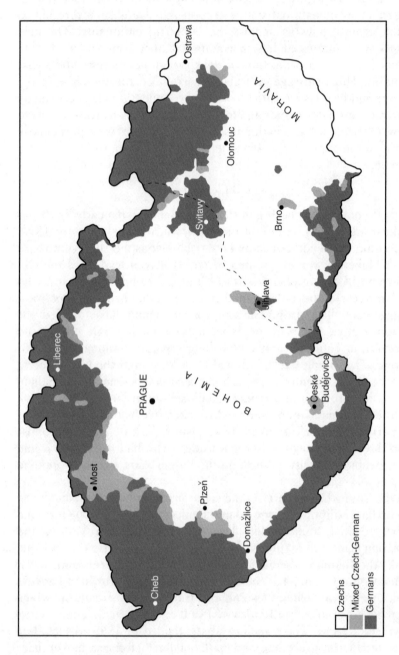

Map 3. Bohemia and Moravia.

parties, particularly among the Germans. Georg von Schönerer, for example, was re-elected to parliament (after an absence of eleven years) from the Cheb (German: Eger) district in north-west Bohemia, and his Pan-German party seated five delegates. The accommodation with the Czechs was to be reached through a language ordinance, published in April 1897.

The Badeni language ordinances applied only to Bohemia (although the intention was to extend them subsequently to Moravia).[7] They allowed the Czech language to be used not only in external communication between citizens and the bureaucracy (the 'outer language') but also in communication among state officials in all parts of Bohemia (the 'inner language'). As a result, all state officials in the affected ministries would be required to gain competency in both languages of the province by 1901. The Young Czech leaders were satisfied with the ordinances, which acknowledged the equality of Czech and German and maintained the territorial integrity of Bohemia. Germans of all political persuasions were opposed to the proposed changes, both because of the ordinances' symbolic attack on German cultural and linguistic hegemony and because, from a practical point of view, they threatened the livelihood of German officials who were not bilingual in Czech. State service was among the most attractive careers for educated German Bohemians, particularly as other aspects of Bohemian life and the Bohemian economy became more dominated by Czechs. Czech officials generally knew German well enough to satisfy the ordinances, but many German officials in Bohemia did not have a sufficient command of Czech.

German reaction to the language ordinances was swift. Formal protests and obstruction in the Reichsrat began in April, as did the mobilization of public opinion through petition drives. It became impossible for parliament to conduct other business when petitions were read aloud in their entirety during sessions, or delegates filibustered and vied with each other to give the longest speech on record. German delegates made it clear that the resumption of normal parliamentary practice depended on the suspension of the language ordinances. Badeni suspended parliament in June and reconvened it in September 1897. In the interim, Czech and German politicians spent the summer mobilizing their supporters in Bohemia. Demonstrations, economic boycotts and street violence were common throughout the remainder of 1897. Efforts to pass the renewal of the Austro-Hungarian *Ausgleich* and the joint budget in the autumn of 1897 failed because of continued parliamentary obstruction, which escalated to the point of violence in November.[8] In an attempt to restore order, the president of the lower chamber of parliament, Julius Falkenhayn, issued an ordinance that permitted the forcible removal of disruptive delegates and their exclusion from parliament for up to thirty days. Demonstrators in Vienna called upon Badeni to resign, which he did in late November. In response, the Czech public initiated its own counter-demonstrations in Prague and other cities in Bohemia, which led to the imposition of martial law in Prague in December.

The consequences of the fight over the language ordinance were felt throughout the final decades of the Habsburg Monarchy. One of the most important results was the undermining of parliamentary government. Delegates had behaved in ways that eroded public respect for them, for the parliamentary process, and for the whole institution of representative government. The Lex Falkenhayn of 1897 compromised the immunity and autonomy of parliamentary deputies. In addition, Prime Minister Badeni was forced to issue decrees under paragraph 14 of the constitution on matters on which parliament had failed to act. Even though parliament later had a chance to ratify those decrees, reliance on paragraph 14 reduced the authority of parliament. Successive prime ministers found it expedient simply to use paragraph 14 to pass controversial legislation, thereby bypassing parliamentary debate. Obstruction also spread from the Reichsrat to the Bohemian diet, where repeated attempts to work out a compromise between Czechs and Germans failed because of nationalist brinkmanship.

A second important consequence of the Badeni crisis was that relations between Czechs and Germans in Bohemia deteriorated. Demonstrations, particularly against German minorities in pre-dominantly Czech areas or Czech minorities in the borderlands of the province, created a siege mentality and strengthened the role of national protection societies. Even respected scholars, such as the Berlin historian Theodor Mommsen, called for violence. In a letter to the *Neue Freie Presse*, Mommsen reminded readers that 'the Czech skull is impervious to reason, but it is susceptible to blows'.[9]

Economic boycotts initiated in 1897 damaged traditional commercial relationships between Czechs and Germans. Some German firms dismissed Czech workers who sent their children to Czech schools. A few German landlords similarly threatened to evict Czech tenants who were involved in national activities. On the Czech side, consumers who frequented German (or German-Jewish) businesses were labelled as traitors and their names sometimes published in newspapers. A climate of fear, distrust and hostility was thus created, particularly in areas along the so-called language border, which prevented the peaceful resolution of differences between the two national groups.

A third consequence of the Badeni language ordinances was that the crisis they evoked led to the radicalization of politics in both the Czech and German camps. Along with the expanded franchise, the crisis contributed to an increase in the strength and number of overtly nationalist parties. It also radicalized both their tactics and their demands. Schönerer's Pan-German party initiated the 'Los von Rom' movement in the summer of 1897 to bring German Austria closer to the Protestant German Reich. Karl Hermann Wolf spoke of '*Germania irredenta*', and hoped that the '*furor teutonicus*' would provoke Germany to intervene in the crisis. In order to retain influence even moderate politicians had to embrace more extreme national demands.[10] The newly formed Czech National Socialist Party gained public support and legitimacy by countering German street demonstrations with their own.[11]

To some extent, the increase in political pluralism was an expected outgrowth of mass politics. The extension of the franchise in 1897 could have brought socio-economic concerns to the forefront of politics, as the German People's Party under Otto Steinwender and the Christian Social Party under Karl Lueger desired.[12] However, this process of political differentiation on the basis of common socio-economic interests was derailed by the intense nationalism evoked by the crisis over the Badeni language ordinances.

In March 1898, Prime Minister Baron Paul Gautsch revised the ordinances. Under the revision, districts in Bohemia were identified as either Czech, German or mixed. The Czech language need only be used in Czech or mixed districts, not in German districts. Czechs such as Josef Kaizl, who served as Finance Minister under the Thun government in 1898, tried to implement the ordinances by appointing and promoting Czech specialists within the bureaucracy. But in reality the languages ordinances were quietly dropped from the government agenda.

Political Realignments, 1897–1914

The early twentieth century saw the coalescence of new political forces in Bohemia. New political parties and alliances were formed, new political platforms were drafted and old ones revised. On the

German side, national and liberal parties continued to try to effect a common platform, which was enunciated in the Whitsun programme of 1899. This programme sought to protect the traditional hegemony of German Austrians against challenges both from other nationalities in Austria and from Hungary. As usual it called for the division of Bohemia, and demanded the establishment of German as the 'inner language' of the Austrian bureaucracy and the general language of communication in society as a whole. Nonetheless, the German political camp was also divided into factions: the Christian Socials sought to focus on the economic needs of the lower middle class in Vienna and Lower Austria and resented the deflection of attention to Bohemian national problems; the German National Party split with the Pan-German party over both goals and personalities; within Bohemia, Germans living in mixed areas like Prague rejected radical demands, such as those put forward in Liberec (German: Reichenberg) in 1906 to create a separate crownland for the border regions of Bohemia.[13] Even the Social Democratic Party was affected by the tendency to splinter. It divided into national parties in 1911, acknowledging the autonomy of the Czech Social Democrats from the Austrian German party.

On the Czech side, between 1897 and 1901, no fewer than five new political parties were formed. These included the State Right Radicals of Karel Baxa and Alois Rašín, the Radical Progressives organized around Antonín Hajn, the Czech People's Party made up of the group of realists around Tomáš Garrigue Masaryk, Václav Klofáč's National Socialists, and the Agrarian Party, which separated from the Young Czechs in 1901 under the leadership of Antonín Švehla. The first three of these parties were led by young progressives, some of whom had been arrested and tried in 1893 as part of the 'Omladina' conspiracy. Thus, they represented a challenge by the younger generation to the by-now-established leadership of the Young Czech Party. Only the Agrarian Party sought to place the economic issues of its constituents in the forefront of its platform, although the National Socialists also claimed to represent the interests of Czech workers.[14]

The fundamental difference among Czech political parties in the early twentieth century was the extent to which Czechs should embrace 'positive politics' of engagement with the Vienna government or should retain an oppositional stance in order to put pressure on the government. Both strategies shared the common aim of gaining concessions from Vienna; they differed mainly on whether small concessions would ever be sufficient to redress the perceived inequality of Czechs and Germans. Karel Kramář, leader of the Young Czechs, was a firm advocate of positive politics. He criticized Czech parliamentary opposition for having prevented the Czechs from benefiting from such programmes as Prime Minister Koerber's economic development and infrastructure investment. From the point of view of his opponents, however, positive politics compromised long-term Czech national interests for the sake of short-term gains. Czech parties also disagreed on whether the historic state right platform, which had been central to the Czech national movement from the 1840s, was still relevant in modern conditions. The National Socialists sought to place the national community of Czechs, both in and outside the Bohemian crownlands, above the state right, while the State Right Radicals (as the name implied) sought full autonomy for the Czechs in a Bohemian state controlled by them. Until 1907, the Young Czech Party continued to dominate Czech parliamentary politics, but, as moderates, they faced increasing challenges to their authority. The Young Czechs responded to the challenge posed by franchise reform by reorganizing the party and revising their platform to focus on specific national goals, such as the demand that a second Czech university be founded in Moravia.

The Austrian franchise reform of 1907 eliminated the old curial system of voting and established universal male suffrage for all men aged 24 and over who had a permanent residence. Franchise reform had been prompted by the Russian Revolution of 1905, which sparked massive demonstrations in favour of franchise reform in Austria-Hungary, as well as by the expectation that a broader franchise would help replace national concerns with social and economic concerns in politics. New elections in 1907 radically altered the composition of the Reichsrat, as the Social Democratic parties won 87 seats, while several new radical parties gained representation for the first time. The number of seats held by the Young Czech Party was reduced from 60 to 21. In response to the challenges posed by universal suffrage, the Young Czechs undertook agreements with other parties in the 1907 and 1911 parliamentary elections not to run candidates against each other in particular districts. This was intended mainly to establish a united front against Social Democrats. They also spearheaded the creation of a Czech Club in parliament as a way of coordinating policy and building a significant voting bloc.

Universal manhood suffrage for parliamentary elections was not, however, followed by comparable electoral reform at either the provincial or the local level. A fifth curia expanded the franchise to the Bohemian diet in 1905, but further reforms were stymied by the entrenched interests of the aristocracy as well as by the inability of Germans and Czechs to cooperate. In local elections, complex electoral geometry enabled towns like České Budějovice (German: Budweis), which had a German majority in the central districts of the city but a Czech majority in the suburbs and the surrounding region, to remain under German control. Curial voting also enabled the more traditional, elite-led parties to maintain their influence in local and provincial affairs.

Austrian officials duly attempted to broker a compromise between Czech and German demands. The Moravian Compromise of 1905, for example, ended direct national competition by establishing three separate houses in the Moravian diet, representing the aristocracy, the Germans and the Czechs. Voters were registered in one of three curias and could only vote for candidates from that group. The Compromise forestalled electoral reform and bolstered the position of the aristocracy and middle-class elites among both Czechs and Germans. However, it was a static solution that precluded additional electoral reform in the future. The Moravian Compromise seemed to promise a possible model for Bohemia, but negotiations for a comparable Bohemian settlement broke down in 1910. Establishing separate houses for German and Czech delegates threatened to lead to the future autonomy of the German regions of the province. Only in the southern Bohemian town of České Budějovice was a compromise on the Moravian model forged in 1914, enabling Germans to retain influence even after the franchise was expanded to include more Czech voters.[15]

The Bohemian diet was subject to repeated boycotts and acts of obstruction in the period from 1883 until 1913. On 26 July 1913, Emperor Franz Joseph closed the diet because Bohemia was insolvent. Although the financial collapse of the province was due in part to an archaic tax collection system that failed to keep pace with the fiscal demands of a modern state, it was also due to the inability of the various parties in Bohemia to work with each other to resolve crucial problems. The diet was replaced by an executive committee of five Czechs and three Germans, whose responsibility was to restore a balanced account in provincial finances. Thus, national strife contributed to the loss of provincial self-governance, one of the key elements of the Bohemian state right programme.

National Defence Activities, 1900–1914

The struggle between Czechs and Germans took place not only in the political realm but also in the spheres of cultural, demographic, and economic competition. The shift from tangible political gains to the less tangible areas of cultural and economic competition had preceded the Badeni language decrees. It was, however, given further impetus by the crisis that surrounded them and their ultimate failure. Street demonstrations and other tactics perfected during the crisis remained an important means of gaining public recognition and support for particular political positions. The breakdown of normal parliamentary government and the continued stalemate in the Bohemian diet meant that national demands were unlikely to be met through normal political channels. This deflected national work from the political arena into the realm of voluntary associations and local efforts, most of which were not under the control of established political parties. By the 1890s, all political institutions had been designated as either Czech or German. The struggle for control over the agencies of local and provincial government had gone as far as it could without significant compromise between Czechs and Germans. For this reason as well, national competition moved into such areas as language, jobs, demography and property.[16]

Voluntary associations to support nationalist activity had been organized from the late 1860s. The law on voluntary associations required that such societies refrain from political activity; instead, national defence associations claimed a cultural or economic purpose. Their activities ranged from raising money to support minority schools, to organizing market fairs to promote local businesses, promoting tourism, establishing employment offices, organizing lecture series, and publishing calendars and almanacs. In addition, some national defence associations engaged directly in small-scale business activities, such as helping to found an agricultural co-operative or purchasing property (such as a farm, mill or pub) that might fall into the hands of the 'other' national group. The oldest national cultural organizations were the *Deutsche Schulverein* (1880) and the Czech Foundation (*Matice Česká*), founded in 1831. The central German Bohemian association, the *Bund der Deutschen in Böhmen*, was founded in 1894. Regional associations soon followed, oriented toward the protection of German minorities in such areas as the Böhmerwald (Czech: Šumava) in south-west Bohemia or Czech minorities in the north.

These associations and their local branches were run by men who had little experience of the compromises required by parliamentary politics. They engaged in highly inflammatory rhetoric that raised the emotional tenor of nationalist disputes. As Jan Křen has noted, the position of each national camp was hardened as 'professional nationalists' invested their reputations and careers in radical nationalist parties and national protection associations.[17]

To attempt to control and coordinate the activities of national protection associations (and nationalist parties), both Czechs and Germans established national councils at the turn of the century. For the Young Czechs, the Czech National Council was a means of asserting their authority outside electoral politics. It was founded in 1900 but remained dormant in its first years. In 1907, after their electoral defeat, the Young Czechs reorganized the Council, which sought to unite all Czech parties (except the Social Democrats) along with the most important national voluntary associations into one organ that could represent Czech interests in such areas as economic development, school policy, migration and foreign relations. German Bohemians created similar structures, establishing a *Deutscher Volksrat* in 1903, an 'above-party' organization to support unified national policies. These central associations were fairly fragile and only modestly effective in an era of intense competition among political parties and nationalist associations, but they represented one way for the formerly dominant (and more moderate) parties among both Czechs and Germans to attempt to maintain some influence.

One of the main aims of national defence associations was to strengthen the economic basis of national development. Rapid economic development after 1900 spurred competition between Czechs and Germans, while the consolidation of wealth in the largest firms and banks created anxiety among the lower middle classes. Thus, much of the nationalist economic propaganda of the early twentieth century was also fuelled by anti-capitalist sentiment. From 1908 to 1910, Bohemia was riven by nationalist boycotts, sparked originally by complaints over the failure of German judges to respond to suits presented in the Czech language. Demonstrations and brawling by university students in Prague followed. The nationalist parties and defence associations quickly issued calls for a boycott. On the Czech side, this fitted a long-standing tradition of promoting economic self-help and self-sufficiency under the slogan '*svůj k svému*' [each to his own]. Germans responded in kind, flying banners that demanded that Germans buy only at German shops. Both German and Czech businesses appealed to the central government to intervene because the boycotts seriously disrupted business in Bohemia. Among the targets were Jewish firms that until now had successfully resisted being labelled as either 'German' or 'Czech'.[18] The boycott of Czech goods spread even to the German Reich, where Czech beer was boycotted.

Despite the boycotts, by the early twentieth century the Czechs had began to establish a modern industrial economy and a full-fledged financial system, including investment banks to support Czech industry. As a result, their reliance on (and contacts with) German firms decreased. Czech industries and banks sought new markets for their goods and services, and they found they were most competitive in other Slavic countries, particularly in the Balkan peninsula. Therefore, Czech business interests supported the Neo-Slav movement, and their orientation toward Slavic trading partners put them at odds with German businesses, particularly those in the north-west of the province, which retained strong economic links to Germany.

Yet despite this competition, Czech firms found many common interests with German companies. Businesses joined separate Czech or German associations, which often worked together to lobby the government for similar concessions. The five Bohemian chambers of commerce cooperated in putting forward a common platform on such issues as the 1907 renewal of the trade treaty with Hungary.[19] Likewise, Czech and German Agrarian parties supported common legislation designed to aid small farmers, and the Social Democratic parties also cooperated closely with each other.

Significant conflict remained around the issue of continued Czech labour migration into German districts in the borderland. In the coal-mining area around Most (German: Brüx), the Czech population quadrupled between the censuses of 1880 and 1900; an unofficial Czech census suggested a six-fold increase in population.[20] Meanwhile, the German population of Prague had decreased from 15 per cent to 7 per cent of the total population of the capital, a decline in absolute numbers from 38,000 to 32,000.[21] Discussions over a Bohemian compromise were increasingly based on the designation of particular districts as 'German', 'Czech' or 'mixed'. This raised the possibility of national censuses (cadasters) of population and property, and heightened the political importance of demographic change. National associations paid close attention to changes in population or property ownership, which were portrayed as major national victories or defeats. For these reasons, the censuses of 1900 and 1910 provoked sharp campaigns among both Czechs and Germans to encourage citizens to declare their language of daily use as either Czech or German.

Political activity followed. German Bohemian demographer Heinrich Rauchberg recommended that Czech workers be encouraged to assimilate to the higher German culture.[22] Franz Jesser, an official in the *Bund der Deutschen in Böhmen*, argued that 'the national struggle is nothing other than a struggle over space. The Czech nation is attempting to increase its living space at the expense of our living space.' Jesser bemoaned the 'physiological degeneration' of the German population, which showed less vitality than the Czech population. At the same time, he noted the higher level of skills and culture among the Germans and complained that Czech workers undercut the wages of German workers.[23] On their side, the Czech National Council and national protection societies actively promoted 'inner colonization' of the border regions and supported the establishment of Czech businesses, schools and national houses (or meeting places) to strengthen the Czech consciousness of these workers.[24]

The relative tax burden of Czechs and Germans was also the subject of great debate: the legal specialist Friedrich von Wieser argued that German representation in the Bohemian diet should be proportional to the higher taxes they paid.[25] The Czech National Council replied that even though the Czechs paid less in direct taxes, they paid more in indirect taxes on consumer goods. In addition, the National Council argued that German income was made possible by Czech labour and that the economic inequality of the two nationalities was the result of centuries of oppression that had yet to be overcome.[26]

In addition to local issues, Czechs and Germans also sought international allies for their struggle. German Bohemians embraced the alliance with Germany and found support from the Pan-German League. Czech political leaders sought foreign support primarily from Russia and France. Karel Kramář advocated a revival of Slavic solidarity, Neo-Slavism, and sought Russian support. The Slavic Conference held in Prague in 1908 had modest results but did lead to cultural and business contacts for the Czechs.[27] Czechs focused on efforts to gain favorable coverage in the foreign press. Because the Bohemian problem was dismissed as an isolated and particular conflict, Kramář attempted to present it as part of a European-wide struggle against Pan-Germanism.[28] The Czech National Council also sought to promote communication with Czech immigrant communities abroad, particularly in the United States. Not only were Czechs and Germans at odds with each other in Bohemia, but they also portrayed their conflict as central to a European-wide clash of Pan-Germanism and Pan-Slavism.

Thus, national conflict in Bohemia was heightened in the two decades preceding the outbreak of the First World War by constant skirmishing over issues of demography, economic development and even the different foreign orientations of Czechs and Germans. National competition was viewed as a 'zero-sum game' in which gains for one nationality represented losses for the other.

The First World War

By the advent of the First World War, the Bohemian diet had been suspended. Czechs and Germans had created separate but parallel societies in Bohemia, and relations between them remained tense. The Austrian parliament had also been suspended in the spring of 1914 by Prime Minister Karl Stürgkh, and it was not recalled until May 1917. Representative government had been replaced by authoritarian rule, which provided an opportunity during the war for the government and its allies among German political leaders to attempt to impose a solution to the Bohemian problem. German Bohemian nationalists such as K.H. Wolf had their own 'internal war aims'[29] and saw Czechs as potential saboteurs. At Easter 1916, they put forward a programme to Germanize the Austrian state by separating Galicia from it (to reduce the Slavic population), dividing Bohemia into Czech and German regions, and declaring German the official state language of Austria. A similar proposal was discussed by ministers in the Austrian government in 1917. Continued Habsburg military dependence on Germany lent credance to Friedrich Naumann's call for *Mitteleuropa*, which many Bohemian Germans welcomed.

Although the majority of Czechs entered the Great War supporting the continued existence of Austria-Hungary, a few, like Tomáš Masaryk, recognized that the defeat of Germany and Austria-Hungary could provide an opportunity to reorganize Central Europe along national lines. Masaryk feared that a victory for the Central Powers would give Germany hegemony over the smaller nations of the region, and therefore, he pledged to work for an Entente victory.

Masaryk, who fled to Switzerland in the autumn of 1914 to avoid arrest on charges of treason, settled in London where he mounted an impressive propaganda campaign to win Allied support for the cause of Czechoslovak independence. In conjunction with Edvard Beneš and Milan Štefánik, Masaryk organized the Czechoslovak National Committee to work for independence. Supporters such as R. W. Seton-Watson in London helped Masaryk gain access to a wide public audience through his lectures at the School of Slavonic Studies, and the journal *The New Europe* promoted Masaryk's idea that small, democratic states in east-central and south-eastern Europe could form a bulwark against German authoritarianism and (after 1917) Russian Bolshevism.

In Bohemia itself, politicians like Karel Kramář organized the 'Mafie' to help support Masaryk's work abroad. The Mafie transmitted information abroad, helped to organize military desertion on the Eastern front, and promoted passive resistance at home. Kramář and his colleague Alois Rašín were arrested in 1915 and sentenced to death for treason; their sentences were commuted by Emperor Karl in January 1917 and revoked in July. When the Reichsrat reconvened in May 1917, the leaders of the Czech Union balanced their declaration of loyalty to the Habsburg state with a demand that Austria be reorganized along federal lines. One radical nationalist however, Antonín Kalina, called for Czechoslovak independence and insisted that the Czechs 'deny most emphatically any responsibility for the war, which was not only forced upon our people, but which was even directed against us'.[30]

The Czech population grew increasingly restive with shortages of basic foodstuffs, restrictions on free speech and assembly, political machinations on the part of German Bohemians, and the loss of life that accompanied military defeats in the war.[31] The example of the Russian Revolution helped to spur increased activity by both national groups and Social Democrats. Public assemblies, such as those celebrating the quincentenary of the death of Jan Hus in 1915 or the fiftieth anniversary of the founding of the National Theatre in May 1918, provided opportunities for the public to demonstrate its opposition to government policy. Economic hardships prompted Františka Plamínková, a prominent Czech feminist associated with the National Socialist Party, to organize an 'economic council' to encourage Czechs to become more self-sufficient economically.[32] The economic basis for Czechoslovak independence was now debated. Economist Jan Koloušek, an ally of Masaryk, outlined the economic basis for future Czech autonomy in the monthly *Naše Doba*.[33] His research provided support for Masaryk's claim that Czechoslovakia had the material resources necessary for independence. Czech Social Democratic leader Bohumíl Šmeral countered that the Bohemian crownlands were not sufficiently industrialized for independence as a socialist state.

Masaryk was convinced that the Czech nation was too small to exist as an independent state without the addition of the Slovaks, and Masaryk's doctrine of 'Czechoslovakism' sought to create a national state of Czechs and Slovaks, whom he saw as two branches of the same nation. In such a state, the Germans would be a minority. For this reason, German Bohemians countered the declaration of Czechoslovak independence on 28 October 1918 with their own declaration of independence for *Deutschböhmen* on 29 October. They hoped that this state, which they saw as a constituent part of *Deutschösterreich*, could become affiliated with Germany.[34] The German Bohemian independence movement was put down with force by the new Czechoslovak army in late 1918 and early 1919, and many symbols of the Habsburg monarchy were destroyed by Czech mobs.[35] Attempts by German Bohemian nationalists to re-organize Bohemian and Austrian government to ensure their own dominance were thus laid to waste, and instead of a majority position, Germans in Bohemia found themselves as minorities in the new Czechoslovak state.

Conclusion

The ongoing and seemingly irreconcilable strife in Bohemia significantly undermined Austrian government from 1897 until the demise of the Monarchy in 1918. It prevented the normal functioning of parliament and thereby diminished the possibility that Austria might develop a political system in which parliament was seen as a full partner in governance. It harmed relations with Hungary by preventing considered debate of joint budgets and trade treaties, particularly in 1897, and allowed the Hungarians to press their own national claims more successfully. The conflict also detracted from the Czech goal of strengthening the self-government of Bohemia. The impasse in the Bohemian diet weakened it as a governing institution. Many political struggles and decisions devolved to the bureaucracy, and Austria became a more emphatically bureaucratic state as a result.

Attempts at compromise had been broached in 1871, 1890, 1897 and 1910. The Hohenwart compromise of 1871 and the Badeni language ordinances sought to make the Czechs equal partners in governing and administering Bohemia. The negotiations for the *Punktace* of 1890 attempted to divide the administrative apparatus of the province so that each national community could enjoy the fruits of self-governance. After the failure of the *Punktace*, German nationalists were split between those who called for the division of Bohemia and those, like Schönerer and Wolf, who sought Germanization. Czech nationalists claimed the right to dominate Bohemia on the basis of historic state right and demographic dominance and were equally unwilling to share power. Any party that attempted to negotiate a compromise after 1897 was accused of betraying national goals. Compromise and cooperation were politically risky in an era when nationalism was seen as the ultimate value.

Much nationalist rhetoric was unleashed not only to attack the opposing side in a conflict, but also (and sometimes more importantly) as a tool by which new parties could assert their legitimacy and gain political support within both the Czech and German camps. This escalation of rhetoric, which included labelling the opposing side as 'our national enemy', contributed to a climate of intolerance.

Outside the immediate realm of politics, the 'small national war' that concentrated on cultural, economic and demographic competition regularly touched the daily lives of Czechs, Germans and Jews in Bohemia. Simplistic negative stereotypes dominated the highly dramatized news coverage of various clashes. The common Bohemian identity that had been shared in the mid-nineteenth century was eroded and replaced by more sharply defined national identities, which negated much of the common experience and interests of the inhabitants of the province. Since both sides could portray themselves as a 'minority' (Germans within Bohemia, Czechs within Austria), they chose to ignore the political processes associated with representative government and engage in cultural work or direct action instead.[36] Language use became symbolic of a whole host of other issues, including access to jobs and education, and cultural and political dominance.

NOTES

1. Jan Havránek, 'Snahy německé buržoazie o rozdělení Čech na sklonku 19. století', *Zápisky katedry Československých dějin a archivních studia* (1961) pp. 19–30.

2. On the designation of nationality by the language of daily use, see Emil Brix, *Die Umgangssprache in Altösterreich zwischen Agitation und Assimilation* (Vienna, 1982).
3. August von Wotowa, *Der Deutsche Schulverein, 1880–1905* (Vienna, 1905).
4. Jan Křen, *Konfliktní společnost. Češi a Němci, 1780–1918* (Prague, 1990) p. 225.
5. Andrew Whiteside, *The Socialism of Fools. Georg Ritter von Schönerer and Austrian Pan-Germanism* (Berkeley, 1975).
6. Lothar Höbelt, *Kornblume und Kaiseradler. Die deutschfreiheitliche Parteien Altösterreichs, 1882–1918* (Vienna, 1993) p. 56.
7. The standard work on the crisis is Berthold Sutter, *Die Badenische Sprachenverordnungen von 1897*, 2 vols (Graz, 1960 and 1965).
8. For a description of parliamentary obstruction, see Mark Twain, 'Stirring Times in Austria', *Harper's New Monthly Magazine*, 96 (March 1898) pp. 530–40.
9. Quoted in Bruce M. Garver, *The Young Czech Party 1874–1901 and the Emergence of a Multi-Party System* (New Haven, 1978) p. 252. The letter appeared on 31 October 1897.
10. See Pieter M. Judson, *Exclusive Revolutionaries. Liberal Politics, Social Experience, and National Identity in the Austrian Empire, 1848–1914* (Ann Arbor, 1996).
11. See T. Mills Kelly, 'Czech Radical Nationalism in the Era of Universal Manhood Suffrage, 1907–1914', (Ph.D. George Washington University, 1996).
12. Judson, *Exclusive Revolutionaries*, pp. 255–57; and John W. Boyer, *Culture and Political Crisis in Vienna. Christian Socialism in Power, 1897–1918* (Chicago, 1995) p. 40.
13. Whiteside, *The Socialism of Fools*, pp. 203–4.
14. Garver, *The Young Czech Party*, chap. 10: 'The Young Czechs and the Successor Parties'.
15. Emil Brix, 'Der böhmische Ausgleich in Budweis', *Österreichische Osthefte* 23 (1982) pp. 225–48. See also the forthcoming study by Jeremy King of České Budějovice.
16. Pieter M. Judson, '"Not Another Square Foot!" German Liberalism and the Rhetoric of National Ownership in Nineteenth-Century Austria', *Austrian History Yearbook*, 26 (1995) pp. 83–98; and Heinrich Rauchberg, *Die Nationalbesitzstand in Böhmen*, 2 vols (Prague, 1905).
17. Křen, *Konfliktní společnost*, p. 274.
18. Catherine Albrecht, 'The Rhetoric of Economic Nationalism in the Boycott Campaigns of the late Habsburg Monarchy', *Austrian History Yearbook*, 32 (2001).
19. Catherine Albrecht, 'Chambers of Commerce and Czech-German Relations in the Late Nineteenth Century', *Bohemia*, 38 (1997) pp. 298–310.

20. Křen, *Konfliktní společnost*, p. 316.

21. Gary B. Cohen, *The Politics of Ethnic Survival. Germans in Prague, 1861–1914* (Princeton, 1981) pp. 92–93.

22. Heinrich Rauchberg, 'Die nationale Besitzstand in Böhmen und die Wanderbewegung', *Deutsche Arbeit*, 2 (1902–3) pp. 585–625; and Rauchberg, 'Die Zählungverhältnisse der Deutschen und der Tschechen in Böhmen', ibid., pp. 1–33.

23. Franz Jesser, *Das Wesen der nationalen Kampfes in den Sudetenländern* (Vienna, n.d. [1912?]) pp. 11–14.

24. See Mark Cornwall, 'The Struggle on the Czech-German Language Border 1880–1940', *The English Historical Review*, 109 (1994) pp. 914–51.

25. Friedrich Wieser, 'Die deutsche Steuerleistung und die öffentliche Haushalt in Böhmen', *Deutsche Arbeit* (1903) pp. 1–28, 117–47, 205–34.

26. *Národnostní poplatnost a zemské hospodářství v král. českém. Odpověd' na úvahu Profa. Dra. Bar. Wiesera* (Prague, 1905).

27. Paul Vyšný, *Neoslavism and the Czechs, 1898–1914* (Cambridge, 1977).

28. Karel Kramář, 'Europe and the Bohemian Question', *The National Review*, 40 (1902) pp. 183–205.

29. Boyer, *Culture and Political Crisis in Vienna*, p. 377.

30. *Naše Revoluce*, VI (1929–30) pp. 157–59.

31. Claire Nolte, 'Ambivalent Patriots: Czech Culture in the Great War', in Aviel Roshwald and Richard Stites (eds), *European Culture in the Great War. The Arts, Entertainment, and Propaganda, 1914–1918* (Cambridge, 1999) pp. 162–75.

32. Albína Honzáková (ed.), *Kniha života, práce a osobnost F.F. Plamínkové. Sborník k 60. narozeninám* (Prague, 1935) pp. 47, 75–76.

33. Jan Koloušek, 'Poplatní síla zemí českých', *Naše Doba*, 22 (1915), pp. 1–6; see also Kaloušek, 'Výživa českých zemí vlastními plodinami', *Naše Doba*, 21 (1913–14), pp. 1079–88.

34. Karl Bahm, 'The Inconvenience of Nationality: German Bohemians, the Disintegration of the Habsburg Monarchy, and the Attempt to Create a "Sudeten German" Identity', *Nationalities Papers*, 27 (1999) pp. 375–405.

35. Nancy M. Wingfield, 'Conflicting Constructions of Memory: Attacks on Statues of Joseph II in the Bohemian Lands after the Great War', *Austrian History Yearbook*, 28 (1997) pp. 147–71.

36. Jiří Kořalka, 'Mehrheiten und Minderheiten in den politischen Vertretungskörpern der böhmischen Ländern', in Kořalka, *Tschechen in Habsburgerreich und in Europe, 1815–1914. Sozialgeschichtliche Zusammenhänge der neuzeitlichen Nationsbildung und der Nationalitätenfrage in den böhmischen Ländern* (Munich, 1991) pp. 126–74.

5

The Hungarian Political Scene

F. Tibor Zsuppán

It may be remembered that, although Hungary had gained consider-able powers of local self-government in 1867 with its own parlia-mentary and local government system, it had not acquired total independence from the rest of the Habsburg Monarchy. The Magyar participants in the formulation of the 1867 *Ausgleich* or Compro-mise had nonetheless been hopeful that Hungary's full independence would, with favourable circumstances, evolve with the passing of time. The Hungarian government's defeat in 1889 over the issue of Lajos Kossuth's citizenship and similar events had served to strengthen hope into near certainty, sapping the ability to govern of the Liberal (*Szabadelvű*) Party itself, which had always emphasized maintaining the *Ausgleich*. As a result, by 1904 opposition parties were united in demanding that Franz Joseph concede greater recog-nition to Magyar sentiment and nationality aspirations in the Common Army, an important step on the road to independence. It was primarily on this issue that the Prime Minister István Tisza was to fight and lose the election of 1905. His defeat, due in large part to his high-minded refusal to conduct yet another electoral campaign of corruption and intimidation like those of the pre-1901 years, would leave Franz Joseph to face fifteen months, in 1905–6, of fruitless attempts to bring changes to the Magyar political scene. Significantly, Franz Joseph's attempt then to introduce suffrage reform would be intended not so much to further democracy, but to combat Magyar nationalism (by enfranchising non-Magyars, among others) and thus bolster the *Ausgleich*. Conversely, it would be principally for that very reason that Magyar nationalists would oppose suffrage reform, as endangering their hoped-for progression towards independence.

Of course, the constitutional crisis of these years was not a sudden one. It had its past history, going back at least to the 1898 difficulty in fixing the 'quota', the ratio according to which Austria and Hungary each contributed to the common expenses of the Monarchy.

Then there were the tariff problems of December 1902[1]; and finally the issue of enlarging the Common Army which erupted in earnest in 1903. This latter issue highlighted more clearly than any other the fundamental flaw in the Dual Monarchy: that the Monarchy's two halves had difficulty in cohabiting within the 1867 *Ausgleich* and that neither the Viennese Reichsrat nor the Budapest parliament represented ultimate sovereignty which, as the 1905–6 events were to show, belonged to Franz Joseph himself. His power was nowhere proclaimed more unequivocally than in Fundamental Law no.145, paragraph 5, of the Austrian version of the *Ausgleich*, where it was stipulated that he exercised 'supreme command over the armed forces' as well as having the 'power of declaring war and concluding peace'. The Hungarian version, Law XII of 1867, paragraphs 12 and 13, nominally weakened the sovereign's rights over the army's reorganization, enlargement and geographical use by making them conditional on parliamentary approval. The discrepancy between the two versions was illuminating.

In September 1903, Franz Joseph insisted that the Budapest parliament pass a bill raising the number of recruits by 20 per cent. The opposition parties countered by using filibustering tactics in the Lower House. When these in turn were countered by the Tisza government bringing in new standing orders for parliament on 18 November 1904, the die was cast for a full-blown constitutional crisis. The vote introducing the new standing orders was pre-arranged as an ambush: at a signal from the president of the Lower House—a raised handkerchief—Tisza's supporters leapt to their feet and the president declared the vote to have been carried by acclamation, and postponed the sitting. On its resumption nearly a month later, the frustrated opposition smashed the chamber's furniture in revenge, an angry turning point followed by a radical abandonment of party loyalties which in effect destroyed the omnipotent Liberal Party. The dissolution of parliament on 3 January 1905 heralded the *de facto* commencement of the struggle between the Crown and the Magyar parties. Three weeks later—and by coincidence almost simultaneously with the events of 'Bloody Sunday' in Russia, whose after-shocks would be felt in Hungary during the autumn—the parliamentary elections were duly held over the customary ten-day period, allowing the authorities to deploy the military to assist the civil power in successive batches of constituencies.

The winter timing and conditions were not the only unusual circumstance of the 1905 general election. István Tisza, the Prime

NEM VÁRT AKADÁLY

'AN UNEXPECTED OBSTACLE': As István Tisza's horse (the Liberal Party) jumps over the river (the Constitution) he is caught by the branch of a tree (Public Opinion). Cartoon from *Bolond Istók*, 11 December 1904.

Minister since November 1903, seeing the growing number of influential defectors from his Liberal Party and the first signs that sections of the countryside's political class were beginning to respond to the defectors' nationalist slogans, confined his intervention, unusually, to issuing circulars to his regional *főispáns* (prefects), merely urging them to maintain law and order for the elections. The customary bribery and cheating at elections, normally coordinated by the government, was this time left in the hands of a myriad of interests at local level, where the desire to maintain the Compromise still largely survived. Despite their efforts, however, the Independence Party and its allies in the Coalition (the Seceding Liberal Party, the People's Party, and the New Party) constituted the majority in the new parliament. Franz Joseph therefore refused to invite them to form the government, lest they insist on enacting such contentious reforms as the introduction of the Magyar language of command into those regiments of the Common Army recruited from Hungary—viewed by him not only as a threat to the status quo, but as a catalyst for nationalist sentiment. A reluctant Tisza was prevailed upon to carry on as prime minister until the middle of June, when Franz Joseph impatiently chose to resolve the constitutional crisis by un-parliamentary means. On 18 June 1905, he imposed a cabinet under a prime minister (Géza Fejérváry) notable mainly for his zealous loyalty to the Crown, and with a minister of interior, József Kristóffy, who was held to be sufficiently adept at political manoeuvring to be able to solve Hungary's endless constitutional wranglings with both Austria and the Crown. The Coalition parties who had won the election were powerless to do other than offer passive resistance.

The plan which Kristóffy presented to the Crown in July 1905 envisaged the introduction into Hungary of universal suffrage, which he judged 'would be in the interests of the Crown' as well as the country. He argued that if the Coalition parties were allowed to make the running, their nationalist demands would disrupt the Common Army, and the very foundations of the dualist system would be undermined. The introduction of universal suffrage, on the other hand, would swamp and 'eliminate the very elements who had opposed the Crown's interests, and the recurrent constitutional wrangles between the two halves of the Monarchy' would come to an end. Such a policy would 'capture the allegiance of the people'—including, crucially, the non-Magyars—with its generosity, and would 'break with those who had usually rallied around the throne in the past', but who now were opposing it—in other words, the Magyar gentry.[2]

We who have enjoyed universal male and female suffrage estab-lished after the First World War find it difficult to grasp the political and social turmoil into which a country, suddenly introduced to the prospect of universal male suffrage, could be thrown. It has to be remembered that the elections held up to this time—from 1848 irregularly, then from 1867 at regular three- and subsequently five-yearly intervals—had invariably been manipulated by the country's political elite of aristocrats, the middle- and lower-ranking nobility, their allies in the urban and rural intelligentsia, and industrial and commercial forces. An electorate formed of a mere 6.5 per cent of the total population and scattered through 413 unequally distributed single-member constituencies could with ease be corrupted or intimidated into supporting socially and politically conservative majorities, whose main motivation lay in preserving or preferably extending ancient privileges against the Habsburgs and the non-Magyars. Equally, there had always been the not entirely negligible argument put forward by opponents of universal suffrage, that Western European nations themselves had refrained from over-hasty political enfranchisement of their own citizens, an example which the Hungarians should also follow, especially as there had been no extension of the suffrage in Hungary since 1874.

The anxiety provoked, therefore, by Kristóffy's proposals brought about the main result desired by the Crown. The Coalition parties did tone down their demands for more Hungarian rights in the Common Army and for an independent Hungarian trading area. At the same time, they were forced in turn to agree that they would legislate a limited suffrage bill if they were actually entrusted with the government. Six months later, on 4 April 1906, it was under just such circumstances that the Coalition was to promise the Crown that its constitutional demands would be suspended until after the new suffrage bill had been put into effect.

During the winter of 1905–6 painful political conclusions had been drawn by the two opposing camps. The Crown was forced to realize that the predominant weight of Hungarian public opinion was not going to accept reforms imposed by Vienna. Groups that could be enticed to come out openly in favour of Kristóffy's reforms were limited to the Hungarian Social Democrats (a section of the Second Socialist International), freemason lodges, radical sociologists and the majority of the politically aware non-Magyar sections of the population. As local government, including the running of elections, was still in the hands of the old Magyar administration, which was itself involved in passive resistance to the unparliamentary government (and with some success, though gradually waning over time), it became clear that Kristóffy's reforms could only be realized through a state of emergency or by a *coup d'état*. The imposition of universal suffrage in both halves of the Monarchy was already being discussed by elements in Franz Ferdinand's circle. Indeed, by now Franz Joseph himself felt that the only resource that he had against the recalcitrant Lower House of the Hungarian parliament was to dissolve it. This, indeed, was shortly effected by an army unit, commanded by a Honvéd general acting as a 'Royal Kommisär', on 19 February 1906.

During the period of passive resistance, which had been announced by the Coalition on 21 June 1905, the Fejérváry government had gradually tightened its control. The salaries paid to local government employees were discontinued (18 November); political freedoms which had gradually been extended since 1867, such as selling newspapers on the streets, were now suspended (6 February 1906); and by March, networks of paid secret informants were being organized in large towns. The 10,000 strong gendarmerie was deployed nationwide to oversee law and order, and now became sole arbiters over the holding of public meetings (hitherto an elected officer of local government or *szolgabíró* had decided such matters). Celebrations planned for 15 March—the anniversary of the outbreak of the 1848 revolution—were banned in advance. Such was the fear among the Fejérváry government's commissioners that they dared not appear in public without armed bodyguards[3]—a feature that had not been seen in Hungarian public life since at least 1860. The events of 1905–6 were not to pass into oblivion quickly, but seemed to herald subsequent oppression, authoritarianism and, ultimately—after 1918—near-totalitarianism. Resorting to the gendarmerie on a large scale would feature again in 1912, when new army estimates were announced, but then continued throughout the duration of the First World War and into the anti-communist and anti-Semitic excesses of 1919–21.

Yet for the time being, the final outcome of the fifteen-month constitutional struggle between Crown and parliament was the compromise of 4 April 1906. In order to avoid the idea of winners and losers, and a repetition of the constitutional crisis, the agreement was not made public until 1909. The new compromise suspended plans and demands on both sides regarding the Common Army, the monarch's sole stipulation being that universal male suffrage should be introduced into Hungary.[4] The uneasy lull continued with the outcome in 1906 of new elections (see Table 2), which gave the Coalition parties another decisive majority, but saw their success offset in parliament by the Crown nominating its confidant, Sándor

Wekerle, as Prime Minister, and Gyula Andrássy the Younger as the Minister of the Interior—the latter entrusted with the stipulated electoral reform. It was this crucial issue that had already been the focus of all the hopes and fears of the respective political forces. The Crown and its supporters saw in it the probable salvation of the *Ausgleich*. Hungarian opinion, however, was less clear-cut. All parties hitherto represented in parliament (Liberals, Independents etc) resented it as an imposed burden, an obstacle on the path to independence—since it would give the non-Magyars an equal voice in affairs—and a threat, in that it would give a voice to the Social Democratic Party, hitherto excluded from parliament. It was therefore an imposition which they fully intended to sabotage.

Although late in development compared to the rest of Europe, the Social Democratic Party, with its base in the trade unions and its links with the Second International, was indeed becoming an element on the Hungarian political scene which could not be overlooked. Its membership was and would remain of a reformist rather than revolutionary persuasion—hence its rift with those left-wing factions who were beginning to flirt with ideas of anarcho-syndicalism. But its overall significance was clear from the fact that trade union membership had quadrupled within a two-year period (1903–5).

A shift in attitudes was also emerging among the peasantry. Even though the socialist leadership paid scant attention to the problems of the small-holding peasants or of the landless agricultural labourers who therefore remained unorganized, the peasantry's underlying dissatisfaction, following the large-scale labour disputes of the 1890s, presented yet another potential threat to the social and political fabric of the unreformed *Ausgleich*. In 1906–8, some unexpected by-election results on the Hungarian Great Plain—few in number but possibly straws in the wind—demonstrated to Andrássy that the peasant voters were becoming ready to abandon traditional deference towards their political betters and vote on class or nationality lines instead.[5] This was a potentially significant development, given that small-holding peasants, living on and amongst latifundia sprawling over one-quarter of all arable land, represented approximately a third of the population.[6]

While, as we saw earlier, in 1906 the pressure against the Habsburgs —for independence—was temporarily abandoned, pressure against non-Magyars was, on the contrary, intensified. This was partly because the Magyar Coalition in power was strongly nationalist, but partly a response to the increasing politicization of the non-Magyars

Table 2. The Elections to the Hungarian Parliament 1905, 1906, 1910

Parties	Seats
1905[1]	
Independence Party	166
Liberal Party (*Szabadelvűpárt*)	159
Seceding Liberal Party (*Andrássy the Younger*)	27
People's Party	25
New Party (*Bánffy*)	12
Independent non-party	14
Romanian nationalist	8
Slovak nationalist	1
Serb nationalist	1
Total	**413**
1906[2]	
Independence Party	254
Constitution Party (*Andrássy the Younger*)	85
People's Party	33
Independent non-party	15
Romanian National Party (*contested 44 constituencies*)	16
Slovak National Party (*contested 18 constituencies*)	7
Serb National Party	2
Total	**412**
1910[3]	
Party of National Work (*Munkapárt—István Tisza*)	258
Independence parties (*three factions together*)	107
Constitution Party (*Andrássy the Younger*)	21
People's Party	13
Non-Magyar deputies (*together*)	8
Democratic Party (*Vázsonyi*)	2
Smallholders' Party	3
Christian Socials	1
Total	**413**

1. The registered electors numbered 1,057, 215 in 1905, whilst in 1906 it was 1,085, 323. Successful Romanian members of parliament attracted 17,613, the Slovak and Serbian members 3,034 and 2,843 votes respectively.
2. Non-Magyar parties contested a total of 79 constituencies and received a total of 65,000 votes.
3. Non-Magyar parties contested 55 constituencies in 1910, receiving a total of 42,590 votes. All non-Magyar registered voters number 432,374, or 40.4 per cent of the entire electorate of Hungary. Even if many must have abstained from voting at all, the majority of the predominantly non-Magyar electorate of the 47 remaining constituencies where the non-Magyar candidates were unsuccessful in 1910 must have voted for the successful Magyar candidates. The explanation for this lies partly in widespread intimidation and venality in many constituencies, but probably also owes much to non-Magyar voters' long-standing perception of the Magyar political class as the appropriate beneficiaries of a parliamentary charade with which non-Magyars were not vitally concerned.

themselves. They had won one or two electoral successes thanks to some extent to the fact that the government had, unusually, practised little of its traditional corruption and intimidation during the elections (a mistake that it would not repeat in the 1910 elections). Thus any concession which the ruling Magyar Coalition might be prepared to make to the non-Magyar nationalities was slight. While the liberal principles which had guided the *Ausgleich*'s 'founding fathers' had emphasized that the non-Magyars were totally equal members of the indivisible Magyar nation, the emphasis had now shifted to the principle of the equality of *individuals*, rather than the equality of nationalities as *groups*. The eventual creation of a Magyar nation state formed of one political nation (the Hungarian) and with a legal basis framed already four decades earlier (in the 1868 Nationality Law), remained the goal, therefore, of the camp of the two Tiszas or that of their opponents, such as Andrássy the Younger, Apponyi, and Kossuth the Younger.

Indeed, economic and demographic developments evident from the 1910 census seemed to offer support for Magyar nationalist aspirations. While the agricultural sector and its population remained of course important, a more significant promise for the future was perceived in the country's increasing urbanization and industrialization. For not only would increasing industrialization diminish Hungary's economic dependency on the Austrian half of the Monarchy; it would also accelerate the process of Magyarization through the usual normative processes (such as education), without the use of expressly repressive measures by the state. Magyar politicians also noted with satisfaction the ethnic picture which emerged in the 1910 census figures. Magyars now constituted 54.5 per cent of the population (a 3.1 per cent increase in relation to 1900); and the percentage of non-Magyars was stagnating or falling, either due to their greater rate of emigration or due to their increasing assimilation to the Magyars through urbanization and industrialization. It has been calculated that between 1890 and 1914, 400,000 Germans, 300,000 Slovaks, 200,000 Jews, 80,000 Serbs and Croats and 50,000 Romanians became Magyars.[7] A further two million non-Magyars were able to speak Magyar—in itself, seemingly a good omen.

In spite of these developments, however, the picture was not uniquely favourable to Magyar aspirations. The trend of Magyarization was perceived to be in danger of slowing down as increasing national consciousness manifested itself among the large territorial blocks of

Hungary's Romanian, Slovak and Serb populations, concentrated on Hungary's periphery close to the actual Romanian and Serbian states. The threat to the integrity of Hungary's borders was evident. And it is noteworthy that even in 1914 the language of instruction in no less than 2,170 primary schools was exclusively Romanian, while in 'Slovakia' 16 per cent of young children received instruction only in Slovak.[8] The latter figure is of course, not high, but it is nonetheless clear that this was not a case of forced Magyarization when compared to the assimilation enforced by totalitarian states of more recent times. Similarly, the free competitive economy of Austria-Hungary was not advantageous only to the Magyars. In Slovakia and Transylvania since the 1880s the growth of Slovak and Romanian financial institutions had markedly contributed to land acquisition by non-Magyars, whereas projects state-financed for purely Magyar nationalist reasons began in earnest only around 1907.

Given therefore the confused implications of the demographic and economic picture, the increasing and diverse national consciousness within Hungary's borders, and the small but significant non-Magyar electoral successes of 1905 and 1906, fears began to grow within the Wekerle ministry that parliamentary institutions in Hungary might soon prove to be wholly unworkable. Meanwhile, István Tisza was ever more deeply convinced of the danger of universal suffrage. In his view the emergence in party politics of class and nationality issues, the latter exacerbated by religious differences which tended to coincide with national ones, could—and here he noted the Austrian example—only diminish and even destroy the prospect of a Magyar nation state.[9] His outlook was shared, among others, by some authors of propaganda, published from 1906 onwards in pamphlet form.[10] This calculated that, should universal male suffrage be introduced in Hungary, as many as 100 non-Magyars and at least 25 socialists would be returned to the Lower House (out of a total of 413), as well as an unknown number of Christian Socials subject to Roman Catholic and, often, anti-Semitic influence.

To the Magyar nationalists, then, it was imperative that attempts at reform be back-pedalled and diverted, and promptly. In March 1908, Andrássy persuaded Franz Joseph to accept introduction of the principle of plural voting on the Belgian model (some men having more than one vote), and in May secured the King's acceptance of the continuation of an open ballot. Andrássy's timing was good: the monarch needed relatively little persuasion, amidst the worries of the Bosnian annexation crisis and the difficulties that had emerged with the multiplicity of parties in the Reichsrat following the introduction of universal suffrage in Austria.[11] It seemed clear that universal suffrage would endanger the Monarchy's internal stability even in Hungary. Andrássy's calculations also took into account evidence that had been gathered suggesting that if the electoral status quo was maintained, the non-Magyar electorate would still vote for official candidates in sufficient numbers as before.[12] For as yet, non-Magyar politicians had failed to unite and act jointly, and were in the event to remain divided until 1915.

In parliament, however, with the abandonment of parliamentary reform at the end of 1908, there was no longer anything to hold the Coalition government together, and the Coalition partners quarrelled. The Independence Party began voicing nationalist demands, especially the setting up of an independent Magyar note-issuing bank. A fraction of that party under Gyula Justh (and later Mihály Károlyi) began to concentrate on the pursuit of democratic reforms, while other reformist groups, such as the Social Democrats, Oszkár Jászi's middle-class Radicals, freemasons and feminists, began to turn to a variety of West European models for the reform of Hungary.[13]

The gradual return now onto the political scene of István Tisza may be seen as symbolically marking the end of the four-year period, from 1906 to 1910, of unsuccessful attempts by Franz Joseph to reform the eastern half of his domain. Tisza represented the continuation of the old, pre-1905 Liberal tradition which could see no prosperity for Hungary other than through the *Ausgleich* and enjoying the advantages of shared status as a Great Power. Upholding the *Ausgleich* would be the main preoccupation of the government he was shortly to form. In February 1910 he founded his Party of National Work (*Munkapárt*) and in June of that year, with about 800,000 males voting in open ballots (and with the presence of about one soldier or gendarme to every thirteen voters), he gained the majority of seats in parliament (see Table 2). Parliamentary time was now concentrated on matters left in abeyance for ten years: legislation on increased army estimates, a higher contingent for the Common Army, emergency wartime enabling measures. Not wishing to appear unmindful of the need for internal reforms, Tisza also had a leisurely electoral bill prepared (eventually passed only in 1913), envisaging a slightly increased electorate and use of the secret ballot in urban constituencies. In the event, the law was never to be put into practice, for Hungary failed to have a general election between June 1910 and January 1920. These bills were, for tactical reasons, handled in the main by figurehead, largely insignificant politicians, supporters of both Tisza and the monarch, such as László Lukács and Karoly Khuen-Héderváry. Tisza himself meanwhile occupied to important effect the most significant position of the time, the Speaker's chair of the Lower House. The chair's authority was exploited in order to silence the Magyar nationalist opposition. Their filibustering, which for so long had delayed legislation, in particular the army estimates, was now put to an end by the introduction of stiff standing orders and by the forcible removal from the chamber of those whose obstruction of legislation 'justified' it.[14]

Yet by June 1913 it was no longer necessary for Tisza to play such a role, and he assumed the office of prime minister (which he was not to quit until May 1917). By this time, on the eve of the First World War, he seems to have been convinced that he alone was capable of prosecuting the Magyar national interest within the Monarchy and steering parliament through the limited reforms that, by now, he was aware were inevitable: the socialists could not be excluded from parliament forever, and non-Magyars' aspirations must be met to some limited degree. To this latter end, Tisza held exploratory talks with leaders of the Transylvanian Romanians in both December 1912 and February 1914. It is significant, however, that one consideration of these talks—the possible position of Romania in the balance of international alignments—reveals the predominance of his old concerns and the tactical element in his discussion of reforms. It is noteworthy too that the reforms he envisaged—and his proposals remained unchanged even after the outbreak of war—were extremely modest, being largely confined to a willingness to respond to Romanian complaints over education and language usage in administrative practice. This the Romanian leaders found inadequate: they demanded in addition the delineation of fifty Romanian constituencies on nationalist lines, the nomination of a number of Romanian prefects, and the creation of some Romanian secretaries of state.[15] These demands Tisza rejected. While the Transylvanian Romanians were not yet themselves, in general, consciously moving towards the goal of a separate territorial entity, Tisza was certainly not unaware of that risk. His approaches in the first half of 1914 to the Croats were likewise rejected. The failure of these conciliatory attempts can hardly have been unanticipated. On the eve of the war the non-Magyars of the country's southern *comitats* (counties) were in a high state of excitement following the Balkan Wars: for example, many young potential recruits were slipping across the frontier to join the colours of their co-nationals in Serbia and Romania, rather than respond to the call-up to Austria-Hungary's Common Army.

Although we now think of Franz Ferdinand's assassination on 28 June 1914 as the thunderclap that heralded the storm to come, in Hungary in fact it stirred little public emotion. He had, after all, been unpopular, particularly since 1912 when the Magyar aristocracy had obtained relatively detailed, and to them highly displeasing, inform- ation regarding the plans which he aimed to implement on acceding to the throne. Recent historiography on the subject, based on the archives of Franz Ferdinand, reveals that the Hungarian political leaders did have grounds for deep anxiety.[16] For the heir to the throne had a close rapport by this time with certain leaders of Hungary's Romanians and Slovaks who submitted various plans to his office. Perhaps the most detailed of these, dated 25 September 1911, by the Slovak Milan Hodža and the Romanian Iuliu Maniu is of particular interest. They envisaged that an uncrowned Franz Ferdinand would effect reforms 'through the Hungarian constitution', but they quickly added that 'from constitutional means it will still be possible to change over to force', whilst the 'reverse would be an admission of failure'. In further parts of their *Promemoria* these nationalist leaders envisaged the suspension of the local government units' adminis- trative competence and the foregoing of all of Hungary's historic rights accumulated over centuries against the Habsburgs.[17]

The news of Franz Ferdinand's assassination produced a tempor- ary stunned indecision inside the Monarchy. This was soon followed, however, by speedy reassessment of the chances for changes which could be made. In Hungary, the heir apparent's death rapidly came to be seen as an advantage, thanks to the universal fear that he had evoked whilst alive. In practical terms, Tisza was automatically elevated into the innermost decision-making circle of the Monarchy. Thereafter, during the 'July Crisis' preceding the outbreak of the war, Tisza alone resisted precipitate action against Serbia. He restrained for a time both the military leaders who wished to declare war immediately and the followers of Franz Ferdinand who hoped to use war to effect speedier reforms inside the Monarchy. Tisza's influence, however, was neither long-lasting nor in the long run constructive. After July 1914 he had no choice but to bow before the united phalanx of warmongers in exchange for valueless assurances on Transylvania's security and empty promises that any territories that might be conquered by Austria-Hungary, notably in the Balkans, would not be annexed.[18]

Tisza's resistance to the onset of war was unlikely in any case to have won much support in Hungary. To the great majority of the population, the oncoming war in the second half of July 1914 was generally welcome—as was the case elsewhere in Europe. There were no pacifist demonstrations and, indeed, were the socialists contemplating such, they would have been well aware that the force of the recent emergency measures[19] would have placed their laboriously constructed organization at risk of dissolution. The non-Magyars themselves, still generally believing in the maintenance of the Dual Monarchy, also raised no protest at the Empire's ultimatum to Serbia and challenge to Russia. Indeed, it was a uniform feature of press comment that the Monarchy would have to be defended against encroaching Tsarist tyranny, and that 'cheeky Serbia deserved a bloody nose'. It was, however, a startling and ominous novelty in the history of *Ausgleich* Hungary when, on 25 July, the army (which, it should be remembered, was a largely autonomous body within the Empire) began widespread internment, accompanied often by atrocities among the Monarchy's Serb citizens, a practice which was to continue more or less for the rest of the war. Romanian inhabitants at first, on Tisza's insistence, largely escaped ill-treatment until the second half of 1915 when a vigorous persecution of the press began. In the autumn of 1916 it was the turn of the invading Romanian army to take the initiative. For six weeks they occupied parts of Transylvania, set up their own administration and, when they were driven out with German help, they took with them not only the bulk of the Transylvanian Romanian intelligentsia but hundreds of Magyar hostages. Now, in turn again, the Magyar authorities took their own reprisals. The final alienation of the population's non-Magyar elements—this time the southern Slavs—was completed in September 1918 when Tisza visited Bosnia and arrogantly rejected the South Slavs' final pleas for autonomy.

On the eve of the First World War the Hungarian parliamentary scene was an embittered one, the opposition aristocrats as well as gentry leaders united only in their dislike of Tisza. Nevertheless, the outbreak of the war soon united all political parties in a *Treuga Dei* or *Union Sacrée*, and the opposition was not without hope that the wartime emergency would make Tisza more willing to form a fully national government in the interests of the nation's survival. These hopes were soon dashed. First Italy's entry into the war in April 1915, and then Brusilov's offensive and Romania's entry on the Entente's side in the summer of 1916, indicated that even such increased peril as these represented was not enough to sway the Prime Minister. The decisive blow to the fragile unity of the *Treuga Dei* occurred when Count Mihály Károlyi split the Independence and '48 Party on 17 July 1916. His new party sought to limit under-standing of the *Ausgleich* simply to a 'personal union' of the two halves of the Monarchy in the person of the Emperor-King, and thus to 'restore the attributes of Hungary's national sovereignty'. The party envisaged 'ending the war with a peace treaty which would realize the country's interests and guarantee its territorial integrity' on these lines.[20] Although at this stage support for Károlyi was slight, the potential implications, especially as defeat seemed more likely, were considerable. The Károlyi Party sought to distance itself in the eyes both of the population and of the Entente from other sections of the opposition, hoping that the latter might be induced to compromise themselves by joining a Tisza-based coalition govern-ment committed to the continuation of the war. In this they were later, towards the summer of 1918, to be partially successful, but only in terms of the effect in Hungary. The Entente was never to make this distinction between the Hungarian parties: Hungarian responsibility for 'war guilt' would prove impossible to shake off.[21]

Previously, in June 1917, the most that could be achieved in that direction was Tisza's replacement as prime minister by a political nonentity, Count Móric Esterházy, thanks largely to the policies of the new King Karl. Into Esterházy's inadequate hands, along with the burden of the war, was placed the long-festering and now resurgent problem of suffrage reform. Indeed, the replacement of Tisza was a hollow victory. The Magyar opposition continued to hope that their country would be fitter to face the changed conditions of a post-war world by the introduction of wide, possibly universal, male suffrage and even the enfranchisement of some categories of women. But they were to be disillusioned. The new King had simply replaced one pro-*Ausgleich* personality with another, albeit a more agreeable one. Tisza's parliamentary majority remained, its cohesiveness and morale rapidly increasing with the realization that no general election on any suffrage basis would be held while the war lasted. Esterházy—weak, respected by few—was replaced within months by the veteran stop-gap politician Sándor Wekerle who aimed simply to continue Hungary's participation in the war and Tisza's basic policies.

Although an Electoral League or Suffrage Bloc was formed in the summer of 1917, including almost all opposition fractions and parties (the Social Democrats, Radicals, left-wing Independents and of course the Károlyi Party), it was, significantly, not joined actively by non-Magyar politicians. Not surprisingly the League failed to provide enough political weight in parliament or, given wartime privations, enough physical presence on the streets to sustain a reformist trend for long. An electoral bill finally reached the statute book in September 1918, but with Wekerle still in office it was so watered down as to be unacceptable to genuinely reform-minded politicians. By this time in any case the right wing of the Electoral League (most noably Vázsonyi) had more or less deserted the genuine reformist movement in response to the contagion of Russia's Bolshevik revolution. From early 1918 Bolshevik ideas were brought into Hungary by soldiers returning from wartime imprisonment in Russia; and they increasingly secured some support in Hungary's industrial and even agricultural population, which was demoralized and desperate in the face of privation, inflation and approaching defeat.[22] The right wing's fear that any genuine reforms in 1918 were likely to 'endanger the maintenance of law, and security of life and property', and to undermine the Monarchy's army as a fighting force, easily outweighed their half-hearted commitment to a reformist trend.[23] Once again, in May 1918, the parties pressing for reform were too varied in their political orientation and had failed to remain united. From now on, internal developments in Hungary would increasingly be dictated by the clash of irreconcilable pressures: those of the Entente on the one hand, and the more extreme of the forces of the Left on the other—as well as those exerted by non-Magyar nationals, who found themselves in positions of increasing strength as the prospect of military defeat faced the Central Powers.

It was after Bulgaria's capitulation on 30 September 1918 that the spectre of defeat could no longer be ignored by Hungarian politicians in view of all that it implied about the destruction of the Monarchy and a creeping realization of non-Magyar nationalist aspirations. It was largely as a last-ditch attempt to counter, or at least channel, these that the Károlyi Party, the Socialists and middle-class Radicals formed a National Council on the night of 24–25 October in Budapest. The individuals and groups involved were once more the familiar adherents of the movement for electoral reform: some parliamentarians, leaders of feminist societies, prominent freemasons, journalists and socialists. It is true that the National Council proclamation demanding that parliament should be dissolved, the country's independence declared and an immediate armistice established, did also acknowledge that 'self-determination of the non-Magyars will have to be established according to the spirit of the Wilsonian principles'. And yet it revealed a continuing blindness to the realities of the situation when it added that the outcome of such self-determination 'would be not to endanger but rather strengthen Hungary's territorial integrity'. The Council's assumption that, once 'parliament was dissolved and new elections held' on the basis of 'universal, equal and secret suffrage', Hungary's non-Magyar inhabitants would be satisfied with their 'local and cultural autonomy', seems to us now staggeringly ill-judged.[24]

Five days of parliamentary turmoil and an increasingly clamorous series of street demonstrations culminating in violence and bloodshed (and the assassination of Tisza by unknown soldier assailants) were to pass before King Karl came to a decision and consented to the appointment of Károlyi as Prime Minister on 31 October. The political takeover itself was now remarkably smooth, since the political leaders of the wartime parliament, fearing the worst, either hastened to remove themselves to foreign countries or retired temporarily, leaving the political field to the extra-parliamentary control of Károlyi's National Council. With that, we enter the new era of revolutions which were to culminate in Béla Kun's short-lived 'dictatorship of the proletariat'.

What we have seen therefore, in this discussion is that the politics of the last decades of *Ausgleich* Hungary highlighted the existence since 1867 of three parallel, but wholly irreconcilable sets of pressures. Of these the first, represented by István Tisza and like-minded politicians, was the determination to maintain *Ausgleich* Hungary within the Monarchy, in the belief that only the maintenance of the Monarchy would be conducive to the strengthening and well-being of Magyar national interests. Non-Magyar national interests, it was held, would also be served by the consequent assurance of their individual development within a prosperous country. The obvious flaw in this position was that it assumed continuity of peace in Europe, or at least that an alliance with Germany would provide a sufficient safeguard for the status quo—something which even István Tisza himself was beginning to doubt in the face of international developments from 1908 onwards.

The second pressure exerted upon *Ausgleich* Hungary in these years arose from the increasing influence exercised, within the traditional ruling circles and politically aware sections of the population, by the Magyar opposition parties who insisted that Magyar national interests were being inadequately served by the Monarchy's policy-makers. Their grievances—regarding, for example, the lack of a note-issuing bank, the neglect of Magyar national interest in the command structure of Magyar regiments of the Common Army, the Court's distance from Budapest, the unjust quota contributions to the common budget—were given a sense of anxious urgency by the growing vociferousness of non-Magyar demands for national rights. This in turn undoubtedly contributed to their over-zealous attempts to Magyarize non-Magyar inhabitants in the years before the war.

This last bring us of course to the third source of pressure: the relatively silent but unshifting and resolute pressure from the non-Magyars. It was sobering for Magyar politicians to note how little the basic demands of the non-Magyars had altered since 1867. Their almost unwavering, resentful boycott of parliamentary elections (their participation—let alone their success—in the 1906 general election was quite unusual) actually strengthened their own national cohesiveness. However much the Magyars may have wanted to Magyarize them through new educational policies,[25] the fact was that they remained largely undisturbed in their economic way of life and in their traditional geographical distribution.[26] In the face of these three opposing and mutually exclusive sets of pressures, it is hardly surprising that attempts to resolve, through reform, the problems that they posed came to nothing.

While historians have in the past been tempted to speculate on how far alternative strategies and limited demographic reform might have succeeded in holding intact either the Monarchy or historic Hungary, the historiography of the last twenty years, based on the newly opened archives of the former Entente powers, has shown the misguidedness of such speculation.[27] For it has become clear that, even had *Ausgleich* Hungary's rulers granted a wide degree of autonomy to its non-Magyar citizens after 1900, this would in no way have sufficed to counteract either the trauma of the World War and its accompanying scramble for new allies by all participants, or the non-Magyars' increasingly irreconcilable hostility to a Magyar national state. It is a matter for sombre reflection, however, that subsequent events demonstrated that the new boundaries of the 'successor states', which largely fulfilled the aspirations of the non-Magyars, simply replaced one instability with another.[28]

NOTES

1. The *Ausgleich* provided a customs and tariff union for the entire Monarchy, with a flat-rate tariff to be levied on the import of goods. The flat rate could work to the disadvantage of the less developed regions of the union. Hungarian opinion remained divided as to the benefits of a customs and tariff union with Austria. For example, as a result of the high tariffs on imported Serbian pigs from 1911 the cost of living rose alarmingly in Hungarian towns. In theory, Hungary was entitled to go its separate way in the economic sphere, and the opposition wished to make political capital out of this option. It is appropriate to note also that comparability existed between the Monarchy's two halves on the levying of excise duties, inland revenues, and the running of the railways. In banking, parity was not achieved until 1878 when the Austro-Hungarian bank was founded.

2. József Kristóffy, *Magyarország kálváriája* (Budapest, 1927) p. 188.

3. István Dolmányos, *A koalició az 1905–1906 évi kormányzati válság idejé* (Budapest, 1976) pp. 258, 272–77.

4. Ibid., pp. 295–330.

5. Hungarian National Archives, Budapest, Andrássy family collection. See K. Nemethy's letter to Andrássy, 23 June 1908; and Gyula Varga's letter to Andrássy, 23 November 1908.

6. E. Kovács (ed.), *Magyarország története*, vol.6/2 (Budapest, 1979) pp. 1116–17. The term 'small-holding peasant' denotes a landholding of a size below 100 acres. In all, around seven million persons belonged to this stratum.

7. László Katus, 'Magyarok, nemzétiségek a népszaporulat tükrében, 1850 –1918', *Historia*, 4, nos. 4–5 (Budapest, 1982) pp. 18–21: 'The two million "new Magyars" between 1850 and 1918 were in various phases of assimilation.'

8. P. Hanák and F. Mucsi (eds), *Magyarország története*, vol. 7/2 (Budapest, 1978) pp. 1007, 1020. See also, Magyar királyi vallás és közoktatásügyi minisztérium, *Education in Hungary* (Budapest, 1908) p. 43: '. . . schools where Hungarian was not employed at all [number] 3154 (19%). Of these, in 2433 Romanian was the language of instruction; i.e. Romanian was used in 14,73% of the whole number of elementary schools.'

9. *Gróf Tisza István összes munkái* (Budapest, 1923) I, pp. 145–236.

10. See for example: A. Szombathelyi, *Képe a magyarországi választókerületeknek az általános választó jog alapján* (Budapest, 1905); T. Dugovich, *Az általános válaztójog és a felvidék* (Túrócszentmárton, 1905); E. Baloghy, *A magyar nyelv és a választási reform* (Budapest, 1908); E. Boreczky, *A választójog kérdéséhez, különös tekintettel a nemzetiségi kérdésre* (Nagyszombat, 1910).

11. Library of the School of Slavonic and East European Studies, London,

THE LAST YEARS OF AUSTRIA-HUNGARY

Diary of Gyula Andrássy (the Younger), entries for 13 June 1907; 4 March, 21 May, 22 October 1908.

12. During the 1901 general election a mere 4.14 per cent of the Slovak electorate voted for Slovak candidates (*Magyarország története*, vol. 7/2, p. 1024). In 1906, out of 110,000 Romanian voters, only 35,000 voted for Romanian parliamentary candidates (ibid., p. 1032).

13. F.T. Zsuppán, *Electoral Reform in Hungary 1916–1919* (Unpublished Ph.D. thesis, London, 1972) pp. 90–130.

14. F. Pölöskei, *István Tisza. Ein ungarischer Staatsmann in Kaiserzeiten* (Budapest, 1994) pp. 71–79.

15. Documents on these negotiations are published in Gábor G. Kemény, *Iratok a nemzetiségi kérdés történetéhez Magyarországon a dualizmus korában (1906–1913)* (Budapest, 1971) pp. 361–73, 546–47. These Romanian demands reflect their desire to restore the pre-1867 status quo. Following the issue of the February (1861) Patent, four Romanian prefects (*főispán*) had been appointed heads of *comitats* in Transylvania and a further four appointed to head *comitats* in Hungary proper. Similarly, the Romanian desire to secure fifty constituencies for their nationality very probably originates from the election results of the summer of 1863 in Transylvania, when 49 Romanian, 44 Magyar and 33 Saxon representatives had been elected—the Romanians very largely from rural constituencies, under the aegis of a centralizing Habsburg administration.

16. Gyula Andrássy diary, entry for 20 January 1912.

17. Kemény, *Iratok*, pp. 222–25. Parallel with the non-Magyars' contacts with Franz Ferdinand, the Magyar political leadership was beginning to take seriously the accumulating propaganda efforts of Slovaks and Romanians in Western Europe and amongst émigrés in the USA. Apart from accusing the Magyars of forceful Magyarization (in no way as severe as the Germans' efforts in Poznania), massacres by gendarmes in Élesd in 1904 and in Csernova in 1907 clearly illustrated the severity of the non-Magyars' oppression. For the latter, see the contemporary influential work by Scotus Viator [R.W. Seton-Watson], *Racial Problems in Hungary* (London, 1908); and for a recent publication: Jan Rychlík, Thomas D. Marzik, Miroslav Bielik (eds), *R.W. Seton-Watson and his Relations with the Czechs and Slovaks: Documents/Dokumenty. 1906–1951*, 2 vols (Prague and Martin, 1995) I, p. 144.

18. John Leslie, 'The Antecedents of Austria-Hungary's War Aims: Policies and Policy-Makers in Vienna and Budapest before and during 1914', *Archiv und Forschung. Wiener Beiträge zur Geschichte der Neuzeit*, 20 (Vienna, 1993) pp. 307–94; József Galántai, *Die österreichisch-ungarische Monarchie und der Weltkrieg* (Budapest, 1979) pp. 251–80.

19. József Galántai, *Magyarország az első világháboruban, 1914–1918* (Budapest, 1974) pp. 152–59.

20. *Magyarország* [the Károlyi Party newspaper], 19 July 1916.
21. Public Records Office, London, F.O.371/2862, 'Intelligence Bureau. Weekly report on Austria-Hungary and Poland', 26 May 1917 (signed by R.W. Seton-Watson): '4. Electoral Reform and Magyarization'.
22. While in 1916 three times as much had to be spent on food as in 1914, this rate surged to over eight times the 1914 level by 1918, while wages rose to a mere two or three times their 1914 level. See *A magyar munkásmozgalom történetének válogatott dokumentai*, vol. 4/2 (Budapest, 1969) pp. 391–94; vol. 5 (Budapest, 1956) pp. 195–209, 213–35.
23. *Vázsonyi Vilmos beszédei és irásai*, 2 vols (Budapest, 1927) II, p. 187: the speech of Vilmos Vázsonyi (the Minister of Justice) in the Lower House, 6 February 1918. On this same day, he uttered the famous sentence which signalled the convergence of middle-class reformers like Vázsonyi himself, with the die-hard reactionaries like Tisza: 'Should there be some who wish to imitate the Russian example, and if as a result, Hungary's frontiers were to remain undefended through lack of fighting zeal in our soldiers, then our enemies would march in and carve this country up so that not even the ruins of Hungary . . . would be left untouched' (*Parliamentary Debates*, 38, p. 227).
24. *Népszava* [the Hungarian Social Democratic Party's daily], 26 October 1918.
25. *Ausgleich* Hungary's attempts to Magyarize its non-Magyar inhabitants almost wholly depended on efforts to teach them the Magyar language. Indeed, during the Monarchy's last thirty years, as many as one million non-Magyars availed themselves of this opportunity without losing their own mother tongue in the process. However, the process was slow, uneven and in places produced a trend contrary to that intended. In early 1918, statistics were produced for the primary schools in Transylvania's 2,623 villages and published in *Magyar Hirlap* (17 March 1918): only 77 villages had Magyar schools, a further 234 villages had no schools at all, while in 841 villages there were non-Magyar schools only. (On the remaining villages, presumably, the newspaper had no information.)
26. This state of affairs held true even though a not insignificant number of Slovaks, Serbs and Croats on the periphery of their traditional homelands were more prone to assimilate to the Magyars or to migrate into towns where assimilation tended to quicken. For the participation of national groups in Hungary's education system at the beginning of the twentieth century, and the ebb and flow of linguistic boundaries, see: Pál Balogh, *A népfajok Magyarországon* (Budapest, 1902) pp. 1008–93.
27. It is debatable how early in the war representatives of the non-Magyars abroad, or the Allies themselves, decided to recognize the desires for independence of non-Magyars and non-Germans in the Monarchy. The western Allies' commitment was variable, but it is generally accepted

that April–May 1918 was the real beginning of their determination to dissolve Austria-Hungary. Amidst the large literature on this, see for example Kenneth J. Calder, *Britain and the Origins of the New Europe, 1914–1918* (Cambridge, 1976); and Tibor Glant, *Through the Prism of the Habsburg Monarchy. Hungary in American Diplomacy and Public Opinion in the First World War* (New York, 1998). That the idea of a 'superstate' or a 'Danubian Confederation' was still entertained in November 1918 by a sober-minded British observer, Captain L.S. Amery, instead of a solution based on 'a chaos of independent sovereignties', was of course untypical of the 1919 peacemakers. Yet Amery was one of the few who envisioned the post-war peacemakers' 'turning of Central Europe into a new Balkans' if they relied on 'nationalism' as the only basis of settlement (Public Records Office, F.O. 371/3136/177223).

28. Documents in the Public Records Office in London show only too well the negative results for democratic institutions, individual rights and minority rights. See especially, the Annual Reports on Romania for 1924 and 1925 by Sir H.G. Dering (both in F.O. 371/10806/170421): 'in the towns of Transylvania (where they not infrequently form an important part of the total population), numbers of Magyar electors are omitted from the electoral lists.'

6

The Southern Slav Question*

Janko Pleterski

I

During the crisis which broke out in Austria in 1897 as a result of the government's attempts to introduce linguistic equality in the Czech lands, all the German bourgeois parties—even the Radicals—created a front of national solidarity, known as the *Deutsche Gemeinbürgschaft*. In 1899, this body adopted a Whitsun programme (*Pfingstprogramm*) for all provinces of Austria, according to which the German national position, threatened by the gradual democratization of the electoral system, would be constitutionally strengthened and even expanded. In response to this, the Slovene and Croat political parties drew closer to one another across the internal state boundaries created by Dualism. In Croatia-Slavonia in 1903, there erupted a widespread agitation in opposition to Magyarization; it led to military repression and the suspension of the constitution. In Dalmatia and the Slovene lands, this caused in turn a dramatic protest in support of Croatia which deepened still further the existing crisis of German and Magyar hegemony within the dualist system. And it was in this year that a respected Viennese newspaper published an editorial entitled 'The Southern Slav Question'.[1]

The writer began with the statement: 'Recently a great political problem has re-arisen, which since the foundation of the dualist form of government seemed to be settled, namely the southern Slav question.' This question was again becoming a problem of concern to the entire Monarchy: 'that distinguishes it significantly from all other nationality questions of Austria and Hungary.' Ostensibly, the great division of the Empire in 1867 had severed the Serbo-Croatian movement on one side of the dualist border from the Slovene movement on the other, while the bulk of Croat Dalmatia had been left to Austria in a constitutional position which was still inadequately

---

*Translated from Croatian by the editor.

119

defined. But in 1903 the Croats, Serbs and Slovenes seemed to be forgetting their various differences and ostentatiously coming together. 'Here there is developing a powerful group of peoples which will one day inevitably break up the dualist state', for

> if these four million[2] ever begin to act under a united leadership, it could be even more threatening to the state as a whole than the Bohemian quarrel ever was for the Austrian half [of the Monarchy]. The Czechs are isolated: a great Slav language island of course, but still an island. But behind our southern Slavs stand the peoples of the Balkans, incessantly restless and insatiable. Should one allow history to be made out of this geographical situation?

If the anonymous writer of this editorial lived until 1918 he would have found an answer to his prophetic question. Already in the years leading up to that time he could have seen that those responsible for the Monarchy's policies were not following the advice given in his article. This was that it was necessary to form the southern Slav provinces and nationalities separately into what he termed 'saturated national existences', to enable these provinces and national units to find 'satisfaction in peaceful isolation' from one another within the existing dualist structure.

From what has been noted already it is clear that the concept of southern Slavdom and the southern Slav question was many-faceted before 1914. It was, in the first place, an ethnic idea which embraced all nationalities of the southern Slav linguistic group (Slovenes, Croats, Serbs, Montenegrins, Bulgarians and Macedonians as well as the nationally still undefined Moslems who used the Serbo-Croat language). But then, as viewed from Vienna, it was a question of those South Slavs who lived in the southern provinces of the Habsburg Monarchy, including from 1908 Bosnia and Hercegovina. For the South Slavs of the Monarchy themselves—the Slovenes, Croats and some Serbs—it was a question of achieving equal political rights with other parts of the Monarchy in a special unit which they themselves termed 'Yugoslav'; but also, in the long run, a question of making closer links and perhaps uniting with southern Slavs outside the Monarchy in Serbia and Montenegro (and Bulgaria until 1913). 'Yugoslavia' and the Yugoslav idea was always a political rather than an ethnic concept. Until 1918 the breadth or narrowness of its definition depended on the continued existence or disappearance of Austria-Hungary's borders in the Balkans.

Map 4. The South Slav Lands of Austria–Hungary.

In the first half of the nineteenth century there had been isolated theories concerning the political organization of the Yugoslavs, but none of them had included all of the South Slavs. In fact these theories were always conceived either within the framework of a solution to the Eastern Question (within the territory of the Ottoman Empire up to the Habsburg borders) or in the context of the constitutional problems of the Habsburg Monarchy (up to its border with Turkey). The first time that a joint scheme for a Yugoslav political structure in a broader sense was formulated was in the years 1866–70. The position of individual southern Slav nationalities within that structure can most simply be defined by the following characteristics. Serbia and Montenegro were in the *East* (bound up with the implications of the Eastern Question); Croatia and its Serbs in the *West* (bound up with all the implications of satisfying Croatia's historic state right within the constitutional system of the Habsburg Monarchy); and the Slovenes in *Germania* (inside the borders of the historic German Empire), as a 'nationality without history' and without any historic state right. In 1866 there was a real possibility of joint action by Croatia and Serbia to eliminate Ottoman rule in Bosnia and Hercegovina, and of attaching these provinces to Serbia.[3] Serbia in turn would unite with Montenegro and eventually form a federation with Bulgaria. Croatia's fate, meanwhile, depended upon the results of the Central European crisis (the Austro-Prussian war) which might destroy the unity of the Habsburg Monarchy.

The question of the Slovenes remained open. It was dependent on the one hand upon Greater Germany's interest in a territorial link with Trieste and the Adriatic, and on the other, upon Italy's irredentist aspirations to these same Slovene territories. The Slovene leaders stressed, through a 'Yugoslav Congress' held in Ljubljana in 1870, that they belonged to the southern Slavs, but among Serbs and Croats there was scepticism about the possibility of their inclusion in any Yugoslav structure. In fact, the expected European 'catastrophe' failed to materialize in 1870 and a similar international situation did not arise until 1914. Instead, the Berlin Congress of 1878 drew up a new map of the Balkans in which both Serbia and Montenegro gained their independence. Bosnia and Hercegovina, however, fell to Austria-Hungary which thereby acquired the right to occupy and administer provinces which formally still remained part of the Ottoman Empire.

By this time, Croats and Slovenes who aspired to be free of Habsburg control faced major obstacles. From the very start their aims clashed with Italy's desire for state unification within broad geographic and strategic frontiers and at the expense of the Monarchy. The Slovenes, as the immediate neighbours of Italy from 1866, based their claims on the so-called ethnic frontier: that is, they sought to fix the boundary along the lower course of the river Isonzo, the old, stable line of contact between the Slovene and Italian peasant populations. Yet on the eastern, Slovene side, such a border would include Trieste, a city which had always enjoyed a special status within Austria but which had an Italian majority. South-east of Trieste in the nationally mixed crownland of Istria, where Croats and Slovenes jointly formed a majority of the population and owned most of the rural terrain, both sides—Italian and Slav—strove to secure the whole region for themselves. As for Dalmatia, Slavs viewed it as part of Croatian territory both historically (the principle of state right) and ethnically, since the Italians there represented a very sparse minority even in the urban centres to which they were restricted.[4]

Italian ideas about Italy's future eastern border were diverse, but all reckoned on obtaining parts of the eastern shore of the Adriatic. If for some this meant crossing the river Isonzo and securing the whole of the Austrian littoral, others certainly envisaged taking the crownland of Dalmatia in its entirety. Very quickly, the Italian idealist Giuseppe Mazzini had abandoned his original stance of 1858 when he had proposed the Isonzo as the natural border for a united Italy in the east. A century later, in the early 1960s, the clash of Italian and South Slav aspirations was summed up by historians from both sides: a group of Italian and Yugoslav academics drew up an agreed text about the nature of the relationship between 1860 and 1920, which might be incorporated into school text-books in both Italy and Yugoslavia.[5] In their introduction they wrote:

There were particularly tough efforts made on both sides to defeat political opponents, since there existed an age-old ethnic, linguistic and cultural relationship between Italians and South Slavs who had mingled and filled the eastern zone of the Adriatic (east of the Isonzo). What made the struggles all the more harsh were the contributory social-economic factors, since the Italian element was almost totally identified with an urban population, while the peasant mass was largely Slav. Yet on both sides there were also more cautious and discerning spirits who set themselves the task of establishing an enduring co-existence between Italians and South Slavs even in an era of national states.

The 'Adriatic question' which was at the core of this relationship not only had a significant impact upon the evolution of the Yugoslav problem inside the Habsburg Monarchy. It also affected relations between the different southern Slav nationalities up to 1918 and beyond.

Yet if Italy's aspirations made a peaceful solution of the southern Slav question more problematic, a more striking obstacle was the dualist structure of the Monarchy. Under Dualism almost all Slovenes fell into the Austrian half of the state,[6] as did a large number of Croats (in Dalmatia and Istria) and the Dalmatian Serbs. The Austrian provinces retained a degree of autonomy and all sent representatives to the Viennese Reichsrat which from 1907 was elected directly on a franchise of male universal suffrage. In the Hungarian half of the Monarchy the historic region of Croatia-Slavonia possessed a degree of autonomy based on state right. The majority of Croats and a significant number of Serbs lived there and were represented by a special delegation in the parliament in Budapest. In 'Hungary proper' (excluding Croatia-Slavonia) there were Serbs in southern regions as well as some Croats, and Slovenes in the south-west. The port of Rijeka (Fiume) had a special status, linked directly to Budapest. In all of Hungary there was a very limited electoral franchise. In 1908 Bosnia and Hercegovina were annexed by the Monarchy and acquired within it a special position, belonging neither to Austria nor Hungary, but being administered jointly by them in a condominium which preserved for the provinces only a façade of autonomy. The emerging political system there was based on a division of the population into three main religious creeds, Orthodox, Moslem and Roman Catholic. Constitutionally, although Bosnia remained in limbo after its annexation, it was granted in February 1910 its own provincial assembly (*sabor*). This was elected on a very complicated confessional and tax-based franchise, and was an advisory body with no legislative power.

The only really representative forum in the South Slav regions of the Monarchy was the Croatian Sabor (diet) in Zagreb. But its own democratic credentials were very thin in comparison to the Reichsrat in Vienna. In 1907, only 2 per cent of the population of Croatia had the vote. In 1910 this was extended to 8.8 per cent, but it remained an open ballot. Furthermore, between 1908 and 1913, Budapest refused to convene the Sabor, preferring to rule Croatia in an 'absolutist' fashion.[7] Political parties were of course still an important factor in Croatian life, but in this system their potential national impact was limited. (The first elections held on the basis of universal suffrage, in 1920, revealed for instance that Stjepan Radić's Peasant Party was the strongest, yet before 1914 its direct predecessor had been one of the smallest groups in the Sabor).

A brief survey of party divisions in the southern Slav regions in the early twentieth century reveals that in the Sabor in Zagreb, the so-called Serb-Croat Coalition of Serb and some Croat parties usually had an absolute majority (see Table 3). It promulgated united national solidarity as the basis for a campaign for full Croatian autonomy within the Empire. The second-largest political grouping were the supporters of Croatia's historic state right. By 1913, these divided definitely into the Pure Party of Right of Josip Frank, and the Starčević Party of Right of Mile Starčević. The former looked to Vienna as a political centre, especially to the 'Great Austrian' reformers (notably the Christian Socials) clustered around Archduke Franz Ferdinand; it opposed recognition of the Serbs of Croatia and

Table 3. Election Results in Croatia-Slavonia 1906–13

	May 1906	Feb. 1908	Oct. 1910	Dec. 1911	Dec. 1913
Serb-Croat Coalition	43[1]	57[2]	35[3]	25	48
'National Party'[4]	25	0	18	22	12
Frankists	20	24	15	27	9
Starčević Party of Right[5]	–	–	9	–	12
Croat Peasant Party (Radić)	0	2	9	8	3
Serb Radical Party	–	2	1	3	0
Non-Party, etc	–	3	1	3	4
Total	88	88	88	88	88

Source: Based on Mark Biondich, *Stjepan Radić, the Croat Peasant Party and the Politics of Mass Mobilization 1904–1928* (Toronto, 2000) p. 95.

1. The Coalition in 1906 consisted of the Croat Party of Right (14), the Serb Independent Party (16), the Croat Progressive Party (3), the Serb Radical Party (3) and non-party or independents (7).
2. By 1908 the Coalition had altered to: the Croat Party of Right (26), the Serb Independent Party (19), the Croat Progressives (4) and the Autonomous Club (8).
3. After 1910, with the merger of the Croat Party of Right and the Progressives, the Coalition consisted of only two parties, the Croat Independents (20) and the Serb Independents (14) with one non-party member. In the 1913 elections the two parties gained 31 and 17 seats respectively.
4. Refers to deputies who supported the Croatian Ban.
5. The Starčević Party of Right split from the Frankists in April 1908, ran jointly with them in December 1911, but not in the 1913 elections.

actively stirred up hatred against them. The Starčević Party, on the other hand, gained in influence all the more because it emphasized Croatian independence from both Budapest and Vienna, and cultivated a new relationship with the Serbs of Croatia on a basis of equal rights. Its significance, moreover, was enhanced through its formal links with kindred Croat parties across the dualist border in Dalmatia and Istria. It also fostered close political ties with the strongest Slovene party, the Slovene Clerical or People's Party, which was expressly allied to the Catholic Church. The Slovenes in Cisleithania, besides this, also possessed parties of a Liberal disposition. These resembled the Serb-Croat Coalition in their national outlook, but lacked any organizational link to the Coalition. In particular the Serbs of the Coalition, under Svetozar Pribićević, rejected ties with the Slovenes, not wishing to make their own position more problematic by removing the dualist border.

In Dalmatia, Croat and Serb bourgeois politicians had begun in 1905 to work together on the basis of recognizing an autonomous Croatia as a common homeland, to which Dalmatia would be annexed and perhaps even Bosnia-Hercegovina. This cooperation signified resistance to Viennese centralization, but it also relied upon the Magyars' own ambitions to make Hungary more independent of Austria. This was the so-called political 'New Course'. It stimulated the creation of the already mentioned Serb-Croat Coalition in Croatia, which was gradually known to have close links with the foreign policy ambitions of the kingdom of Serbia. As for the southern Slav politicians of Bosnia-Hercegovina, they competed with one another to impose on these provinces a Great Croat or Great Serb political programme. Both Serbs and Croats aspired to control Bosnia at an unspecified future date, but for the present they focused their efforts on encouraging Moslem inhabitants to opt for the Serb or Croat nationality respectively. The Moslems, however, were increasingly developing a separate political identity of their own and taking on the characteristics of a distinct nationality.

In all the southern Slav lands there also existed socialist parties, which at first had been organized within the Austrian and Hungarian Social Democratic parties. Later they founded their own: in 1894, the Social Democratic Party of Croatia and Slavonia; in 1896, the Yugoslav Social Democratic Party (for the Slovene lands with Istria and Dalmatia); and finally in 1909, the Social Democratic Party of Bosnia and Hercegovina. Rather naturally, these labour parties did not promote nationalism, but tried in their own way to respond to the challenge posed by the national question. Thus, they formally accepted the resolution of the London Congress of the Second International (1896) on a nation's right to self-determination. They also approved the programme of Austria's Social Democratic Party (1899), advocating the creation of linguistically defined and culturally autonomous regions in the Monarchy.

At the same time, they independently developed their own theories on the need for 'a common struggle by the Yugoslav poor', aiming to create a united Yugoslav social democracy with no reference to existing dualist or provincial borders. In 1909, at a joint congress in Ljubljana, the South Slav socialist parties agreed in particular a programme of their own for solving the Yugoslav question. This 'Tivoli resolution' even conceived of some future Balkan federation, but it chiefly viewed the national question in cultural-linguistic terms rather than as a political goal. Here they differed from the social democrats of Serbia who envisaged creating a larger national state as one element in a federation of Balkan national states. In 1910, the difference was openly expressed during the Balkan Socialist Congress in Belgrade, which South Slav socialists from the Monarchy also attended.[8]

The kingdom of Serbia (a principality until 1881) had, after the Congress of Berlin in 1878, conducted its foreign relations for a quarter of a century under the shadow of Austria-Hungary. In domestic affairs absolutism was revived from 1893, when King Aleksandar Obrenović established a dictatorship. For twenty-five years Serbia's role in the West, in relation to the South Slavs of the Monarchy, was effectively paralysed; in the East, however, in 1885, it had launched a war against Bulgaria and was defeated. The turning point for Serbia came only in 1903. In the so-called 'May revolution' (according to the old calendar), some officer-conspirators murdered the king and queen, and with widespread public support a temporary civilian government restored constitutional rule. A large assembly offered Petar Karadjordjević the throne. In international affairs Serbia now encountered serious difficulties; Great Britain even broke off diplomatic relations for three years. But domestically, it was transformed into a constitutional monarchy. In spite of the diplomatic boycott, in which the Habsburgs did not participate, Serbia from 1903 managed to break away from Austria-Hungary's political and economic domination. It rapidly restored its traditional political ties to Russia, opened new markets in Italy, and bound itself politically and economically to France where in 1906, in defiance of

Austria-Hungary, guns were commissioned for the Serbian army. By that time the Monarchy had already begun an economic blockade of Serbia, the so-called 'Pig War', which lasted until 1910 but ended in failure for the more powerful neighbour. In these years Serbia was also rapidly modernizing. The existing high school in Belgrade was transformed into a university in 1905, ushering in the 'Pericline Age' of Serbian education and culture. So a democratic, independent Serbia acted like a magnet for the southern Slavs of the Habsburg Monarchy.

In turn, the Monarchy's annexation of Bosnia-Hercegovina in 1908 aroused great excitement amongst the Serbian public. They generally felt that these provinces should, on the elimination of Turkish sovereignty, be united with the Serbian state. Russia's restraining influence encouraged the Serbians to accept the new situation. Since Bosnia and Hercegovina were now definitely allotted to the *West*, the idea of unifying the various branches of the Serb 'nation' gained an increasingly western, Yugoslav orientation. Yet such a course could only fully materialize in a situation similar to that of 1866–70: if there was a 'catastrophe' or a European war. Until then, Serbia's foreign policy revolved around settling accounts with European Turkey. In 1912, the formation of a Balkan league with Bulgaria, Greece and Montenegro led directly to the first Balkan War in which Serbia was very successful on the battlefield, but failed to achieve its main goal, an outlet to the Adriatic through northern Albania. The Great Powers decided to create an Albanian state on the Adriatic coast. Serbia however emerged from the war significantly enlarged and gained, via the Sandžak, Kosovo and Metohija, a territorial link with Montenegro. To the south, Serbia liberated from Turkish rule and retained Vardar Macedonia, to an extent greater than had been agreed with its former League allies. This was a blatant provocation to the Bulgarians who themselves began the second Balkan War (June 1913) against all the other Balkan states. Bulgaria's defeat and the establishment of new state boundaries in the Balkans was confirmed by the Treaty of Bucharest (10 August).

Serbian territory now doubled from 39,000 to 87,000 square kilometres with a total population of 4.5 million. Serbia was no longer an ethnically homogeneous state, for its borders embraced a large number of Macedonians and Albanians. The need for internal consolidation made the Serbs reluctant to engage in any new international conflict, especially with Austria-Hungary; they knew moreover that Russia was not ready for war. In February 1914, the Serbian Prime Minister, Nikola Pašić, secretly informed politicians of the Serb-Croat Coalition in Zagreb that they need not solve the Yugoslav question, for it would be solved by Serbia together with Russia—but that at present neither was ready for war. Pašić's message in fact had a deeper significance. He was concerned less with a time-scale for dealing with the problem, more with reserving for Serbia alone the right to play the role of a Yugoslav 'Piedmont' in the future. Ignorant of Pašić's views, the leading Slovene Clerical politician Janez E. Krek concluded at this time that Serbia desired peaceful relations with Austria-Hungary and that the only realistic course was for the Yugoslavs of the Monarchy to solve their own problems independently.[9]

In the southern Slav regions of the Monarchy people were conscious, within the broad framework of a German *Drang nach Osten* [thrust to the east], also of a certain Austro-German pressure which came to be known as the *Drang nach Süden* [south]. Certainly, from an economic point of view it was not particularly effective, for Viennese and Budapest capital was meagre and could not bring about a rapid influx of modern industry. But on the other hand, the 'thrust' was notably strident in its political ambitions, in its pronouncement of Austro-German but also Magyar predominance in the region. In Bosnia-Hercegovina, a narrow-gauge railway was built and there was much talk of plans to construct a normal railway line across Bosnia towards Turkey.[10] There was also much talk of linking Dalmatia by rail to Zagreb and Budapest, across Bosnia-Hercegovina, but this too remained on paper. The only significant line constructed in the twentieth century was that built in 1908 across Carinthia, Carniola and Gorizia (the *Tauerbahn*) as another connection to Trieste. It was intended to meet the needs of southern Germany and the western (Alpine) Austrian lands, but in the south to cater especially for the needs of Trieste itself, as a port and industrial centre. Nevertheless, the Croat and Slovene lands as a whole experienced very sluggish economic development, resulting in an enormous emigration of population to the Americas. It was the obvious need to decide independently about their economic development which brought the South Slavs into increasing conflict with the efforts of Vienna and Budapest to strengthen their political predominance.

As part of the political 'New Course' in 1905, Croats from Dalmatia had tried to secure support against Vienna in Italy as well. Officially of course Italy remained an ally of Austria-Hungary (the Triple Alliance). The Dalmatians therefore got into contact with the Italian opposition. This meant the grouping on the democratic Left

which had continued the tradition of the Risorgimento and consequently had anti-Austrian designs. Yet at the same time it had kept
up a tradition of Adriatic irredentism (of Ricciotti Garibaldi). With
regard to this tendency, the Dalmatians proceeded to propose—
without Slovene agreement—an 'Adriatic compromise' by which the
Austrian littoral would be divided up. To the Italian sphere would be
conceded a substantial amount of Slovene territory in the hinterland
of Trieste, together with Trieste itself and western Istria. In 1906,
Slovenes in Trieste and Croats in Istria finally found out about the
terms of this deal when the Italians themselves sought their consent.
They duly rejected the emissaries from Rome, arguing that they
would rather stay under Austrian protection and wait for things to
improve, than attach themselves to Italy where 'national death'
would surely await them. This was a significant episode which made
Slovenes all the more anxious that the Croats (and Serbs in Croatia)
might be willing to sacrifice them to Italy in order to secure their own
special interests.[11]

It was such fears which convinced many in the Monarchy's
southern Slav regions before 1914 that individual solutions to the
South Slav question would not work. Rather, the problems of the
area had to appear on the Monarchy's agenda as an entity, as a
Yugoslav question. In 1911 the British scholar R.W. Seton-Watson
dedicated his book, *The Southern Slav Question and the Habsburg
Monarchy*, to the Austrian statesman who might possess 'the genius
and the courage necessary to solve the South Slav Question'.[12] The
leaders of Austria–Hungary, however, were not qualified for such a
role, nor, at the same time, was the authority of the army, aristocracy
or church adequate any longer as a basis for maintaining the Empire's
integrity. To those Germans and Magyars who wielded political
power, the Monarchy itself was the instrument or the goal of their
ambitions; a democratic alternative, of transforming the Empire
into a federation of nationalities, was never their intention. Nevertheless, until the First World War the forces which could destroy the
Monarchy had still not gained the upper hand. Indeed, for the
individual national movements of the 'subject peoples', Austria-
Hungary continued to be seen as a lesser evil than the dangers which
might come to the fore through its dissolution: Greater Germany for
the Slovenes and Czechs, Tsarist Russia for the Poles and Romanians,
and Italian irredentism for the South Slavs on the Adriatic coast.[13] As
for the ruling circles, they hoped to maintain the existing structure of
the Monarchy; and they did not see the Yugoslav problem as an issue

legitimately raised by contemporary events. Instead, they labelled the problem in the usual bureaucratic language as a matter of 'Slav intrigues' (*slawische Umtriebe*). They qualified this only by referring to 'Great Serbian irredentism' in the south of the Monarchy, stating that there were treacherous forces at work there rooted in Serbophile convictions. This appraisal of the situation determined a pragmatic conservative policy.

In 1908–9, the odium in this policy was directed particularly against the Serb-Croat Coalition in Croatia-Slavonia. Mass treason trials were launched which in the end backfired on the governing elite itself, for it was established that the alleged plots were based on falsified documents (the Friedjung trial).[14] This aggressive action was supported in the South Slav lands only by the Frank Pure Party of Right, while the other parties, though politically opposed to the Serb-Croat Coalition, found ways to distance themselves from the trials. The Serb-Croat Coalition itself, however, did not respond with more radical policies, for already it was adopting an opportunistic stance. True, it remained faithful to the principle of cooperation between Serbs and Croats in Croatia, but it still sought support amongst the ruling circles in Budapest, opposed to a Greater Austrian programme, in order to preserve the constitutional conditions which gave it a majority in the Sabor.

It was the dissatisfaction of the generation of young intellectuals with this opportunism which was one of the main reasons for the appearance of national revolutionary (*omladinski*) movements in the Empire's Yugoslav territory. In different variations, these movements envisaged a united Yugoslav nation, and planned to solve the southern Slav problem by seceding from Austria-Hungary and creating, with Serbia and Montenegro, an integral and independent Yugoslav state. The victory of the Balkan allies in the war against Turkey in 1912–13 positively encouraged these aspirations. The youth movement was not accepted by the official parties—on the contrary. But it in turn did not identify with Serbian ruling circles either, not even with the bellicose organization of Serbian officers, *Ujedinjenje ili Smrt* (unofficially termed *Crna Ruka*—the Black Hand). The latter, partly following the example of the Russian 'terrorist' *Narodniki*, favoured assassination—the 'murder of a tyrant'—as a tactic.[15] Meanwhile, even the revolutionary enthusiasm of the *omladina* in Croatia began to fade in the years before the war, in conditions where to all intents and purposes there was a *modus vivendi* which was secretly counselled by the Serbian government. In May 1914 in

Zagreb, the young Ivo Andrić, later a Nobel Prize winner for his novel *The Bridge on the Drina*, sarcastically characterized the political climate: 'All of Croatia is snoring in an unseemly sleep. The only people awake are poets and assassins.'[16]

Yet the quick-witted Andrić had not noticed another broad political movement which had been visible since 1911. Like many other liberal Croats and Serbs of the time, he was blinded by political and ideological prejudices. He and others, for example, viewed the concept of Croatia's historic state right primarily in negative terms; in other words, they characterized it as the Croats obstructing any political recognition of a Serb people within the Croat nation. They also excluded *a priori* the possibility that even a modern form of Catholic clericalism could emerge as a factor to be reckoned with in the national movement. And finally, they did not feel themselves sufficiently strong to be able to espouse including the Slovenes in a solution of the Yugoslav question, thereby cutting across the dualist border between Austria and Hungary. Andrić, for example, had failed to notice that events were in train which in 1912 resulted in the first joint South Slav party of 'Slovenia' and Croatia, something which the Serb-Croat Coalition had not conceived of, nor perhaps desired either. 'The diaphragm was pierced which divided the Slovenes, concentrated in Austrian territories, from the Croats.'[17] In this way a precedent was set for that anti-dualist concentration of Yugoslavs which occurred in the Monarchy during the final crisis of 1917–18.

The creators of the new party were the Starčević Party of Right, the only one to draw adherents from all the historic regions inhabited by Croats, and the Slovene People's Party, which encompassed the great majority of Catholic Slovenes. This combined Croat-Slovene party promulgated the unity of the Croat and Slovene peoples, aiming to reorganize the Monarchy in a way which would form the South Slav lands into a special state entity. Such a demand became known as 'Trialism' (as opposed to Dualism), although the party was not in principle against a general federalization of the Empire. To achieve these political aims it turned to the heir apparent, Archduke Franz Ferdinand, and his circle. Yet, as an autonomous and widely organized movement, the party was effectively at odds with the Archduke's Greater Austrian ideas which were based on the legitimacy of the ruler, had little sympathy with national sovereignty, and above all absolutely rejected the notion of separating the Slovenes from Austria. Of course, another weakness for the party was its own composition. There were those within it who stressed a Great Croatian ideological tendency, something which had no chance of ever being supported by Serbs and was also wholly unacceptable to German and Magyar nationalists. In 1913, the outright Serbophobes (the Frank Pure Party of Right) split off from the united Croat-Slovene party. In the latter there were increasing calls for a new, positive relationship with the Serbs and for cooperation with the Serb-Croat Coalition to protect Croatia's constitutional regime against Hungary's absolutist aspirations. Here a notable role was played by the Croat-Slovene Club which the party created in the Viennese Reichsrat. Indeed, the tradition which was cemented by this anti-dualist Slovene-Croatian political cooperation would be crucial when in the course of the war Yugoslav political forces began to concentrate in and between Ljubljana and Zagreb.

Until the First World War there was no uniform Yugoslav programme, either within the Habsburg Monarchy or in connection with Serbia and Montenegro. The Yugoslav movement in effect was multi-centred with each one of those centres conceiving the Yugoslav idea as a broad framework which might possibly benefit the realization of their own basic national interests. But there was arguably a genuine 'Yugoslav' quality in their respect for each other's rights and their readiness to adapt to each other's interests.

II

One can detect the differences between the southern Slav political parties in the way that they reacted to the danger of war in the crisis after the Sarajevo assassinations. Later, when war had already been declared against Serbia, these differences were officially suppressed. In Croatia, it was the Frank Pure Party of Right and the small Peasant Party of Stjepan Radić which adopted a hostile attitude towards Serbia. A similar stance was taken by the Croat Clericals both in Dalmatia and Bosnia-Hercegovina, and, in Slovene territory, by the Clerical party of Carniola. It was a mood which socialists summed up as *furor patrioticus*. Apart from feeling indignant at the actual deed of assassination, these parties' reactions reflected their conviction that the death of the heir apparent had ruined all hope of an anti-dualist reform of the Empire stimulated by his personal drive. Liberal and social democratic elements, on the other hand, while condemning the murder itself, emphasized that the real reason for it ought to be sought in government policy which was oppressing South

Slav aspirations. They condemned in no uncertain terms the persecution of Serbs within the Monarchy.

After Austria-Hungary had attacked Serbia, the Empire's southern
Slav lands were subject to repressive treatment at the hands of an
absolutist military regime. (In Hungary absolutism was not formally
introduced, but repression was still widespread.) The methods and
intensity of repression varied. It ranged from direct physical violence
against Serb inhabitants, especially in Bosnia-Hercegovina and
Vojvodina, to the elimination of all Yugoslav political links under the
pretext of suppressing 'Serbophilia', to attempts by local authorities
to settle accounts with undesirable nationalist movements. Karl
Heinold, the Austrian Minister of the Interior, observed on 10
September 1914 that the authorities in Styria 'already seem to see in
every person of Slovene nationality a politically unreliable individual'.[18] In such circumstances all political parties stressed their
loyal attitude, as did the mobilized Slovene, Croat and even Serb
soldiers; only in Bosnia-Hercegovina were there noticeable Serb
desertions to Serbia. Traditional military loyalty to the Emperor
seemed to be very much alive, but military intelligence still noted the
apathy of the civilian population as well as signs of anti-militarism.
It came to the conclusion that it would only be possible to clean up
the political situation in Carniola, the Littoral and Dalmatia if,
instead of civil authorities, military governors were immediately
installed.

The attitude to the war of southern Slav civilians and soldiers
altered to some extent after Italy's entry into the war in late May
1915. As we have seen, Italy's aspirations in the eastern Adriatic had
been public knowledge for a long time, and in the secret Treaty of
London (26 April) they were recognized by the Entente, one of the
essential prerequisites for Italy's entry into the war on their side. To
quote again the words of the Italian-Yugoslav historians who drew
up a joint text in the early 1960s: 'The London Pact suited Italian
political and military circles for it guaranteed Italy security against
Austria-Hungary, while if Italy were defeated it also protected her
against the "Slav danger", namely against Russian expansion into the
Balkans and the Near East.'[19] The treaty, however, alienated Slovenes
and Croats from the Entente. Its disclosure proved to be the final
stimulus for the founding on 30 April in Rome of a Yugoslav
Committee, composed of Slovene and Croat leaders who had fled
from the Monarchy to the West. In the long term, the treaty had a
potentially damaging impact on Italy's image in Europe since it

suggested that Italy was oblivious to the rights of small nations. Even before the pact was signed the Italian government had been warned about its consequences from influential quarters. Tittoni, their ambassador in Paris, cautioned that if Italy were to incorporate Slovene and German elements (the latter in south Tyrol), it would create inside the country 'two irredentist nests'—one Slovene and one German—which could become a pretext for future wars and would force Italy to be permanently armed for any eventuality.[20]

Aside from this potential Italian danger, Slovenes and Croats in the Monarchy were faced with more immediate challenges to their national existence. In Austria, they were forced to take stock due to the repressive nature of military absolutism, and especially the blatant efforts by the German nationalist parties to have constitutional changes enacted during the war. However, none of the South Slav political parties expressed their views publicly. Instead they made secret soundings, already before the end of 1914, about creating a separate state entity. This applied also to Croatia in the Hungarian half of the Monarchy, where political conditions were somewhat more liberal. The Serb-Croat Coalition, with its majority in the Sabor, cooperated with the Ban (the monarch's representative in Croatia) and the Hungarian government in order to preserve constitutional conditions, prevent the Sabor's dissolution, and thwart the ambitions of Frank's Pure Party of Right which remained tied to ruling circles in Vienna. This famous 'Coalition opportunism' which continued until the last months of the war, had—as we have seen—been agreed with the Serbian government in 1914. It was a strategy which actually constituted a great obstacle to the creation of any Yugoslav movement in Croatia. As for the politicized Catholic circles, from August 1914 some of the clergy in Croatia were already inclining to the idea of union with Serbia; they perceived especially that this could eliminate the danger of Italy's territorial pretensions. In the last phase of the war, it was from the ranks of this section of the clergy that the leading activists of the Yugoslav movement emerged: Vjekoslav Spinčić, Fran Barac, Janez Krek and Anton Korošec. Meanwhile, the young lay clerical intelligentsia in 'Slovenia' persistently reproached the episcopate for not seeing that the real threat came not from the Orthodox Church but from German Protestantism. In the end, the Bishop of Ljubljana, Anton B. Jeglič, was to be converted to the Yugoslav political ideal by the reality of nationalist and social developments, even though he thereby put himself directly at odds with the Vatican which continued to support the Habsburg state.

Since neither Russia nor little Serbia itself were ready for war with Austria-Hungary and its allies, it is logical not to blame the Serbian government for the assassination of Archduke Franz Ferdinand on 28 June 1914. As it turned out, Serbia against all expectations mustered enough forces to be able to withstand successfully the Monarchy's aggression.[21] But the situation was still extremely grave. Nikola Pašić's government declined the Serbian High Command's advice of offering peace to Austria or of simply doing nothing, and instead in November 1914 resolved to fight on to the bitter end. This decision was interlinked with that of determining Serbia's war aims. On 7 December at Niš, the Serbian government announced that Serbia's great defensive campaign 'once begun, had become simultaneously a struggle for the liberation and unification of all our oppressed brothers—Serbs, Croats and Slovenes'. Serbia thus equated the struggle for its own nationalist goals with Yugoslav objectives. Yet this behaviour was at first intelligible only because the Yugoslav programme offered Serbia, both in wartime and for the future, the best prospects.[22] Everything was staked on an Entente victory and the assumption that Austria-Hungary would crumble and disintegrate. Serbia's war aims were thereby in direct conflict with Italy's aspirations, but also with Entente diplomacy which was trying by this time to gain Italy as an ally. Through the Serbian government's Niš Declaration the Yugoslav question officially acquired an international character, but in a very particular way: it impinged on the war aims not only of one, but of both hostile groupings of Great Powers.

In 1914, and until much later, the Entente governments had no intention of breaking up the Habsburg Monarchy although it was obvious that they would eventually be faced with the question of reorganizing the map of central and south-eastern Europe: a return to the pre-war status quo was already impossible. All Yugoslav hopes would certainly be dashed if the Central Powers were victorious. And yet, this did not stop the Austro-Hungarian High Command from thinking in 1915–16 that Croat and Slovene soldiers' enthusiasm to fight against Italy might be enhanced if certain non-binding hints were dropped about domestic reforms which would take place after the victory. Furthermore, as far as left-wing parties in central Europe were concerned, it is clear that their revolution—which they never attempted—would not have resulted in Yugoslav unification. Rather, it would have led to separate solutions of the southern Slav question, on the one hand within the historic framework of Austria and

Hungary, on the other in the Balkan region. Thus, if the Central Powers were determined to destroy any chance of a Yugoslav state emerging, the concept of Yugoslavia did not feature in the plans of the Entente or of any European workers' revolution either.

In the autumn of 1915 the fortunes of the World War turned against Serbia. Bulgaria declared war on Belgrade, and there followed German military intervention in the Balkan theatre. Serbia was occupied but never surrendered; together with the remnants of the army, King Petar, the government and the Skupština (the Serbian parliament) fled with enormous hardship across Albania to reach Allied sanctuary. An upturn in fortunes occurred in Russia by 1916 where groups of volunteers—South Slavs from the Monarchy—were being organized as part of the Serbian army; in this way 'Serbia' contributed to the Allied cause on the Eastern front in the Dobrudja (Romania). In Greece too, on the borders of Serbia and Bulgaria, a large sector of the Allied Salonika front was eventually occupied by reorganized Serbian forces. Already in the autumn of 1916 an Allied offensive here liberated Bitola (Monastir), a town in occupied Serbia. Yet in 1917 even the Serbian leadership did not completely reject the idea of a separate peace with Austria-Hungary, particularly since they knew that Vienna had begun secret negotiations with the Entente. Evidence exists to show that the Regent Aleksandar also favoured this idea. This would partially explain the trial held in Salonika of members of the Black Hand, who were condemned to death and executed; they were accused of conspiring against the Regent, but it was generally known that Vienna blamed them in particular for the Sarajevo assassinations.[23] There was however no separate peace with the Monarchy.

In the West, as we have noted, anti-Austrian émigrés from the southern Slav areas of the Empire had formed the Yugoslav Committee (*Jugoslavenski Odbor*). This was above all dominated by Croat politicians from Dalmatia who in mid-1915 had fled to Paris from persecution in Italy. Its leaders, Ante Trumbić and Frano Supilo, aimed from the very beginning at uniting the Serbs, Croats and Slovenes of Austria-Hungary with the kingdoms of Serbia and Montenegro. They sought support not only from the Entente, but particularly from the Serbian government of Nikola Pašić. But they remained unsure as to whether the latter would accept their Yugoslav programme and not simply expand Serbia's borders to those regions of the Monarchy where Serbs lived in direct proximity to Serbia and Montenegro. The situation had of course altered to some extent after the Niš Declaration of December 1914. Pašić then actually encouraged Yugoslav émigrés to set up a special committee which would propagate Serbia's as well as their own Yugoslav programme in the Allied lands, for in this way he hoped to safeguard Serbia's role as a 'Piedmont' for the future Yugoslav state.

Bogumil Vošnjak, a Slovene member of the Yugoslav Committee, painted at this time one vision of 'Yugoslavia' for the British and American public. It merits attention because he highlighted some essential expectations about its future which were not realized after 1918 nor after 1945:

> The variety of creeds, the mixture of North and South, West and East, will make Jugoslavs into an extremely interesting melting-pot of the neighbouring civilizations. But the leading aim will be the full assimilation of the political methods and the chief political rules of Western civilization. We will search for models, not in a bogus civilization such as that of Vienna and Berlin, but we will go to the extreme West for social aspirations and prototypes. Only a society grown up in civic liberty can be a model for young nations loving civic liberty more than any other treasure . . . As the Western Power of the Balkans, . . . Jugoslavia will be a living symbol of the reconciliation of two great human directions of civilization of West and East . . . [Jugoslavia] will have a tremendous task in international life in endeavouring to reconcile the Western and Eastern Churches, to bring Rome nearer to Constantinople and Moscow . . . It will be easy for a state of this kind, absolutely unimperialistic, so similar to Phoenicia, to be a faithful guard against false German Imperialism created by Junkerdom and servitude.[24]

Despite such idealism, most of the Yugoslav Committee were not so preoccupied with how their new state would be organized, but more with the threat posed by the Italians, their expansion on the Adriatic and their wholly negative stance towards the creation of Yugoslavia.[25] However, at the very start of their activity, the Croat émigrés were compelled, when considering the question of Croatia's future relationship with Serbia in Yugoslavia, to make up their minds about one more unresolved matter: namely, should the Croats favour union with the Slovenes or remain within the framework of a 'Balkan Yugoslavia' based upon the Serb and Croat nationalities? Although Russian diplomats stressed that 'Slovenia' could not be included in any solution of the Yugoslav question, Supilo and Trumbić maintained that Croatia's orientation could not be separated from the fate of the Slovenes, since without them most Croats would prefer to establish their own state than fall under the rule of a Serbian king.

As a result, Supilo and Trumbić invited the Slovenes to send representatives to join them abroad. For the Slovene leaders it was especially important that the Croats had definitely decided upon an ethnic border with Italy on the Isonzo river, and were opposed to ceding Slovene territory to Italy or indulging in any territorial bargaining with Italy over Slovene heads. It was in this spirit that Trumbić had advised Slovene and Croat politicians, who before Italy's entry into the war had met secretly in Trieste on two occasions, that any Italian occupation should be met with armed resistance. This would apparently necessitate the creation of volunteer units within the Habsburg army itself, similar in some ways to Józef Piłsudski's Polish legions which were already engaged on the Eastern front against Russia. Such an idea was thwarted by non-official Russian diplomacy intervening, since for Russia too Italy's participation in the war as an ally was of greater importance.[26] However, this did not prevent Slovene, Croat and even Serb soldiers of the Austro-Hungarian army from feeling that the new front against Italy was a bulwark for the southern Slav territories against Italian imperialism. Their behaviour, though lacking any real political basis, amounted to a kind of anonymous resistance to the Italians; abroad, their great sacrifices were simply viewed as a sign of Austrophilia.

The Entente governments were undecided over the whole question of whether the Slovenes should be included in a Yugoslav settlement. But already in 1916 Vošnjak, their most prominent publicist abroad, had tried to point out to the West the significance of this 'detail':

Not unless the new Jugoslav state is permitted to include the Slovenes will it be able to enter completely into the world of Western culture and gradually to discard the last remnants of oriental manner and Byzantine traditions. A rigidly centralistic regime would evoke a never-ending series of misunderstandings, the revival of half-forgotten prejudices . . . Through living in constant mutual relations with the great cultured nations of the West, not only the Germans and Italians, the Slovenes became a Western people. They were educated in discipline and order [. . . under] the influences of centuries of regular administration . . . The Slovenes would contribute much that is valuable to the future Jugoslav community. They would represent the sound element of labour, organization and economic occupation.[27]

Such sentiments won little sympathy in Italy. Although the Italian Foreign Minister, Sidney Sonnino, felt that Hungary with Croatia could be separated from Austria (something expressed in the Treaty of London), he did not reckon on the break-up of the Monarchy itself. Still less was Rome prepared to agree to Croatia, and certainly not 'Slovenia', uniting with Serbia and Montenegro. If a unified Yugoslav state was created on the eastern shores of the Adriatic it would represent a fundamental obstacle to Italy's aspirations in this region and to its influence in the Balkans. Serbia had not been officially informed about the provisions of the London pact as far as it profited Italy's territorial aims, but Pašić nevertheless objected to the treaty. Because of this the Yugoslav Committee in many matters bowed to the wishes of the Serbian government. This in turn explains to a large extent why the Yugoslav Committee did not insist on being recognized by the Allied governments as an international body similar to the Czechoslovak and Polish National Committees. It did not achieve this even in 1918, when the Allies had finally resolved upon the 'nationality principle' (i.e., the destruction of Austria-Hungary).[28] Serbia itself therefore remained the internationally legitimate standard-bearer for the creation of a Yugoslav state, something which had serious consequences not only at the time of the Peace Conference when Serbia represented 'Yugoslavia', but also for domestic relations within the new Kingdom of Serbs, Croats and Slovenes after the war.

In 1916, the political hopes of Slovenes and Croats reached their lowest ebb. Serbia was occupied. Italian forces captured the town of Gorizia and on the famous battlefield of Doberdo came perilously close to Trieste. While the German nationalist parties in Austria announced their programme of creating by decree or *oktroi* a new constitution (to set Austria on a firm 'German course'), the censor prevented Slovenes and Croats from publicizing their political demands. Within the Slovene People's Party, which supported cooperation with the Croats, a split emerged since its leader, Ivan Šušteršič, behaved as an Austrian patriot and opposed political activity as long as the war lasted.[29] New possibilities for change arose only from the end of 1916 when re-convocation of the Austrian Reichsrat was impending and political parties in both halves of the Empire were forced to decide upon the nature of their 'address' to the new monarch. From the very beginning, Emperor Karl blocked all demands which were aimed against Dualism. He immediately took the oath to the Hungarian constitution, which it was known that

Franz Ferdinand would have refused, but postponed taking the oath to the Austrian constitution; thereby he left open the chance of implementing German demands by *oktroi*. In this way he prevented any comprehensive settlement of the Yugoslav question, but also effectively forestalled the possibility of any improvement in the position of Slovenes and Croats in Austria.

The Entente note on war aims of 10 January 1917, although it too failed to recognize the need to solve the Yugoslav question as a whole, was of major importance. It divided the issue into, on the one hand, the restoration of Serbia and Montenegro, and on the other, the liberation of Austria-Hungary's 'Slavs'; this could only mean the Croats, Slovenes and Serbs, since the Poles and Czechoslovaks were mentioned separately. In contrast, the Austrians could interpret the American President's proposal of a 'peace without victors' as proof of his interest in preserving the Dual Monarchy. However, Woodrow Wilson's announcement that the peace conference would have to decide upon the internal reorganization of the Empire immediately encouraged the South Slavs to prepare constitutional demands for that occasion.

Since the Serb-Croat Coalition remained passive, the initiative continued to lie in the hands of the Starčević Party of Right in Croatia, and the Slovene-Croat parliamentary club in Vienna. Their link across the dualist border had been steadily maintained since 1912. The club, headed by Anton Korošec of the Slovene People's Party, became the basis for a concentration of all Slovene, Croat and Serb deputies to the Reichsrat and, with the new name of 'Yugoslav Club' it formed one more centre for Yugoslav agitation. On 30 May 1917, at the start of the first wartime session of the Austrian parliament, the Yugoslav Club announced its programme. It aimed at unification 'under the sceptre of the Habsburg-Lorraine dynasty' of all lands inhabited by Slovenes, Croats and Serbs in one territorial entity, which would be 'free of any national domination by foreigners and constructed on a democratic basis'. The very nature of this 'May Declaration' was incompatible with the dualist system. All the nationalist declarations at this time in the Reichsrat envisaged that it would be through some domestic reform that the new monarch would set out on the road to conclude peace. The real historical significance of the Yugoslav Club's declaration was that it was the first joint programme in the Habsburg Monarchy to treat the Croats, Serbs and Slovenes on an equal basis. It did not represent a complete solution of the Yugoslav question, nor did it presuppose an Entente victory, and therefore it was not an anti-Habsburg programme. On the other hand, it certainly did not assume that Austria-Hungary would win. Rather, it favoured a compromise peace.

Since these expectations of a compromise peace were not fulfilled, the May Declaration gained new historic importance through its anti-dualist tendencies. It became the basis for a broader movement of self-determination, which started in July 1917 and then grew steadily in the southern regions of the Monarchy. In evaluating this movement in September 1918, French experts on the Supreme War Council at Versailles concluded that, alongside Serbia, a second South Slav centre had come into being: one inside Austria-Hungary. The goal of this centre, they surmised, was not so much to achieve an internal federalization of the Habsburg Monarchy, but rather to create an independent southern Slav state.

The radicalization of South Slav politics in Austria in mid-1917 occurred in ignorance of what was happening at the same time on the Greek island of Corfu. There in July, the Serbian government and the émigré Yugoslav Committee came to an agreement on a joint 'integral' Yugoslav programme, linked of course to an Entente victory and the disintegration of Austria-Hungary. The Corfu Declaration was itself a product to some extent of international developments. The February revolution in Russia and the American entry into the war against Germany had made the Serbian government more flexible with regard to recognizing the Yugoslav Committee as something of a partner.[30] The Declaration was a compromise as far as internal organization of the state was concerned. But in relation to the Entente, it meant that Serbia was now actively pursuing a broad Yugoslav programme and that the Committee was to be seen as the representative of the Habsburg South Slavs in their struggle for self-determination. Later, when Serbia's position improved, Pašić strove to eliminate the principles agreed on Corfu.

In Croatia meanwhile, the Yugoslav Club's May Declaration was taken up and adopted by the Starčević Party of Right. In its statement to the Sabor on 6 June 1917, the party particularly urged Serbs of Croatia to associate themselves with the Croats and Slovenes. The Serb-Croat Coalition, however, stuck to its old dualist standpoint. It emphasized that the Yugoslav Club's demands would mean 'a complete break with prevailing political conditions, creating a scenario which would threaten Croatia-Slavonia's autonomous position' in Hungary (the *Nagodba* of 1868); in contrast, it argued, Slovenes and other South Slavs in Austria had nothing comparable to lose.[31] As for the other parties in the Sabor, Stjepan Radić for the Peasant Party reacted positively towards the Yugoslav Club's declaration, while the Frank Pure Party of Right simply reasserted its demand for a Croatian state. The fact that it now seemed impossible to postpone some solution of the Yugoslav question caused some of the most prominent Serb members of the parliamentary majority to secede from the Coalition because of its continued reserve. On behalf of Serb 'dissidents of the Coalition', Srdjan Budisavljević told the Sabor on 1 August that unification of the Slovene, Croat and Serb peoples could only come about outside Dualism; therefore, one ought to follow the Starčević Party's appeal and agree to the May Declaration. On this occasion Budisavljević significantly neglected to mention the Habsburg dynasty.

In Bosnia-Hercegovina as well, the Yugoslav Club's activity, and especially the work of Korošec, helped to reanimate political life, enabling almost all the political parties there to adopt a Yugoslav programme. For the May Declaration posed the question of Yugoslav unity on a political basis which was different from the pre-war theory of Trialism but also rejected Dualism. While the Serb and Croat parties in Bosnia reorientated their programmes in a Yugoslav direction, the Moslem politicians added their voice later when on 20 September 1918 they expressed the same Yugoslav stance to Count Tisza in Sarajevo.[32]

Meanwhile in 'Slovenia' and to some extent in Istria and Dalmatia, there developed from late 1917 a broad nationalist agitation known as the 'declaration movement', which took as its political basis the May Declaration.[33] By means of petitions, proclamations by parishes and societies, public meetings and demonstrations, this agitation pressed as its minimum goal for the right to self-determination as defined in the May Declaration. At the same time it was a movement for peace, better social conditions and against the 'German war'. Its increasingly radical demands contributed in May 1918 to the revolts of Slovene soldiers, in garrisons at Murau, Judenburg and Radkersburg, which proved to be the most significant rebellions in the Austrian hinterland. The organizers of the revolts were soldiers who, as a result of the peace treaty of Brest-Litovsk, had returned from Russian captivity only to be sent almost immediately back to their units rather than being allowed extensive leave. Already earlier in the year there had been a naval mutiny in the Bay of Cattaro; sailors of all nationalities had taken part, but many Slovenes on that occasion had publicly displayed symbols of the 'declaration movement'. In May 1918 the Slovene Social Democrats joined the movement as well. Thus the slogan of *Jugoslavija* had become a symbol of both national and social aspirations.

In January 1918 Serbia's war aims had faced their most critical test when Wilson and Lloyd George seemed to abandon the 'nationality principle' by announcing that the Dual Monarchy would be preserved. Pašić then tried to secure at least Bosnia-Hercegovina for Serbia, but without success. Yet, at this decisive moment, Serbian diplomats were able to counter the statements of the Great Powers by pointing to the agitation in Austria as proof that the Empire's South Slavs were clearly moving towards independence and unification on the Italian model; in other words, they wished to secede from Austria and unite with the 'new Piedmont' (Serbia). Indeed, the issue of Yugoslav unity and independence at this time revolved around two separate but still inter-linked questions: first, whether at the end of the war Serbia would be amongst the victors who would dictate the peace; and second, whether domestic unrest would cause the disintegration of Austria-Hungary. A compromise peace would frustrate the first of these possibilities, but also probably the second as well.

From the autumn of 1917 the mounting agitation based on the May Declaration had not diminished in the southern Slav regions. Neither the victory of the Central Powers at Caporetto in October, nor the statements made by Lloyd George and Wilson, had restrained the unrest. On 31 January 1918 the Yugoslav Club addressed a memorandum to the peace conference at Brest-Litovsk, demanding that the question of self-determination for Slovenes, Croats and Serbs of the Monarchy should be internationalized. In early March, politicians from the Empire's Yugoslav regions met in Zagreb to try once again to bring about some concentration of all their parties on the basis of self-determination. However, the Serb-Croat Coalition was still reserved and did not participate, something which delayed the formation of national councils (to prepare for the new state) in all the South Slav regions but especially in Croatia-Slavonia.

Throughout this time Austria-Hungary's ruling elite remained wedded to Dualism. In May 1918, just at the moment when the western Allies were returning to the nationality principle and beginning to think of a victorious peace and the dissolution of Austria-Hungary, the Austrian government of Ernst von Seidler tried to prohibit the Yugoslav Club's activity. Seidler declared that the Slovene regions would always remain in the same state structure as the German territories. In similar fashion, Emperor Karl when meeting a

German delegation from Slovene regions on 25 May guaranteed that they would not be separated from the German parts of Austria and that the authorities would manage to suppress the Yugoslav movement. All Slovene political parties reacted immediately, issuing a statement two days later in which they insisted that the Slovene people had a right to self-determination and that they were not prepared to commit suicide, not even for the Emperor. On 16 August a National Council was finally established in Ljubljana, representing 'Slovenia' and Istria, but with local branches in Maribor, Klagenfurt, Gorizia and Trieste. It announced in advance that it was only part of a future joint national council in Zagreb, but such a body continued to be thwarted by the opportunism of the Serb-Croat Coalition. The Coalition's stance only altered when in late September Allied and Serbian forces broke through on the Salonika front, Bulgaria surrendered, and Serbian territory was rapidly falling into Allied hands.

On 11 October Emperor Karl summoned Anton Korošec, president of the Yugoslav Club, and told him that the Monarchy could be transformed as the Club desired. Korošec answered: 'What has happened already is enough to make us mistrust you.'[34] Indeed, the Imperial Manifesto of 16 October still aimed to reorganize the Empire within the dualist framework. Only at the last recorded meeting of the Austro-Hungarian Common Ministerial Council on 22 October [see Appendix] did the ruling elite concede for the first time that the southern Slav regions of the Monarchy might be grouped together outside the dualist structure. But this resolution was stillborn.

Meanwhile in Zagreb on 6 October the joint National Council of Serbs, Croats and Slovenes had finally been established under Korošec's presidency. The Slovene and Croat socialist parties joined it, as did the Serb-Croat Coalition two days later. Secession from Austria-Hungary was executed on 29 October, simultaneously by the Sabor in Zagreb and by a large national gathering in Ljubljana. Thereby an independent state of Serbs, Croats and Slovenes was created, its representatives pronouncing themselves 'ready to form a joint state with Serbia and Montenegro'. While the exiled Serbian government now recognized the existence of this second centre for Yugoslav unification, those who had openly opposed it bore the consequences. Ivan Šušteršič, the leading Slovene Austrophile who from 1917 had been a dissident in the Slovene People's Party, formally acknowledged the *fait accompli* but fled to Vienna in fear for his life. In Zagreb, the small Vienna-orientated Pure Party of Right dissolved itself, only to re-form a few days after the foundation of the united Kingdom of Serbs, Croats and Slovenes (1 December 1918). A decade later it would become the basis for Ante Pavelić's Ustaše movement.[35]

Field Marshal Svetozar Boroević, the Austrian commander famous for his battles against Italy and chief of the army group stationed nearest to the new Yugoslav state, had planned to intervene at the last minute. He intended to move on Vienna with his forces and rescue the Emperor and his regime. However, as a result of the Yugoslav revolution there was complete confusion to the rear of Boroević's armies; already on 1 November he too was forced to bow to the reality of the events created by Ljubljana and Zagreb. As one Austrian military historian has written, he was compelled to abandon his dream of repeating Ban Jelačić's celebrated march on Vienna during the 1848 revolutions.[36] This small episode shows only too clearly the fundamental changes which had taken place in the Habsburg Monarchy in the seventy years from 1848 to 1918.

NOTES

1. *Die Zeit*, XXXV Nr 452 (Vienna, 30 May 1903).
2. This of course is written before the annexation of Bosnia and Hercegovina in 1908.
3. The joint actions might have developed due to the contacts in 1866–67 between the Serbian Prime Minister, Ilija Garašanin, and Bishop Josip Juraj Strossmayer: see Vojislav Vučković, *Politička akcija Srbije u južno-slovenskim pokrajinama Habsburške monarhije 1859–1874* (Belgrade, 1965).
4. For example, in the census of 1910, the nationality of the population of Istria was recorded as being 43.52% Serbo-Croat, 38.14% Italian and 14.27% Slovene; in Dalmatia the census recorded 96.19% Serbo-Croat and 2.84% Italian.
5. The discussions between 1960 and 1964 were led by Franco Valsecchi and Jorjo Tadić. The text was subsequently published in *Cultura e scuola*, no. 37 (Rome, January-March 1971); and in *Jugoslovenski istorijski časopis*, br. 3–4 (Belgrade, 1975) pp. 85–124.
6. They were divided between the crownlands of Carniola, Styria, Carinthia and the Austrian Littoral of Gorizia, Trieste and Istria. Only in Carniola did the Slovenes have an overwhelming majority (94.36% in the 1910 census).
7. See R.W. Seton-Watson's contemporary account: *Absolutism in Croatia* (London, 1912).

8. See Vlado Strugar, *Jugoslavenske socijaldemokratske stranke 1914–1918* (Zagreb, 1963).

9. Janez E. Krek, 'O Jugoslovanskem vprašanju', *Zora*, XX (Ljubljana, 1913–14) pp. 70–81.

10. See for example, Peter Sugar, *The Industrialization of Bosnia-Herce-govina 1878–1918* (Seattle, 1963).

11. See Janko Pleterski, 'Politika "novog kursa", jadranski kompromis i Slovenci', *Jugoslovenski istorijski časopis*, br. 3–4 (Belgrade, 1975); and for the wider context the standard work: Rene Lovrenčić, *Geneza politike novog kursa* (Zagreb, 1972).

12. R.W. Seton-Watson, *The Southern Slav Question and the Habsburg Monarchy* (London, 1911) p. v.

13. Fran Zwitter (with Jaroslov Sidak and Vaso Bogdanov), *Les Problèmes nationaux dans la Monarchie des Habsbourg* (Belgrade, 1960) pp. 146–47.

14. See Hugh and Christopher Seton-Watson, *The Making of a New Europe. R.W. Seton-Watson and the Last Years of Austria-Hungary* (London, 1981) pp. 68ff., 76ff.

15. See Vladimir Dedijer, *The Road to Sarajevo* (New York, 1966).

16. Mirjana Gross, 'Nacionalne ideje studenske omladine u Hrvatskoj uoči svjetskog rata', *Historijski Zbornik*, 21–22 (Zagreb, 1969) p. 138.

17. Leo Valiani, *La Dissoluzione dell'Austria-Ungheria* (Milan, 1966) p. 58.

18. Österreichisches Staatsarchiv Vienna, Verwaltungsarchiv, Ministerium des Innern, Präsidialakten karton 2137, Heinold to Styrian Statthalter, Z.11816/M.I., 10 September 1914.

19. See note 5.

20. *I Documenti Diplomatici Italiani. Quinta Serie: 1914–1918*, III (Rome, 1985), p. 142 no. 172: Tittoni to Sonnino, 23 March 1915.

21. For Serbia's attitude on the eve of war see Mark Cornwall, 'Serbia', in Keith Wilson (ed.), *Decisions for War, 1914* (London, 1995) pp. 55–96; he particularly challenges the idea that Russian support in the July Crisis stiffened Serbian resolve to resist Austria's demands. For Austria-Hungary's initial campaign against Serbia in 1914, see Rudolf Jeřábek, *Potiorek. General im Schatten von Sarajevo* (Vienna, 1991).

22. Andrej Mitrović, *Srbija u prvom svetskom ratu* (Belgrade, 1984) p. 163.

23. See David MacKenzie, *The 'Black Hand' on Trial: Saloniku 1917* (New York, 1995) pp. 70–72.

24. Bogumil Vošnjak, *A Dying Empire. Central Europe, Pan-Germanism and the Downfall of Austria-Hungary* (London, 1918) pp. 133–35.

25. See the classic study by Dragovan Šepić, *Italija, Saveznici i jugo-slavensko pitanje 1914–1918* (Zagreb, 1970).

26. The non-official diplomacy was by a secret agent of the Russian government, Vsevolod Svatkovski, active and accepted among the Croatian political émigrés in 1915.

27. Bogumil Vošnjak, *A Bulwark against Germany. The Fight of the Slovenes, the Western Branch of the Yugoslavs for National Existence* (New York and London, 1919) pp. 278–79.
28. See Gale Stokes, 'The Role of the Yugoslav Committee in the Formation of Yugoslavia', in Dimitrije Djordjević (ed.), *The Creation of Yugoslavia 1914–1918* (Santa Barbara and Oxford, 1980).
29. On Šušteršič, see now Janko Pleterski, *Dr Ivan Šušteršič 1863–1925. Pot prvaka slovenskega političnega katolicizma* (Ljubljana, 1998).
30. The Serbian government had now lost Russian (Tsarist) support, while the United States' entry into the war had strengthened the hand of nationally representative bodies like the Yugoslav Committee.
31. Bogdan Krizman, *Hrvatska u prvom svjetskom ratu. Hrvatsko-Srpski politički odnosi* (Zagreb, 1989) p. 111, note 60.
32. Hamdija Kapidžić, *Bosna i Hercegovina pod austrougarskom upravom* (Sarajevo, 1968) pp. 248–53.
33. For more on this crucial grass-roots movement, see below p. 189. It receives no mention in John R. Lampe, *Yugoslavia as History. Twice there was a Country* (Cambridge, 1996), which as an otherwise seminal work is singularly weak on the period of the First World War.
34. Arhiv Republike Slovenije, Ljubljana: Vladimir Ravnihar, *Mojega življenja pot* [memoirs].
35. See Hrvoje Matković, *Povijest nezavisne države Hrvatske* (Zagreb, 1994).
36. Oskar Regele, *Gericht über Habsburgs Wehrmacht. Letzte Siege und Untergang unter dem Armee-Oberkommando Kaiser Karls I— Generaloberst Arz von Straussenburg* (Vienna and Munich, 1968) p. 166.

7

The Eastern Front

Rudolf Jeřábek

Despite all efforts by the Army High Command (*Armeeoberkommando*—AOK) in the First World War, Austria-Hungary's war against Russia never gained the same degree of popularity among the Empire's nationalities as did, surprisingly, the wars against Serbia and Italy. Before 1914, Franz Joseph and the ruling elite might well recall the Holy Alliance of a century earlier, when Austria and Russia had shown solidarity against the forces of social and national upheaval; or the military aid which Tsar Nicholas I had despatched to save the Habsburg dynasty in 1849. The Habsburg elite were only too aware of the potential dangers of a war against Russia: Archduke Franz Ferdinand, for example, expected that both empires would suffer both revolution and destruction if it ever came to a major armed conflict between them. Moreover, in its role as the Panslav protector, the great eastern neighbour was known to enjoy considerable sympathy among many sections of Austria-Hungary's Slavic population. Against this danger, in the event of war, might be set the reality that prior to 1914 Russia seemed to be stirring up less irredentism in the Monarchy than either Serbia or Italy.[1] There was also a good deal of ignorance in Austria about conditions beyond the Galician borders; for most of the general public the vast Russian Empire undoubtedly seemed much too antiquated and rotten to merit much fear or attention.

Indeed, after Russia's defeat by Japan in the war of 1904–5, the Triple Alliance Powers no longer tended to regard Russia as a real danger anyway, despite the myth of Russian invincibility which had existed ever since Napoleon's retreat in 1812. However, when it became obvious that the Russians were quite able to restore and then enlarge their military forces in a very short space of time, Russia's Polish territories, which projected far into Central Europe, became once again an uncomfortable and by no means negligible factor in the strategic planning of the Austrian military leaders. Even so, the

Austro-Hungarian military paid less attention to the Eastern theatre of war than they devoted to their traditional enemies, France, Italy and Serbia. In the latter cases, the shorter distances and denser lines of communication held out some hope of a quick victory in the style of Moltke in the 1860s. The maxim that there would be a 'battle of encirclement', a new 'Cannae',[2] preoccupied the brains of the general staff officers to a degree which made them seriously underestimate the importance of the Russian front. Relying on the 'indolence' of the Russian state and its military machinery, the Austrian and German general staffs failed almost completely to agree on a coordination of their operations.

The agreement between the two general staffs merely consisted of a letter from the younger Moltke, German Chief of the General Staff, giving vague promises that Germany would launch an offensive across the river Narev in the direction of Siedlec into the rear of the Russian armies attacking the Austrians.[3] More importantly, it contained the promise that Germany would have defeated the bulk of the French army by the fortieth day of mobilization so that its main forces could be sent to the east; up to that point Austria-Hungary would have to bear the chief burden of the war against Russia. In fact both these expectations were to remain unfulfilled. But the AOK was not able to realize its own initial war plans either. At the beginning of the war the Monarchy put even fewer troops into the field against Russia than had originally been planned.

For a Great Power, Austria-Hungary's forces were much more lacking in uniformity than might have been expected. They consisted of three parts: the Common or imperial and royal Army (*k.u.k. Armee*), recruited from all parts of the Monarchy, and the imperial-royal (*k.k.*) Landwehr and the royal-Hungarian (*k.u.*) Honvéd, recruited respectively in the Austrian and Hungarian halves of the Empire. Although the terms Landwehr and Honvéd were akin to 'territorial army', these were not at all second-line troops. As a result of the Hungarian nationalist struggle from the mid-nineteenth century, both halves of the Monarchy maintained their own armies and ministries of defence alongside the Common Army and War Ministry. The Honvéd's official language—the language of command —was Hungarian, whereas in the other two parts of the armed forces it was German. Equipment and organization were practically homogeneous, but according to their areas of recruitment there were many regiments with more than one regimental language. Only 142 units of the Common Army had a single regimental language, whereas 163 units had two and twenty-four units even three regimental languages. In fact, up to four or five languages were used in certain regiments, making the officers' task of coordination very difficult.

According to official figures on national composition, the rank and file in the Common Army was composed of 25 per cent Germans, 23 per cent Magyars, 13 per cent Czechs, 9 per cent Serbs or Croats, 8 per cent Poles and Ruthenes respectively, 7 per cent Romanians, 4 per cent Slovaks, 2 per cent Slovenes and 1 per cent Italians. In contrast, the officer corps looked rather homogeneous: among every 1,000 career officers there were 761 Germans and 107 Magyars, 52 Czechs, 27 Poles, and 27 Serbs or Croats. The proportions altered for the reserve officer corps where there were only 568 Germans compared with 245 Magyars, 106 Czechs, 33 Poles, and 19 Serbs or Croats. However, István Deák has convincingly questioned the reliability of some of these official statistics. For career officers, he argues that within the 'German' assignation there were concealed many who were non-German by birth but 'Austrian' by conviction within the standing of their profession. Among the reserve officers, he suggests that there was a similar concealment of nationality (this time due to assimilation among Romanians, Slovaks or Ruthenes) even if the Germans, Magyars or Czechs were more educated and therefore most likely to be well represented as one-year volunteers. The figures therefore have their limitations and highlight to some extent the degree to which the military were 'ethnically-blind' when it came to recruitment. At best perhaps, they are useful in showing us how the army would be affected when more nationally minded individuals— of the reserve officer corps—were thrust into the shoes of the career officers once the latter were decimated in the first few months of the war.[4]

Altogether in 1914 Austria-Hungary would put forty-nine infantry divisions [ID] and eleven cavalry divisions [KD] into the field. This was in no way excessive since Russia opened the war with about a hundred IDs and thirty-five KDs. The Monarchy, furthermore, had to divert at least eight IDs against Serbia, which left only forty-one IDs and eleven KDs for the Russian theatre. This resulted directly from the fact that Vienna had fallen seriously behind in the arms race. The following figures show the number of infantry divisions which the Monarchy would have been able to put into the field if it had milked its population potential to the same extent as its European competitors: 80 (Germany), 100 (France), 150 (Bulgaria), 162 (Serbia).[5] This lack of a really powerful military machine prevented Vienna from adequately backing up an aggressive foreign policy. Relatively small sums had been spent on armaments in a state which was economically weak anyway, but where army bills were often blocked by 'national obstruction' in the parliaments. In 1906 14.6 per cent of the imperial budget was spent on defence; later it rose slightly: 15.7 per cent by 1910. This was in marked contrast to the 1906 figures in other countries: 20 per cent in Russia, 23 per cent in Serbia, 25 per cent in Italy, 28 per cent in France, 29 per cent in Britain and 50 per cent in Germany. The military expenditure per head amounted to a mere 14 crowns (*Kronen*) compared to Germany's 43.7, France's 39, Britain's 38.4 and Italy's 16.9 crowns per head.[6] Only Serbia (12 crowns per head) and Russia (10.7) were spending less than the Monarchy. The Russians of course not only utilized their population potential on a relatively small scale, but clearly lacked the finances to increase their forces at a faster rate in the wake of the Japanese defeat (after which they completely rearmed with modern war material). But the potential for mobilizing their army was particularly strengthened by the improvement of the railways: the AOK was to be greatly surprised by the speed of the Russian mobilization.

In the summer of 1914, the AOK, by mismanaging its own army's mobilization, even succeeded in exacerbating the ratio of forces on the Eastern front. Its plan, which had been regarded as particularly flexible, designated that most of the armed forces (*A-Staffel*) would be sent to the Russian front no matter what happened, while Serbia would supposedly be contained by the small *Minimalgruppe Balkan*. Additionally there was the *B-Staffel*, the divisions of which were to be sent against Serbia only in the case of a confrontation with Serbia alone ('Case-B'). If Russia entered the war, *B-Staffel* would, instead, have to strengthen the *A-Staffel* forces in Galicia. The following table shows the composition in each of the three groups mentioned above and also numbers the so-called *Marchbrigaden* (marching brigades) which were third-line troops comparable to the Austrian Landsturm.[7] The marching brigades consisted only of reservists and were inadequately equipped with either machine-guns or artillery.

	IDs	KDs	Marching brigades
A-Staffel	28.5	10	21
Minimalgruppe Balkan	8	–	7
B-Staffel	12	1	6

When war was declared on Serbia on 28 July 1914, the Chief of the General Staff, Franz Conrad von Hötzendorf, fatally hastened to put his cherished dream of Case-B in motion, which meant that the *B-Staffel* was immediately directed to the south as well. However, Russian mobilization on 31 July, and the declaration of war against Russia on 6 August, made it imperative suddenly to divert the *B-Staffel* to Galicia to join the *A-Staffel*. The AOK was naturally frightened that such a radical upsetting of the military railway time-table would provoke chaos (a scenario precisely forseen by railway experts in the winter of 1913/14). Therefore it had to gamble that there might be time enough to gain a decisive victory against Serbia with the help of the second army, which formed the larger part of the *B-Staffel*, before diverting the victorious troops northwards. In fact, in the Balkans, the Habsburg forces under General Oskar Potiorek were to face one defeat after another, something again which Austrian war-games in the six months before hostilities had accurately predicted. In the east, meanwhile, the Russians succeeded in completing their mobilization and assembly a week earlier than expected by the AOK. The outcome of all this AOK bungling, caused largely by Conrad's rigid adherence to a supposedly flexible plan, was that three divisions more than originally planned were detained in the Balkans: and the ratio of forces on the Eastern front became even more unfavourable for the Austrians.[8]

At the start of operations 46.5 IDs and 18.5 KDs on the Russian side were confronted on the Austrian side by only 37.5 IDs and 11 KDs.[9] This meant that on average about two Austrian IDs had to fight three Russian IDs. On closer inspection this ratio became even more disadvantageous for the Monarchy. A Russian division was composed of a greater number of battalions, guns and machine-guns, resulting in a superiority of 60–70 per cent in infantry, 90 per cent in light and 230 per cent in heavy field artillery; thirty-two machine-guns of a Russian division faced twenty-four of an Austrian. Last but not least, the Russian artillery possessed a larger quantity of ammunition and the range of their guns was far superior. In the field of tactics too, the Russians enjoyed a substantial advantage. They had learnt much from the disastrous experiences of 1904–5, something which the Austro-Hungarian war attachés, delegated to observe the Russo-Japanese conflict, had warned Vienna about in vain. A crucial Austrian failing was to be the lack of coordination of infantry and artillery. While their infantry tended to attack in dense formations, often failing to overcome enemy troops who were already firmly entrenched, their artillery were deployed in the open and fired without cover, fighting their own private battle against the hostile batteries. A disastrous enthusiasm for attacking without exploiting the terrain would cause huge losses on the Austrian side.

This error of trying to solve all problems by relying unquestionably on the offensive possessed not only the front-line officers, but even the Austro-Hungarian general staff—and especially Conrad himself. This character of charismatic reputation was politically and militarily obsessed by the thought of offensive. His life's mission was to break the ring of enemies at home and abroad (the irredentists and the men behind them in the neighbouring states) with one great blow, even at the risk of placing the Monarchy's existence at stake. As he noted later, it was a choice of drawing the sword or simply allowing the Empire to disintegrate.[10] Accordingly, Conrad stuck to his offensive plans against Russia even though his initial force in Galicia had been considerably weakened. Hoping to hit the Russian armies in their assembly stage, he ordered the Austrian 1st and 4th armies to march northwards into Poland. The 3rd army and some units of the 2nd army (which had arrived from the Balkans) had to cover the sector to the east and therefore started moving too.

In the event, Dankl's 1st army was successful at Kraśnik (23–25 August) and Auffenberg's 4th army at Komarów (26 August—2 September), but the 2nd and 3rd armies were beaten east of Lvov [Lemberg] and had to retreat, threatening in the process to expose the rear of the two victorious armies. While the Galician capital actually had to be evacuated on 2 September, an ambiguous war-bulletin that 'Lvov is still in our hands' (*Lemberg ist noch in unserem Besitz*) caused consternation in Vienna. Hastily a bridgehead was built there on the northern bank of the Danube, and the authorities even contemplated moving the state archives into the catacombs of St Stephen's cathedral. Meanwhile, the 4th army had turned its front eastwards, coming to the aid of the beaten eastern group; but the 1st army with the assistance of a German second-line corps was unable to hold off the steadily increasing Russian menace and so fell back into Galicia. The 2nd, 3rd and 4th armies were then beaten again at Lvov-Rawa Ruska (6–11 September) and retreated further to the line of the river San. Conrad's initial campaign had been a disaster, losing the Monarchy 100,000 dead and 150 miles of territory in the Bukovina and Galicia including the city of Lvov.[11] Many Habsburg generals were reported to have suffered nervous breakdowns.

To the north in contrast, the Germans under Hindenburg had been victorious at Tannenburg in late August and the Masurian Lakes in the first half of September; but their thrust towards the Polish town of Siedlec, which Conrad had expected, never materialized. As mentioned above, the fortieth day of mobilization was supposed to be the deadline for shifting the German main-weight from west to east. Yet, in spite of knowing by 25 August from the Austrian liaison officers at the German High Command (DOHL) that there would be no German supporting offensive, Conrad was still not inclined to a more cautious strategy in the east. Indeed, he was very much at fault for failing to prevent Brudermann's 3rd army from beginning an offensive on 26 August which could only end in disaster.

In response, Conrad first pressed Moltke repeatedly for a German relief attack, and finally appealed to the DOHL to send German forces directly to aid the Austrians in their predicament. However, the first two German corps from the west were rolling towards Prussia. Only after the battle of Rawa Ruska was direct support at last forthcoming from the Germans. This could not be on anything like the expected scale after the Schlieffen plan had failed at the battle of the Marne (5–12 September), something incidentally which the DOHL tried to conceal from the Austrians. The new cooperation of the two allies in the east also caused more friction when it came to the employment of troops and the issues of command. The Austrians increasingly felt that Germany was winning its victories at the expense of the Monarchy which had had initially to carry the main burden of war against Russia. In turn, the Germans' reproachful attitude towards their ally for its lacklustre performance was encapsulated in General Ludendorff's dismissal of Austrian generals as 'childish military dreamers' for whom he had nothing but 'contempt'.[12] Such a mentality was to marr relations between the Central Powers until the end of the war, making their temporarily productive association one which was always fraught with suspicion and unease.

Conrad and Hindenburg's new partnership in the east rapidly led, in keeping with their joint mania for attack at all costs, to another offensive. In their first joint campaign the troops advanced to the rivers San and Vistula and were temporarily able to relieve the besieged fortress of Przemyśl (6 October). But already a month later a set-back forced another retreat. The ring around Przemyśl was closed again as the Russians advanced on Cracow, the fortified city of western Galicia. Nevertheless, the Central Powers continued to insist on the offensive. A new attack with its main (German) weight on Polish soil soon petered away and was followed by even greater losses of territory. Only a flanking attack on the advancing Russian 3rd army south-east of Cracow—the battle of Limonawa-Łapanów (1–13 December)—brought the desired relief for Austria, enabling the allies to advance both in Poland and in Galicia up to the Dunajec river where they entrenched themselves. If this might suggest that the military alliance was finally effective, the priorities of the AOK and the DOHL were almost always at loggerheads. Conrad, given the Austrians' limited resistance to the Russian 'steam-roller', as well as the urgency of impressing neutral Italy and Romania with a victory, viewed the Russian theatre as his prime concern. Falkenhayn, the new German Chief of Staff, was averse to diverting fresh troops to the east, demanding instead that Hindenburg should release forces for more pressing concerns elsewhere.

The now developing Carpathian campaign, which lasted from 23 January to 14 April 1915, was probably the most brutal chapter of the war between Austria-Hungary and Russia. Przemyśl had now become a watchword for the Monarchy both militarily and politically: on its relief or fall depended the attitude of neutral countries (Italy and Romania) and the morale of the Austro-Hungarian population. Months of dogged fighting in the snow-covered passes of the Carpathians—with Austrian forces already supported by a whole German army—resulted, in the face of an enemy which was well entrenched, in no gain of ground but in a tremendous waste of men and material. Thus the 2nd ID, which had numbered 8,150 combatants on 23 January, was left with 1,000 by 2 February. It mattered less that the percentage of prisoners taken by the Russians was relatively small, even if some cases of mass desertion by Czech and Serb soldiers were occurring,[13] for frostbite and death through freezing were the order of the day. Finally on 23 March the fortress of Przemyśl had to be abandoned when 3,500 officers and 120,000 troops surrendered to become prisoners of war. As the Russians entered the town they were faced with a horrifying sight, as one officer explained:

> Everywhere one saw the bodies of freshly-killed saddle horses, some of them animals that must have been worth many thousand roubles. Around the bodies were groups of Hungarian soldiers tearing at them with knives; with hands and faces dripping with blood, they were gorging themselves on the raw meat. I have never seen in all my experience of war a more horrible and pitiable spectacle than these soldiers, half crazed with hunger, tearing the carcasses like famished wolves.

The American journalist who reported these words was quickly convinced that Przemyśl had surrendered through sheer hunger.[14]

Yet despite this mounting plight of the Central Powers, the sequel was to be their most successful action of the whole world war. Although Falkenhayn was convinced that the war could not be settled in the east at all, in April he agreed to reinforce the Galician front by eight divisions from the west. In return, German generals took over the commands there in decisive places. On 2 May, there took place the breakthrough at Gorlice which snowballed into a vast gain of territory. On 4 June Przemyśl was recaptured (by German troops), on 22 June Lvov followed. The allies swiftly advanced 360 kilometres, pushing the Russians almost out of Galicia to a shortened and therefore more densely concentrated front. But then problems with supplies, largely caused by difficulties in restoring the rail network, put an end to the campaign on 8 August.

The allies now went their separate ways in the east again. Falkenhayn wanted to relieve the hard-pressed Turks, which made it necessary to open up the land connection by knocking out Serbia, something which was achieved in the autumn of 1915 with the aid of Bulgaria.[15] Conrad, for his part, had suffered in 1915 from his increasing dependence on German forces. He and the AOK felt that the Germans had slighted both them and their Empire by publicly monopolizing the victories in the east. But the AOK's 'solo-tour', the Rowno campaign of 26 August to 14 October, billed as a *Schwarzgelbe* or black-yellow offensive to finally free eastern Galicia from Russian occupation, ended in disaster with a loss of 230,000 men. One of Conrad's key advisers commented that the 'entire operation belongs among the most shameful in the annals of what we have been able to accomplish in leadership'.[16] Indeed, the self-confidence of the AOK and their troops, the restoration of which had been one of the main aims of the offensive, now cracked up even more. Austria-Hungary's reputation in the Balkans—with Bulgaria, but especially with Romania —suffered decisively. The result was a further deterioration of the Monarchy's position within the alliance, particularly the relationship of the AOK and the Ballhausplatz to their German counterparts.

Already in the Carpathian campaign the flower of the peacetime Habsburg army had perished. Whereas at the start of the war there had been 1,612,000 men in the field, by the end of 1914 2,232,000 had been sent to the Eastern front, of which 979,000 were already counted as losses. According to these figures, 12 per cent of the men and 14.7 per cent of the officers were dead, while 27.8 per cent of the men and 12.8 per cent of the officers were prisoners of war. From 1 January to 30 April 1915 alone, 793,000 officers and men had been lost, of whom 358,000 were dead, captured or missing. Throughout 1915 an enormous supply of manpower was to remain imperative in view of the losses of the Gorlice and Rowno campaigns—500,000 and 230,000 respectively.[17]

An even more alarming phenomenon for the AOK became apparent by late 1915. Slav troops, although proving reliable when placed under German command, were failing to perform adequately under Austro-Hungarian leadership, a fact which seemed to be documented by the extraordinarily high numbers of prisoners taken—100,000 during the *Schwarzgelbe* offensive. Entire Czech, but also Ruthene and Polish battalions were surrendering to the enemy without a fight.[18] Signs of a decline in morale were obvious. Most alarming, however, was the transformation of the officer corps. While 5.2 per cent of German army officers lost by late 1915 were missing or captured, the corresponding figure in the Austro-Hungarian army during the Rowno campaign was almost 30 per cent, and in the 4th army it was even 33 per cent. Similarly, if in the German army the proportion of wounded to sick officers was in a ratio of 2.4:1, among the Monarchy's forces it was 1:1.6. The structure of the Austrian officer corps had undergone a considerable change since the beginning of the war, both in character and personnel. The proportion of reserve officers had steadily increased which meant that more and more non-German and non-Magyar officers were holding positions of power at a tactical level. A large number of the career officers were also needed in the hinterland—indeed, they were striving for such placements. This produced striking phenomena at the front. For instance, in June 1916 the newly formed 70th Honvéd ID numbered only nine career officers in its four regiments with two of the regiments possessing a single career officer. The same deficiencies were evident among the reserve officer corps.

In December 1915, the AOK exploited the let-up in activity on the Eastern front to shift its attention at last to the Italian theatre of war. Since territorial gains in the east seemed highly unlikely, Conrad had come to regard the Russian front as a millstone round his neck, preventing him from fulfilling his ambitions against Italy. Above all, the Austrians' successful defence against superior Italian forces had matched their expectations far more than events in the east. A defensive victory in Bukovina at the turn of the year served only to increase the AOK's dismissal of the Eastern theatre where it was felt installing huge numbers of shelters or 'fox-holes' would be the best remedy against further Russian attacks. This ostensibly defensive stance dealt yet another blow to morale: Austro-Hungarian troops began to lack fighting practice on a front which was generally passive, while the tactical training in which they engaged was erroneously still geared towards attack and not defence. Although manpower losses had been recouped, with peak levels reached in the number of men, the Eastern front by 1916 was being steadily weakened in favour of the Italian theatre in terms of ammunition, heavy artillery and machine-guns; and most units which were viewed as elite troops were transported to Tyrol.

The result in the east came on 4 June 1916. General Brusilov, already a notorious figure to the Austrians, began a bombardment at Lutsk (Volhynia) against Archduke Joseph Ferdinand's 4th army and in Bukovina against Pflanzer-Baltin's 7th army, swiftly overwhelming the opposing forces. Perhaps three quarters of a million Austrian soldiers were lost, including half the 4th army. The Habsburg officers and commanders had blundered disastrously, with Conrad himself now subject to the severest criticism from both Berlin and Vienna. Having already failed in his May offensive against Italy, he was faced with chaos in the east and could no longer oppose full subordination to the German military. On 3 August a German common command was created under Hindenburg for most of the Eastern front, only a first step towards the installation on 13 September of a joint High Command with Kaiser Wilhelm—in fact Hindenburg and Ludendorff —at its head. This development was actually welcomed by many in the Austrian and Hungarian leadership, by opponents of Conrad, and even by the Habsburg commander-in-chief Archduke Friedrich who for a long time had wanted to excuse himself and retire. It is thus clear that the AOK's status in the Monarchy was in a shaky condition even before the change of Habsburg monarchs in November when, by introducing a new constitutional regime, the AOK's influence was undermined even more.[19] If the AOK's failings had important implications with regard to the power structure within the Monarchy, it also of course decisively affected relations with Germany: not only militarily, but in the way that it laid the basis for that economic and political dependence from which Emperor Karl would seek to extract himself in the Sixtus Affair.

In the wake of Brusilov's victory the whole of Bukovina and the eastern part of Galicia remained under Russian occupation with the front moving perilously close again to Lvov. This had domestic repercussions in the Monarchy. An increase in strikes was followed from the summer of 1916 by a mounting display of Panslav tendencies. A further military consequence was Romania's entry into the war on the side of the Entente (27 August). Although the Central Powers cooperated and conquered most of Romania in a relatively short period—September 1916 to January 1917—the balance sheet for Austria-Hungary by the end of the year was striking. In 1916 the Empire had lost over a million officers and men in the east, 60 per cent of their total losses, proving indeed that this theatre was a fundamental drain on resources while at the same time offering nothing of advantage for the future.

Indeed, the Monarchy's permanent engagement in the east only brought new dangers. On 1 July 1917, the 'Kerensky offensive', the only offensive of revolutionary Russia, began and specifically exploited to good effect the national disunity of the Habsburg forces. Kerensky employed the Czechoslovak Brigade, recruited from Czech and Slovak prisoners of war, against Habsburg regiments of the same nationality, producing a breakthrough in eastern Galicia and in Bukovina on a front of 300 kilometres and to a depth of 65 kilometres.[20] The AOK had to rely on German help again in order, in a rapid counter-thrust, to expel the Russians almost totally from Habsburg territory, thereby diminishing any military importance of the campaign. More important was its political effect. Already in 1915–16 Slav troops had aided early Russian successes, but to a degree greatly exaggerated in the accounts on both sides, reaffirming all the more the Czechs' reputation as 'grave-diggers' of the Monarchy. The battle at Zborów on 1–2 July 1917 then boosted this image at home and abroad: and it was to become an essential component in the mythology of the post-war Czechoslovak state.

By the end of August 1917, the 'North-Eastern front'—as it was termed by the AOK—had slipped back into a certain uneasy calm. With only sporadic local engagements, the AOK was able to withdraw some units or relieve them with exhausted troops from the other theatres. Thus, for the imminent offensive on the Isonzo it was possible to transfer to Italy three Austrian and four German divisions from the Austro-Hungarian section of the Eastern front. The Bolshevik Revolution then produced a two-month armistice which the AOK had been anxiously trying to effect in the east since the fall of Tsardom. One result of this transitional period in the winter months, when delegates from the Central Powers and the Bolsheviks were haggling over the slogans of 'annexation' and 'self-determination' at Brest-

Litovsk, was a peace treaty with Ukraine which had seceded from Russia. For Vienna the key purpose of what was termed the 'bread peace' was economic, to secure grain supplies for the Monarchy. But there were serious military repercussions after the Bolshevik armistice collapsed and confusion reigned in Ukraine: the Austrians, after some initial resistance, were forced to bow to the DOHL and participate in the invasion of Ukraine. While this might have seemed to some as an extra lever with which to secure the promised grain supplies, the reality for Austria was to confirm that operations in the east simply wasted manpower while bearing few fruits. Instead of supplying the one million tons of grain agreed to by the Ukrainian treaty, only 46,225 tons could be imported into the Empire during 1918. Most of the food requisitioned in Ukraine was needed to supply the forces of occupation.[21]

From the start of the war, events on the Eastern front had been closely intertwined with the issue of food supplies for Austria-Hungary's civilian population. Only on the Eastern front were large agricultural regions of the Empire transformed into battlefields or immediate war zone. This caused a crop failure in Galicia for years, and it came after bad weather had already diminished the Austrian crop (minus Galicia) of 1914 by 37 per cent. This alone was an immense threat to Austria's civilian population since the Monarchy in the years preceding the war had failed to cover its food require-ments and depended on the import of wheat and corn which was now closed due to the Entente blockade.[22] Galicia, while possessing 28 per cent of Austria's population, had produced a sizeable propor-tion of its cereals, including wheat (20 per cent) corn (21), barley (22), rye (29) and oats (29). The crownland had also owned more than half of Austria's horses, an especially crucial resource in wartime. With the opening of hostilities much of the Galician population had fled westwards from the Russian 'steam-roller' and thenceforth had to be supported by the state; this, at a time when harvest yields in the rest of Austria were fast decreasing due to the lack of manpower, cattle, seeds and fertilizer.

In this wider food crisis, which the Galician predicament had exacerbated, there was to be no cure from the direction of Hungary which still had a considerable food surplus. Within the Empire, Hungary had normally sold most of its considerable agricultural surplus (about 85 per cent) to Austria, the remainder abroad. But from the first negotiations about food coordination in June 1915, the Hungarians had insisted on prioritising a per capita supply to their own population based on peacetime consumption. The result was that whereas Austria had major headaches in feeding its own civilians and refugees as well as raising its own share of the army's supply, Hungary proceeded to provide its army share out of the surplus which it had formerly sold to Austria. So the war in the east contributed in its own way to the dualist system's economic disintegration and was unable, either from Ukraine or Romania, to provide anything but temporary succour for Austria's predicament.[23]

The 'bread peace' between Austria-Hungary and Ukraine in February 1918 was followed, after a short burst of hostilities, by those with the Bolsheviks on 3 March at Brest-Litovsk, and with Romania on 7 May at Bucharest. While these treaties enabled some troops to be transferred to the Italian front, none of them brought any relief of significance to the Monarchy's food crisis. It can be said that they acted negatively also in that they further stimulated war-weariness and national and social unrest. Moreover, if the Bolshevik slogan of 'self-determination' had intensified Slav agitation in the Monarchy, the imperial elite had themselves contributed to alienating their subjects in the north-eastern provinces. While the Ruthene nationality as a whole had been treated as suspect from the start of the war, by February 1918 the elite had turned this policy on its head in order to secure a Ukrainian peace: they promised a Ruthene crownland in eastern Galicia—and as a result alienated the Poles who had previously been an element steadfastly loyal to the Habsburgs. An equally disturbing result of the treaties in the east was the stream of prisoners of war who began to enter the Empire. These 'home-comers' were not only unenthusiastic about returning to the front-line to risk their lives again, but had come into close contact with Bolshevik propaganda. Whereas many soldiers of the non-German nationalities became strengthened in their national consciousness, the largest number of disgruntled soldiers were those who had been infected with socialist-revolutionary ideas. From April 1918 there were a series of revolts by returning soldiers which reached their peak in May and June.[24] The seeds of disintegration which the home-comers brought with them played a considerable role in the final collapse in the autumn of 1918.

The Eastern front was a theatre of the world war which did not decisively influence the outcome of the war through its battles, nor even by the peace treaties signed at the front. Its decisive influence on the course of events was that it severely restricted Austria-Hungary's capabilities in military, political and economic terms. Being dependent on the help of its much more powerful ally Germany, the Monarchy was deprived for most phases of the war of its sovereignty. All its attempts to regain some freedom of manoeuvre ended in disaster: the Tyrol offensive of May 1916, the Sixtus Affair of 1917–18, the Piave offensive in 1918. The real military significance of the Eastern theatre was that it absorbed not only Habsburg troops from other theatres, but also a large quantity of German forces from the Western front. The Western front was the only place where a final end to hostilities could be decided, while the peculiarities of the Eastern front—most notably its sheer expanse—prevented any real decision which might favour the Central Powers. As a result of this, the Russian collapse brought no great relief in military or economic terms to the Monarchy; rather it produced a whole new set of national and social dangers. It was a steady drain on resources, playing its part in exhausting an Empire which could not cope with a four-year experience of 'total war'.

NOTES

1. See however Count Berchtold's concern in 1914 about Russia's impact among the Ruthenes of eastern Galicia: Z.A.B. Zeman, *The Break-Up of the Habsburg Empire 1914–1918* (Oxford, 1961) p. 12.

2. In 216 BC at Cannae in southern Italy, Hannibal had defeated the Romans with a double envelopment of a superior enemy, one of the greatest tactical manoeuvres of military history.

3. Rudolf Jeřábek, *Die Brussilowoffensive 1916. Ein Wendepunkt der Koalitionskriegführung der Mittelmächte*, 2 vols (Phil.Diss. Vienna, 1982) I, pp. 3, 12. On Austro-Hungarian military coordination, see two articles by Norman Stone: 'Moltke and Conrad: Relations between the Austro-Hungarian and German General Staffs, 1909–1914', in P. M. Kennedy (ed.), *The War Plans of the Great Powers 1880–1914* (Boston, 1979) [reprinted from *The Historical Journal*, 9 no. 2 (1966)]; and 'Die Mobilmachung der österreichisch-ungarischen Armee 1914', in *Militärgeschichtliche Mitteilungen*, Nr 16 (Freiburg, 1974), pp. 67–95. For more recent reassessments, see Holger Herwig, 'Disjointed Allies: Coalition Warfare in Berlin and Vienna, 1914', *Journal of Military History*, 54 (1990) pp. 265–80; and Graydon A. Tunstall Jr, *Planning for War against Russia and Serbia: Austro-Hungarian and German Military Strategies, 1871–1914* (New York, 1993).

4. István Deák, *Beyond Nationalism. A Social and Political History of the Habsburg Officer Corps 1848–1918* (Oxford, 1992) pp. 178–189. For the official statistics: Maximilian Ehnl, *Die österreichisch-ungarische Landmacht nach Aufbau, Gliederung, Friedensgarnison, Einteilung und*

nationaler Zusammensetzung im Sommer 1914, [Ergänzungsheft 9 of *Österreich-Ungarns letzter Krieg*] (Vienna, 1934) p. 14; *Österreich-Ungarns letzter Krieg 1914–1918*, 7 vols (Vienna, 1930–8) I, p. 44 and II, Beilage I.

5. Oskar Regele, *Feldmarschall Conrad. Auftrag und Erfüllung 1906–1918* (Vienna, 1965) p. 161.

6. Ibid., pp. 163, 169. Although the broad thrust of these figures remains accurate, see the new detailed assessment by David Stevenson, *Armaments and the Coming of War. Europe 1904–1914* (Oxford, 1996) pp. 1–9.

7. The Landsturm consisted of older, long-retired reservists. Landsturm units were worse equipped (fewer machine-guns for example) than the ordinary troops and had originally been designated for security tasks in the rear-zones.

8. For new material on the Monarchy's misguided war plans and its early campaigns against Serbia, see Rudolf Jeřábek, *Potiorek. General im Schatten von Sarajevo* (Graz, Vienna and Cologne, 1991) pp. 97ff.

9. *Österreich-Ungarns letzter Krieg*, I, p. 177.

10. Franz Conrad von Hötzendorf, *Private Aufzeichnungen. Erste Veröffentlichungen aus den Papieren des k.u.k. Generalstabs-Chefs*, ed. Kurt Peball (Vienna and Munich, 1977) p. 91.

11. The atmosphere in occupied Lvov was observed in December 1914 by Bernard Pares (*Day by Day with the Russian Army 1914–1915* (London, 1915) pp. 75–76): 'Lvov is taking on more of the character of a Russian town. Many of the Jews have left. The Russian signs over new restaurants, stores, etc, meet the eye everywhere. Of the Little Russian [Ruthene] party which supported the Austrians, many have now returned and are making their peace with the new authorities . . . Numbers of Russian priests are pouring into Galicia, but not fast enough for the Uniat[e] villages which have embraced Orthodoxy; as soon as they arrive, peasants come with their carts and take them off to their parishes, without waiting for any formal distribution.'

12. Holger Herwig, *The First World War. Germany and Austria-Hungary 1914–1918* (London and New York, 1997) p. 148.

13. Notably on 3 April 1915 when Czech soldiers of k.u.k. infantry regiment 28 not only put up no resistance to the Russians but surrendered *en masse*, as a result of which their sector of the front collapsed. The subsequent investigation revealed a string of blunders and mishandling of the regiment by Hungarian officers while it had been in the hinterland; and the behaviour of the regiment at the front must be seen as a logical consequence of that experience. See Richard Plaschka, 'Zur Vorgeschichte des Überganges von Einheiten des Infanterieregiment Nr. 28', *Österreich und Europa. Festgabe für Hugo Hantsch* (Vienna, 1965).

14. Stanley Washburn, *The Russian Campaign, April to August 1915* (London, 1915) pp. 31–32.

15. On Falkenhayn, see the study by Holger Afflerbach, *Falkenhayn. Politisches Denken und Handeln im Kaiserreich* (Munich, 1994).
16. Major Karl Schneller, quoted in Herwig, *The First World War*, p. 147. Herwig notes that Conrad had once again asked too much of his armies and ignored climatic conditions.
17. *Österreich-Ungarns letzter Krieg*, II, pp. 118, 141, 270, 279 and Beilage I; III (Vienna, 1932) p. 181.
18. Jeřábek, *Die Brussilowoffensive 1916*, I, p. 109.
19. Manfried Rauchensteiner, *Der Tod des Doppeladlers. Österreich-Ungarn und der Erste Weltkrieg* (Graz, Vienna and Cologne, 1993) pp. 362–68.
20. For a thorough analysis see Karel Pichlík, Bohumír Klípa and Jitka Zabloudilová, *Československští Legionáři 1914–1920* (Prague, 1996).
21. Alfred Krauss and Franz Klingenbrunner, 'Die Besetzung der Ukraine 1918', in Hugo Kerchnawe (ed.), *Die Militärverwaltung in den von den österreichisch-ungarischen Truppen besetzten Gebieten* (Vienna, 1928) p. 389; *Österreich-Ungarns letzter Krieg*, VII (Vienna, 1938) Beilage 2.
22. *Österreichisches Statistisches Handbuch für die im Reichsrate vertretenen Königreiche und Länder*, ed. k.k. Statistische Zentralkommission, XXXI 1912 (Vienna, 1913) p. 73.
23. Hans Löwenfeld-Russ, *Die Regelung der Volksernährung im Kriege* (Vienna, 1926) pp. 146–58; Löwenfeld-Russ, *Im Kampf gegen den Hunger. Aus den Erinnerungen des Staatssekretärs für Volksernährung 1918–1920* (Vienna, 1986) p. 37.
24. Richard Plaschka, Horst Haselsteiner, Arnold Suppan, *Innere Front. Militärassistenz, Widerstand und Umsturz in der Donaumonarchie 1918*, 2 vols (Vienna, 1974) I, pp. 278–90.

8

Disintegration and Defeat
The Austro-Hungarian
Revolution

Mark Cornwall

In March 1918, General Karl Tersztyánszky, a former commander on the Eastern front but now demoted to a largely ceremonial position at the Imperial Court, pictured the Habsburg Monarchy in extremely gloomy colours. 'Unfortunately', he wrote to a fellow-general, paraphrasing *Hamlet*, 'so much is rotten in the state of Denmark that the door stands wide open to pessimism.'[1] On the Italian front, now Austria-Hungary's main military theatre, the Habsburg armed forces in spite of their sweeping success over Italy at Caporetto the previous autumn were stationary and starving. In the interior of the Empire the situation, in Tersztyánszky's view, had never been so bad. There had just been widespread strikes in all the major cities as well as a serious naval revolt in Dalmatia. In Hungary the politicians were carrying on in time-honoured fashion, pressing for more economic and military independence from the rest of the Monarchy. In Austria (Cisleithania) meanwhile, Polish, Czech and South Slav politicians were behaving in a positively treasonable fashion, and yet were still receiving overtures from the government of Baron Ernst von Seidler. Even in Vienna, the dynastic capital, Tersztyánszky could find few hopeful signs. He crept around in civilian dress in order to avoid abuse from the Viennese. On the tram he listened, horrified, to malicious jokes about the Imperial family or to soldiers' banter which made his hair stand on end.[2] He could not imagine what the future would bring:

The war has brought our old Monarchy nothing good . . . I have never been a pessimist, but I am fast becoming one. Everywhere you see only

opportunism and frivolity; everything, everything, is different from what
it once was. The poor old Emperor can have no rest in his grave, for
his whole life and governmental work is basically destroyed and the
new establishment is already now creaking in every joint.

How Austria-Hungary in wartime had reached this state of affairs,
and why the Empire disintegrated in its own 'Revolution' in October
1918, are the themes which will be explored in this chapter. Clarity
is vital to make sense of the divergent conclusions reached by historians as to why dissolution occurred. For while there is consensus that
the war itself was fatal for the Monarchy's survival, the issue of what
weight to give the myriad disintegrative forces is still highly debatable. If we are to agree with Jean Bérenger, 'the dissolution of Austria-
Hungary is not explained by the question of nationalities, the oppression of the Slavs and the Romanians, or even the tremendous tensions
created during the war. . . . The political catastrophe is largely
explained by external factors.'[3] In complete contrast, Alan Sked suggests that 'its dissolution was not brought about by the Allies' but by
'the peoples of the Monarchy [who] at long last demanded their
rights'.[4] Apart from setting up this dialectic on the impact of internal
and external threats to Austria-Hungary's existence, we also need to
examine the 'staging posts' towards disintegration during the war.
Just as one might easily ascribe the demise of the Monarchy to factors
at work long before 1914, so in studying the war years—and the
short-term causes of the collapse—we can highlight specific elements
which sustained or weakened the imperial body. Through this we can
better understand why the Habsburg Empire disintegrated when it
did—not sooner or later.

To begin with the apex of the imperial structure is apt. For in July
1914 citizens of Austria-Hungary went to war principally to defend
the prestige and honour of the Habsburg Emperor, Franz Joseph. His
dynasty continued to be the main ideological glue for the Empire.
Those thousands who were mobilized into the armed forces and
other sectors of the war effort temporarily supplied a new common
bond of sacrifice on behalf of the imperial mission: and over a million
would die for that cause during four years. It was not surprising that
defeat in war would in itself (as in the 1860s) gravely weaken
dynastic power, this time leaving a vacuum which only new 'nation-
states' could fill at the dynasty's expense. Franz Joseph contributed to
this scenario because, as recent biographers (nudging aside the
nostalgic image) have noted, he did not possess the imagination or

the will to give his Empire a non-dynastic *raison d'être* in the decades before 1914.[5] As we will see, in the increasingly ideological conflict of 1914–18 the Habsburg state entity was then not equipped with adequate or vibrant arguments with which to perpetuate its mission and oppose the propaganda of its nationalist enemies.

Even so, the death of Franz Joseph in the middle of the war was in itself a blow to that mission. His great-nephew Karl, the new Emperor-King, could hardly fulfil the dynastic role embodied in his predecessor for seventy years, or indeed command the same respect, even if he regularly toured his subjects at the front and in the hinterland. Tersztyánszky's words above hint at this. One of the quips which Tersztyánszky overheard in Vienna recounted how, on a visit to the new Emperor at the High Command 'you hope to meet a 30–year old there, but you find a man with the appearance of a 20–year-old youth, who thinks, speaks and acts like a 10–year-old boy'.

Yet it was not just Karl's youth and inexperience which caused rumblings of discontent amongst many of the military and political elite. It was the fact that, unlike Franz Joseph, he was determined to introduce change to the Monarchy. Here he was bound to step on many toes, both of those who were conservatively inclined and of those who felt he was not moving far enough. Events were to show that a policy of weak compromise or indecision was the worst possible one to adopt during wartime among subjects already depressed by economic hardships and war-weariness. It was undoubtedly better either to push through swift, radical measures by decree, making serious adjustments to the Monarchy which would satisfy more of its constituent national leaders; or to shore up the bureaucratic-military regime which had existed since the beginning of the war. Both of these 'options' in themselves avoided consensus while posing obvious risks for the future. Neither of them were effectively pursued. The first was impossible largely because of the obstinate outlook of the German-Austrian and Magyar elites who increasingly wished to use the wartime emergency to reinforce their own threatened national and social status. The second was not one which Karl himself wanted to pursue, but which he could never wholly escape.

For Karl's 'liberal' leanings, or his desire for any imaginative 'federal' restructuring of the Empire which would redistribute power more evenly, should not be exaggerated. Certainly he wanted to bring the 'sorely missed blessings of peace' to his peoples (an early announcement which hardly enhanced the war effort) and to restore 'constitutional government' to Austria. Both ideas were given an added urgency by the February revolution which toppled the Tsar in Russia and sent a dire warning to the Habsburgs. He was also duly keen to push though suffrage reform in Hungary (the burning political issue in Budapest). But at the same time, as one might expect from a man ensconced among Franz Ferdinand's former advisers, Karl could not avoid a semi-autocratic outlook at times. Witness his inclination to install a 'ministry of generals' during the social crisis of spring 1918. Then there was his unilateral secret peace-feeler to the West in March 1917 through his French brother-in-law Prince Sixtus. When the move became public a year later as the 'Sixtus Affair', Karl—unmasked before an outraged Germany—felt bound to deny his own role; in Robin Okey's words, he was pushed into the position of a 'mendacious autocrat'.[6]

Notwithstanding his vague talk of federalizing the Monarchy, Karl gave no serious lead in the direction of reforming the imperial structure. Rather, he himself helped to confirm the rigid dualist system. Immediately on his accession in November 1916, he acceded to István Tisza's wish for a swift coronation in Budapest, where he took an oath to preserve the integrity of the Hungarian lands. At the same time he aroused justifiable suspicion about his intentions in Austria through declining to take the oath to the Austrian constitution. The door was left open for what Czernin, his enigmatic principal minister, was keen to implement: namely to impose, by *oktroi* (decree) and before any recall of parliament, a 'German solution' for Austria. Austria would be restructured to give the Germans decisive control, paralleling that of the Magyars in Hungary. The fact that such an oktroi (in other words, use of paragraph 14 of the constitution) was abandoned in April 1917 was certainly due in part to Karl opposing it. Like Tsar Nicholas II, Karl's indecisiveness—which would be so evident in the last days of the Empire[7]—was at times overtaken by a sharp streak of obstinacy or resoluteness on certain principles. But it did not mean the disappearance of this 'German course': it quickly resurfaced and would decisively exacerbate national tensions in Austria in the last year of war. The new Emperor, amidst all the talk of a 'new regime', was unable to think far beyond the governmental framework he had inherited.

Among the Monarchy's elite it was the military in particular who could feel disgruntled at Karl's 'new broom'. Karl was determined to weaken its influence and soon began making major changes at the High Command (AOK: *Armeeoberkommando*). Many staff officers may not have regretted the dismissal of the prickly Conrad von

KAISER KARL AND HIS GENERALS
(including, seated far-right, Conrad von Hötzendorf)

Hötzendorf as Chief of the General Staff and his replacement by the far more congenial Arz von Straussenburg. They were probably more irritated by the spartan conditions now imposed at the AOK (which deprived them of their usual supply of cream cakes).[8] More serious was Karl's assumption of the post of commander-in-chief in place of Archduke Friedrich whose post had long been a 'fiction' from which he was keen to be relieved. The monarch now directly interfered in the conduct of the war, assuming more responsibility for the army's successes or failures, and slowing the decision-making process since the AOK was now often forced to be mobile, following him around. Those with the outlook of Conrad (now dispatched to command the army in southern Tyrol) were endlessly critical of the new laxity of approach, epitomized by the abolition of two forms of punishment (tying up and chaining up) which they felt to be vital as a means of disciplining the ranks.

Far more disturbing, however, was the new regime's encroachment upon the military sphere in the hinterland. It is important to empha-size that for the first two years of the war the military had wielded considerable powers in the Austrian half of the Empire, which was effectively run as a bureaucratic-military dictatorship. In late 1916 after the murder of Count Karl Stürgkh (the Austrian Prime Minister), Conrad and others, who had constantly jostled with Stürgkh to

171

secure more influence (in Bohemia for example), pushed yet again for an intensified militarization of Austria. It was a rearguard action since the military hierarchy, as one Austrian historian has stressed, was already a shell of its former self because of the disasters on the Eastern front.[9] It would never recover its former power, and so would always be able to blame the political authorities in Austria or Hungary for the fracturing of control which occurred in the final years of the war. Karl's half-measures towards a more inclusive regime for the Empire not only undercut the special powers of the military, but unleashed a barrage of criticism against them. One example was the Emperor's amnesty for political prisoners in July 1917 which allowed convicted 'traitors' like the Czech leader Karel Kramář back into the community. Until the end of the war the amnesty was viewed by the military elite as a major stimulus to desertion; as Conrad himself put it, 'the men expect with certainty that when peace is concluded the amnesty will be extended to deserters to the enemy as well'.[10] The amnesty of course was only a small part of the restoration of some governmental 'normality' in Cisleithania in mid-1917. Most notable was the convocation of the Reichsrat in May and the concomitant relaxing of press censorship in the Monarchy as a whole. While the Reichsrat became a veritable forum for nationalist discontent, the greater freedom of information was crucial in diffusing nationalist ideas which had earlier been subsumed beneath a forced show of 'patriotic consensus' towards the Habsburg war.

From the summer of 1917 at least, social discontent in the hinterland began to play a greater role in sapping the morale of the armed forces. This was entirely natural since the more the army became a body of 'civilians in arms', the more it mirrored those trends spreading elsewhere in the Monarchy. Front and hinterland constantly interacted. It is useful to keep this in mind when weighing up the old argument, still popular among some historians, which lauds the Habsburg army for doing its duty and fighting on till the bitter end while the Empire collapsed around it. Certainly there were few open revolts at the front until the last days, and a surprising degree of cohesion and discipline was maintained in most units. But Alan Sked's idea that the army was not 'overwhelmed by the nationality question' is misleading.[11] By the summer of 1918 the army, like the Empire, was fast disintegrating and certainly could not have faced another winter of war. The resemblance to the Russian war machine a year earlier was striking. Thousands of Austro-Hungarian soldiers were exceeding their leave and remaining in the hinterland; indeed, their number has been set as high as 250,000, roughly the same as the number of troops serving in the front-line against Italy. If they were motivated in part by simple war-weariness and doubts about further sacrificing themselves for a questionable cause, they were also increasingly enveloped in the social and nationalist unrest, which they first heard about, and then experienced.

One could argue from this, as military circles were wont to do, that the Habsburg army was being 'stabbed in the back'. It was denied adequate food supplies and could not remain unaffected by mounting disturbances in the hinterland. But this argument cannot be taken too far.[12] While it is clear that the Monarchy eventually collapsed from within, the internal disintegration went hand in hand with the army's lacklustre military campaigns and its basic inability to win the war. This failure, a key underlying reason for the Empire's dissolution, owed a great deal to the mistakes made by the High Command itself.

From the start of the war the AOK had helped to put its own troops at a disadvantage in relation to the enemy. Already Austria-Hungary had fallen seriously behind in the arms race in comparison to the other Great Powers. But this deficiency—for which the military for once were not responsible—was then compounded by grave miscalculations in military planning. Both the competence of Serbia's forces and the difficulties of a Russian campaign had been under-estimated by Conrad who had put his faith in a supposedly flexible plan of operations which, just like Germany's Schlieffen plan, proved to be remarkably inflexible. Austria-Hungary's mobilization was then bungled and inadequate forces were sent both to the Balkan and Eastern theatres. As a result, Serbia (like France) was not quickly eliminated from the war, while the Eastern front simply became a bottomless pit into which the Monarchy's resources were thrown. It thereby diverted these resources from Conrad's favourite objective— 'perfidious Italy'. Although even Conrad had tried desperately to prevent Italy entering the conflict in May 1915 and opening up a third front for the Monarchy (which he predicted would lead to its eventual collapse), he soon brushed aside his doubts and pushed for that theatre—'these scoundrels' the Italians—to be made a priority for the Habsburg war effort.[13] There was some realism here in that, arguably, a Habsburg victory, with its implications of French encirclement, might have seriously affected the course of the war. But there was also a strong streak of Social-Darwinist fatalism. In June

1914 Conrad had written to his lover that the approaching conflict would be 'a hopeless struggle, but even so it must be undertaken, for such an ancient monarchy and such a glorious army cannot perish ingloriously';[14] in the July crisis he had been the key figure in pressing for a military solution against Serbia. In the same stubborn and fatalistic spirit he pressed constantly during the war for the offensive. In June 1918 he was the prime architect of Austria-Hungary's disastrous last offensive against Italy at a time when his fellow-commanders were advising against any further straining of military resources.

The Monarchy's early military disasters had fatal repercussions especially in the field of manpower. There were losses of 600 officers and 22,000 men in the first confused campaign against Serbia alone. By the end of 1914 the figure totalled over a million on all fronts and it mounted steadily during the fruitless Carpathian campaign of early 1915 and in subsequent months. By 1916, with a monthly loss at the front of 224,000 men, the march-formations which every month carried reserves to the war zones were no longer covering gaps in the manpower. This placed increased burdens upon existing troops in the front-line and a degree of restricted leave which damaged morale.

This was then exacerbated by the nationality issue which undermined unit cohesion as well as throwing up a host of questions about the kind of war in which the Empire was engaged. Increasingly, for example, there were not enough Croat officers to command predominantly Croat regiments or insufficient 'national' reserves for a particular division. The military compounded this deficiency by stereotyping certain nationalities as 'reliable' (German, Magyar, Slovene, Croat) or 'unreliable' (Serb, Czech, Ruthene). This threw a new element into the equation when it came to deploying 'suspect' troops in sensitive areas of the homeland or the front. Even so, because of the mass deaths, those who were promoted into trustworthy positions were often precisely those ex-civilians who had strong nationalist sympathies or only a shaky allegiance to the Habsburg cause. We should stress that many educated soldiers undoubtedly retained a 'dual allegiance'—to their nationality and 'homeland', but also to their Empire. But commitment to the latter was threatened as the war continued without end. Paradoxically, when an enemy was knocked out—Serbia (1916), Romania (1916) or Russia (1917–18)—the effect was not always beneficial, for certain troops then began to question the purpose of the war and to look forward to a speedy peace. The Habsburg cause also looked shakier as the nationalist debate in the hinterland became more polarized. When in mid-1918 the army finally began a programme of 'patriotic instruction' in the ranks, it found it hard, particularly at such a late stage, to muster many attractive arguments with which to raise morale.[15] It was no match for the nationalist propaganda that was circulating through the domestic press, reinforced by an imaginative propaganda campaign directed against the Monarchy from Italy.

Mention of the latter introduces us to the question of external threats to Austria-Hungary's existence. How far did they contribute to the collapse and then to disintegration? Most of the countries with which the Empire was at war either had designs upon Habsburg territory (Serbia, Romania and Tsarist Russia on Bosnia, Transylvania and Galicia respectively); or were finally prepared to exploit the Empire's national tensions in order to win the war (Britain and France). For Italy, the two objectives coincided forcefully by 1918. Both the United States and Bolshevik Russia viewed the Monarchy ideologically: as a reactionary imperialist target which needed to be transformed through a 'liberal' or a socialist upheaval. In other words, the potential of all these external threats emanated directly from Austria-Hungary's own unsatisfactory internal situation, lending emphasis to the primacy of domestic circumstances in its fate. Only by exiting early from the war could the Empire have been saved from mounting encirclement by enemies whose agendas increasingly mirrored or exploited the social-nationalist unrest within its borders.

Here, historians have rightly emphasized Austria-Hungary's satellite relationship to its over-mighty ally, Germany, as a fatal ingredient. The German alliance helped tie the Monarchy into the world war when, by early 1916, it had subdued Serbia and completed its major war aim. Military dependence became just one strong thread in the German strait-jacket from which the Monarchy could not extricate itself. Early in the war, after the initial disasters on the Eastern front, the Germans had mooted the idea that Ludendorff should assume overall command of allied forces in the east; Conrad would be subordinate to him though still in charge of the Austro-Hungarian sector at the front. Conrad managed to resist this for, though committed to the German alliance—'the fixed guideline for all my behaviour' as he wrote later[16]—he was equally determined to assert the Monarchy's military independence and prestige; all the more so, since it soon became abundantly clear that Austria-Hungary's military priorities (notably Italy) in no way tallied with Germany's.

This was reflected in Conrad's tense relationship with Falkenhayn, the German Chief of the General Staff, and in his efforts, when possible, to 'go it alone': for instance, in the *Schwarzgelbe* campaign in late 1915 and the Trentino offensive of May 1916.

It remained a fact, however, which Conrad's deep umbrage at German contempt for the Monarchy's performance could not diminish, that Austria-Hungary was the junior military partner. The Monarchy simply lacked the resources to pursue a war successfully on several fronts. Thus, all of its major military breakthroughs— Gorlice (1915), Serbia (1915), Romania (1916) and Caporetto (1917)—came about when the allies combined forces. When Conrad tried to be too independent, the result was usually disastrous. In June 1916, when Brusilov broke through in the east, Conrad and Falkenhayn were predictably pursuing separate goals in Italy and at Verdun respectively. This, together with careful Russian preparation and the incompetence of the Austrian commanders, enabled Brusilov to wipe out two of Conrad's armies. Conrad now could not resist Germany taking over control of the whole of the Eastern front. Austro-Hungarian forces there became completely intertwined with their German counterparts, the latter acting as 'corset strings' for the Habsburg forces.[17] Nor could the Austrians object when Kaiser Wilhelm in September assumed overall command of the Central Powers' military operations. This effectively subordinated the Habsburgs to the Hohenzollerns and increasingly meant that military policy for both allies was dominated by Germany's generals.

It is important not to dismiss the Monarchy as wholly in Germany's military shackles after 1916. The Austrians, for example, still retained almost full control on the Italian front, which after 1917 became 'the front' for all intents and purposes. Yet in other ways the nature of the relationship was all too apparent, symbolized by the frequent visits made by the AOK to German Headquarters (and not vice versa). Karl might well want to loosen a strait-jacket which Franz Joseph at the end of his life had come to accept, but he could never do so except surreptitiously. In terms of military operations, it meant that the Austrians had no influence over Germany's decision to begin unrestricted submarine warfare in 1917; nor could Karl prevent German rather than extra Austro-Hungarian troops being used in the Caporetto offensive, any more than he could resist German pressure for joint operations against Bolshevik Russia in early 1918 or German demands for Austrian divisions to be sent to the Western front in the summer. When in August 1918 Karl and Arz visited German Headquarters at Spa for the last time, Arz urged the need for peace, but was overruled by the German military. This incident was really just a postscript to the Austrians' more fateful pilgrimage to Spa on 12 May. On that occasion, in the wake of the notorious Sixtus Affair, Karl had been forced to subordinate his Empire, politically and economically, to German plans for a *Mitteleuropa*. Arz and Hindenburg in turn signed a famous *Waffenbund*, promising to coordinate their armies more closely than ever before. One German newspaper, the *Frankfurter Zeitung*, proclaimed the significance: 'With the new alliance, Austria-Hungary ceases to be an independent state and becomes a region of the German Empire.'

This blatant subordination reinforced the image of the Monarchy, at home and abroad, as being fully committed to Germany's war effort. It thereby stepped up that national and ideological polarization, internally and externally, which in six months would tear the Empire asunder. For the British and French leadership, it was final confirmation that there was no point in trying to preserve an Empire which was simply a German satellite. For about a year until March 1918, Britain and France had been flirting with Vienna to try to secure a separate peace, leaving the Monarchy intact. Both had also, in the course of the war, behaved in a way which implied some future weakening or restructuring of the Monarchy. Thus Serbia, Romania and Italy had been promised big chunks of territory (Italy, in the Treaty of London, a whole swathe from Tyrol down to Albania); while Poles had been assured of independence and unity, most notably by the French in late 1917. Yet none of the western Allies had stated that their aim was to destroy the Habsburg Empire (nor would they ever officially). Indeed, at the turn of the year, both Lloyd George and Woodrow Wilson, in hoping for a separate peace, emphasized that such a break-up was 'no part of our war aims'.[18]

By May 1918 the atmosphere had changed and break-up by implication was increasingly the card on the table. In this process, the threat which Britain and France (and the United States) posed to Austria-Hungary came above all from their public pledges to the Czechoslovak émigré movement over the summer. Not only were the Czechs by far the most efficiently organized of the émigrés (with much less internecine strife than in the Yugoslav or Polish camps). They now came with their own fighting machine—the Czechoslovak Legion—as proof of their 'readiness' to spill blood for the Allied and their own national cause. The Legion's military exploits, in Italy and France but especially against the Bolshevik menace in Siberia, soon brought political rewards. London, Paris and Washington tripped over themselves with mounting commitments. In late June, the French not only promised to support an independent Czechoslovakia but mentioned a future Yugoslav state for the first time; the Americans in turn declared that 'all branches of the Slav race should be completely freed from German and Austrian rule'. But it was British recognition (on 9 August) that the Czechoslovaks and their armies were 'Allies' which particularly sounded a siren to all. In the Allied camp, it encouraged ever more commitment to the Czechs, but also to other less clear-cut 'national' causes like the Yugoslav and Romanian. In the Monarchy itself, it stimulated nationalist Czech politicians to be bolder, while serving belated notice on the Habsburg authorities. If at this eleventh hour the elite did not make concessions on the national issue, a 'Czechoslovak' entity might well take shape, carved out of the two halves of the Monarchy. The western Allies' statements did not make this inevitable, but certainly gave an extra push towards such a scenario if the Habsburg authorities lost their legitimacy.

The Anglo-French-American ideological stance therefore played a catalytic role. The United States' commitment to 'self-determination', as outlined in Wilson's 'Fourteen Points' in January 1918, publicized an American mission with a particular moral edge. Both nationalist leaders and the Habsburg elite could in fact draw comfort from this message since it advocated national autonomy within the Empire (not national independence). The Habsburg authorities were rather more anxious about 'British intrigues'. In February, Lloyd George had publicly appointed Lord Northcliffe to head a campaign of propaganda against the Central Powers. Despite the myths which surrounded Northcliffe's organization,[19] Vienna's attention was thereby deflected from an enemy Power which arguably posed a greater direct threat to Austria-Hungary's survival: Italy. Not only was Italy, with its obsession with territory, one of the major obstacles on the Allied side to Austria's peace talks of 1917. In the last year of war, after the shock of the Caporetto disaster, Italy became the key centre committed to the 'nationality principle' as a means of winning the war against the Monarchy. It expressed this commitment through public displays on behalf of the émigré cause, such as the Rome Congress of Oppressed Nationalities (April 1918); but above all militarily, by permitting a Czech legion at the front and by launching a major propaganda offensive in the enemy trenches.

Ironically, the latter campaign was partly inspired by the Austrians themselves who had used the weapon of 'front propaganda' against

Russia in 1917 and then turned it on Italy. Now it was targeted on the Monarchy itself with the specific aim of fomenting nationalist agitation. Official Italy's own moral stance on behalf of the 'oppressed nationalities' may have been wafer-thin when it came to supporting a Yugoslav cause which clashed with Italy's own territorial claims. But by September 1918, for the purposes of winning the war, Italy's front propaganda was publicizing as a 'war aim' both the destruction of Austria-Hungary and the creation of an independent Yugoslavia.[20] This vigorous campaign was an increasingly dangerous phenomenon for it played on the reality of national polarization in the Monarchy and did so on the latter's doorstep. There was a tangible impact. The Rome Congress was echoed a month later in Prague when ('oppressed') nationalist leaders gathered to celebrate the Czech national theatre's fiftieth anniversary. Meanwhile, millions of nationalist manifestos were being scattered over the front, over Zagreb and the Croatian littoral; and the presence of Czech legionaries in the front-line was proof of Czech allegiance to the Allied cause. All these elements encouraged waverers at home to believe that an alternative to 'German-Magyar dominance' was possible if the Monarchy lost the war. In the most dramatic gesture of Italy's propaganda campaign, the poet-adventurer Gabriele D'Annunzio on 9 August flew into the heart of the Empire and dispersed manifestos over Vienna. It was a gesture symbolic of Austria-Hungary's vulnerability against an ideological challenge being stirred from within and without.[21]

This penetration from the west was matched by a complementary threat from the Russian east, so that in the last year of war the Monarchy was caught in an ideological vice. The eastern threat however was largely the result of peace, not war. Certainly, pre-Bolshevik Russia had flirted with wielding the 'national weapon' (for example, by successfully employing a Czechoslovak brigade in the 'Kerensky offensive' of summer 1917). Its intermittent occupation of Galicia (1914–17) was also lastingly destructive, for it cut Austria off from its richest agricultural region at a time when the West's economic blockade was biting. But it was especially the Bolshevik Revolution, followed by peace talks at Brest-Litovsk, which galvanized social unrest in many of the Monarchy's urban centres and mobilized new layers of the population. While the Bolsheviks proclaimed peace and 'self-determination' for all peoples, stringing out negotiations in order to foment revolution abroad, the German military were determined to annex vast tracts of territory in the east. As the talks stalled, expectations of peace rose sharply in the Monarchy. The Bolsheviks' example had already provoked major socialist demonstrations (10,000 people in Budapest on 25 November); and their call for self-determination, which seemed in such contrast to the arrogant Prussian-Austrian stance at Brest, was taken up by Czech politicians in an 'Epiphany declaration' (6 January). The socialist and pacifist notes were then to the fore in the strikes and food demonstrations which erupted across the Monarchy from 15 January.

Although the Austrian and Hungarian Social Democratic leadership brought the protesters to heel in return for government promises, the lessons of this mobilization were important: workers' councils for example had temporarily been set up in many Hungarian towns. Nor did danger from the east diminish when peace was finally concluded at Brest. The Habsburg authorities were paranoid about the spread of Bolshevism—a parallel in their minds to enemy propaganda from the west—yet they still failed to cope with the chief by-product of the peace. When ex-prisoners of war began to return home from Russia, they were coldly processed for signs of Bolshevism and then expected to rejoin their former units almost immediately. The head of military intelligence would judge later that the apparatus to deal with these 'homecomers' had been a 'too widely meshed sieve' to counter Bolshevism.[22] In fact, it was the apparatus itself which bred much of the disillusionment with their old homeland. Among the 500,000 who had returned by June, most homecomers naturally did not want to continue the war, many deserted and hid in the cities; others formed the core of the six major military rebellions which occurred in the hinterland in May 1918. Peace in the east, therefore, threw up as many problems as it solved because it did not mean an end to hostilities. It had offered a false dawn to thousands of civilians who had long ceased to believe that the war was being fought on their behalf. As such, it contributed to the breakdown of Habsburg legitimacy.

This internal breakdown, however, had begun in the first months of the war. It is there, if not before, that we already find many of the ingredients which produced the disintegration of 1918. Evidence from the summer of 1914 suggests that individuals had responded to the war with mixed emotions, some with joy and excitement, others with anxiety, others with sullen obedience to authority. In Vienna, Edmund von Glaise-Horstenau observed the wild enthusiasm which contrasted with his own misgivings about the future. In Prague, Franz Kafka noted a certain euphoria (chiefly from Germans), but also the soldiers with their 'rigidly silent, astonished, attentive black faces'. In Zagreb, a young Josip Horvat was surprised at how all seemed enveloped in the war-fever: Croat soldiers sang of avenging the Sarajevo murders as they marched off southwards, while young women strewed flowers before them.[23] For all those who were enticed by the adventure or who felt a duty to defend the Empire against Serbian-Russian aggression,[24] there were others who obeyed grudgingly or from the start did not view this as their war.

The same pattern is clear in the behaviour of the press. Under the force of patriotic spontaneity, a strong degree of self-censorship was apparent. Social Democratic organs like *Arbeiter-Zeitung* in Vienna or *Népszava* in Budapest soon toed the line which had immediately been adopted by loyalist papers such as *Neue Freie Presse*. For those journalists who stepped out of line there was a 'sword of Damocles' hanging over them in the shape of the regional censor office. Some papers, such as the Prague-based *Čas* managed to walk the tightrope for a year before being closed down for 'an inadmissible style of writing'. Others, for instance all thirty-one Serb-language papers in southern Hungary, were simply banned at the outset.[25]

Indeed, alongside the façade of patriotic unity one must set the types of regime which were introduced into Austria, Bosnia and Hungary in the early months of the war. In analysing them, it seems difficult to speak about a 'domestic truce' in any broad sense,[26] for these regimes were actively discriminatory against major sections of the population. Through a heavy-handed approach, they reinforced prevailing national and social discrimination (the unsolved pre-war issues) and made it very difficult to reach any compromise later on. In Austria, for instance, the Prime Minister Count Stürgkh, had been ruling by decree since adjourning the Reichsrat in March 1914. In view of his experience of parliament he declined to recall it, judging that 'every political debate will damage Austria more than a lost battle'.[27] As a result, until 1917, Austria remained unique among the major belligerents in lacking any parliamentary forum (since regional assemblies also remained closed). This suited many German-Austrian nationalist MPs who had a keen eye on what they might achieve for themselves with the goodwill of the Stürgkh regime. But it was a formidable blow to Vienna's relationship with Slav politicians, who were denied any official forum where they could express their views, critical or otherwise, on the Habsburg war.

Instead, the Austrian half of the Empire was run as a bureaucratic-military dictatorship.[28] Under the emergency laws, which Stürgkh pushed through by decree in late July 1914, the political authorities secured arbitrary powers to intern dissidents, suspend associations and curtail press freedoms. The same laws placed substantial power in the hands of the military. In the hinterland their instrument was a newly created War Surveillance Office (*Kriegsüberwachungsamt*), attached to the War Ministry in Vienna, which soon gained a sinister reputation for intervening in non-military spheres in order to curb dissent. Meanwhile, to the rear of the fronts, certain regions were designated as 'war zones' where the military had overriding control. These included Bosnia-Hercegovina, Galicia, Bukovina and parts of Moravia, and from May 1915 they were extended to cover most crownlands near to Italy; indeed, in Cisleithania only the German and Czech lands remained outside the war zones. Under this regime, the Slav and Latin peoples whose settlements happened to lie in or near the war zones not only faced a more uncomfortable existence, but also increasing discrimination by authorities who had a fixed view of 'loyalty'. In the south, the Serb population was naturally viewed as unreliable (Serb property in Zagreb and Sarajevo had been vandalized after Franz Ferdinand's assassination). By September 1914, over a thousand political suspects had been transported out of Bosnia, while in Bosnia itself much of the Serb leadership was interned. When General Stjepan Sarkotić became governor there at the end of the year he sensed that he was 'sitting on a volcano' and resolved 'with God's help to prevent any outbreak of lava': he banned all political activity and dealt ruthlessly with Serb associations, culminating in the Banjaluka trials of 156 Serbs in early 1916.[29]

The same label of 'unreliability' was quickly stamped on the Ruthenes of eastern Galicia and the Italians of Tyrol. In each case, even if military suspicions of trafficking with the enemy were somewhat natural and justified, the authorities' blanket approach helped to fuel national stereotypes and discrimination, while alienating potential support for the Habsburg cause. Nor could such heavy-handedness purely be ascribed to the priorities of war. By late 1914 hundreds of community leaders from the Slovene lands and Dalmatia had also been arrested, including the Reichsrat MPs Franc Grafenauer, Josip Smodlaka and Ante Tresić-Pavičić. At the same time in Bohemia, almost a thousand Czechs had been locked up for political offences and thirty-two societies dissolved. In Bohemia, which was not in the 'war zone', the military had a particular tussle with Stürgkh for influence, especially after two Czech regiments deserted on the Eastern front in April 1915. The upshot came a month later when the military arbitrarily arrested the Czech leader Karel Kramář, put him on trial and sentenced him to death. It was a major error of judgment, a 'great stupidity'.[30] As in Serb, Ruthene or even Slovene communities, such behaviour stimulated a nationalist response, encouraged individuals to take stock, and created martyrs. If Czechs too were now viewed as 'unreliable' by many of the authorities, the bureaucratic-military regime of 1914–16 did much to shape that stereotype. It presaged an inevitable backlash against the regime in 1917 when military powers were reduced and their 'victims' were allowed a voice.

The situation in the Hungarian half of the Empire was equally authoritarian.[31] The Magyar oligarchy, while able to block the level of military interference so characteristic of Austria, possessed their own emergency laws in order to maintain firm state control. Certainly, the public show of patriotism endured longer than in Cisleithania. The Budapest parliament also continued to exist as a 'national' forum where elected politicians could debate and spar, maintaining an uneasy truce until Mihály Károlyi broke away and formed his own party in July 1916. Yet this all belied the deep social and national fissures in Hungarian society which slowly expanded under the strains of an all-embracing war. Tisza himself refused to restructure his government into a 'national coalition'; and even after his dismissal by Karl in May 1917, his influence remained strong behind the cabinets of the wily Sándor Wekerle. It was a blinkered outlook, obsessed until the very end with upholding the Magyar gentry's national and social dominance within the dualist structure of the Monarchy. Although this was achieved as long as the war lasted, it came at a heavy price. Even in the last eighteen months of the war, when Károlyi's party allied with the extra-parliamentary Social Democrats to form a coalition which would replace the ruling elite, the latter still made only minor concessions. There were severe repercussions from this (not least for Tisza himself). First, it meant that when the regime surrendered its authority to the coalition (renamed the National Council) in late October 1918, the revolution was far more turbulent than elsewhere in the Empire. Second, by persistently blocking any change to Dualism or to the borders of greater Hungary, the Magyar elite limited the options for reform elsewhere in the Monarchy. In so doing, they contributed substantially to its final disintegration.

For the Magyar oligarchy, both in government or opposition, the real 'national question' was that of Dualism: of Hungary's relationship to the rest of the Empire. The heated wartime parliamentary debates over this issue steadily boiled over, as Hungary's economic and military sacrifice was scrutinized by Tisza's opponents. It was an unrelenting clash over what were Hungary's 'real interests', and it would only find its *dénouement* when Tisza and his elite were toppled at the end of the war. In a backlash, the National Council then abandoned Dualism altogether and tried to take greater Hungary towards independence.

However, alongside this vibrant interpretation of the national question there was also the latent issue of Hungary's non-Magyar nationalities. For most of the war they remained passive, their behaviour dependent on the fate of Magyar authority. In the case of autonomous Croatia, there was a certain degree of political consensus. In June 1915, the Croatian diet (Sabor) was allowed to reopen, providing some Croatian legitimization for the war's continuation. Yet in their common Sabor statement at the time the Croatian leaders also indicated that their support for the Habsburg cause was not unconditional. Loyalty to it was now juxtaposed with an open demand for greater Croatian unity in a restructured Empire. In this way the ruling Serb-Croat Coalition sent a clear message to Budapest, but then maintained an opportunistic stance. Only in the last month of the war would they jump ship and join Croat radical elements: when it was clear that Magyar authority was vanishing along with the Empire itself.

In contrast, Hungary's Slovaks and Romanians were largely quelled by force, hardly raising their heads until disturbed from outside the kingdom. While Budapest was at first prepared to tolerate some faint Slovak stirrings (and the military viewed Slovaks as 'reliable'), they were suppressed from 1915 when evidence mounted that some Slovaks welcomed the idea of unity with Czechs across the dualist frontier. Not until May 1918 would the small Slovak intelligentsia feel confident enough to speak out for self-determination and Czechoslovak unity. Similar stirrings from the Hungarian Ruthenes (who fell into the 'war zone' in late 1914) did not begin until after the war.

The Romanians of Transylvania were as usual more problematic. With them Tisza's regime trod softly for a much longer period, anxious lest neutral Romania should be provoked into attacking. Budapest even secured some patriotic endorsement for the war from certain Romanian religious and political leaders. However, the stance of both sides was tested to the full when Romania finally invaded in the summer of 1916. Neither the Transylvanian leaders nor the normally passive Romanian peasantry hesitated to nail their colours to the Romanian mast. As a result, when the enemy forces were driven out, about 80,000 Transylvanian Romanians fled with them, effectively draining the principality of its keenest minds. Severe Magyar repression followed, with the internment of about 3,000 intellectals in a camp at Sopron. It was this demographic upheaval which enabled a military intelligence officer at Koloszvár to report as late as May 1918 that 'the Romanian population in the countryside behave calmly, stoop to no anti-Hungarian comments and no longer dream about being united with Romania'.[32] Any Romanian intellectuals who remained behind were cautious and reserved, giving no lead to the peasantry until the last months of the war.

In both Austria and Hungary, therefore, the entrenched mentality and extreme coercion of the two regimes from 1914 limited the options for reconciliation later on. It would prove impossible for either authority to re-mobilize opinion behind the war effort, as occurred for example in Britain, France and Italy in 1917–18. But we can go further: for large sections of society the Austro-Hungarian regimes were of weak legitimacy anyway (made weaker, as we have seen, by their own wartime behaviour). They made little effort to rally their civilian populations behind a common goal of endurance. Apart from the methods of coercion and censorship, common to all the belligerent states, the output of official patriotic propaganda in Austria-Hungary was very limited and overly German-Magyar in tone.[33] Simply to construct any effective and all-embracing propaganda was undoubtedly impossible anyway, since it lacked the firm backdrop of social or national consensus: the headaches experienced with 'patriotic instruction' in the armed forces in 1918 showed this. Among civilians it was never tried. Instead, rival nationalist arguments could slowly fill the vacuum and supply the alternative 'solutions' which the Habsburg authorities could not.

The rising support for these alternative solutions, notably from the summer of 1917, cannot be divorced from the Monarchy's wartime economic catastrophe. That experience shows us again the impact of foreign pressures on domestic inadequacies. Even though the authorities had moved quickly to adjust to a war economy, setting up on the German model a range of 'centres' to try to manage raw materials and food supplies, this never compensated for the lack of pre-war economic planning. The results of the Allied blockade (a topic which requires more research) were felt already by October

1914, and could only get worse when Russian troops occupied Austria's 'bread-basket' of Galicia while Italy blocked off markets to the west. By March 1915 there was bread or flour rationing in all regions, coal production had dropped substantially, and any integrated transport system had collapsed. As the governments resorted to printing money to meet military costs, inflation spiralled to a degree—especially in Austria—which exceeded most of the other major belligerent states.[34]

The situation was then exacerbated by the economic impact of Dualism, and the Monarchy's inability to function as an economic unit. The Hungarian authorities, upon whom Cisleithania was increasingly dependent to make up its own food deficiencies, balked at any coordinated 'food office' and looked to their own needs first. Admittedly, Hungary's own resources were not abundant: food riots occurred already in June 1915; the harvest of 1916 was a severe disappointment; and by November only 7,800 pigs remained compared to the 30,000 which had been exported monthly to Austria at the start of the war. But the Austrian-Hungarian disparity sharpened the national stereotypes and divisions. By May 1916 there were the first hunger riots in Vienna itself, where daily 54,000 people were attending soup kitchens. The beleaguered mayor, Richard Weiskirchner, fell back on lambasting the Magyars who were 'more interested in seeing us starve than the English'. Further south, the picture deteriorated markedly, with famine slowly encroaching in Istria, Dalmatia and Bosnia. By mid-1918 in central Istria, the postal censor reported a complete breakdown in food provisioning with locals 'preparing for their meals not only nettles but also all kinds of edible and inedible grasses'. Those who could, stole across the dualist border into Croatia where, one observer noted, 'everything swims in fat and the black-market blossoms'.[35]

With these economic realities, it was not surprising that the domestic disintegration of the Monarchy was much clearer in Austria than in Hungary. From 1917 it was in Austria particularly that national-political polarization could intensify. The dictatorship of 1914–16 gave way to a regime which, though more constitutional, offered many of Austria's Slav politicians a bleak future where the Germans would dominate. From early 1915, the German nationalist parties had been drawing up proposals for a 'German solution' for Cisleithania, culminating in their infamous Easter programme (*Osterbegehrschrift*) of 1916. This was designed once and for all to solidify German control of Austria. While retaining Dualism, Galicia would be given a special autonomous status in the Monarchy (sub-dualist) and excluded from representation in the Reichsrat; through this removal of the Poles and Ruthenes, the Germans of Austria would at last gain a comfortable majority over the remaining Slavs. German security would further be enhanced by dividing up the administration of Bohemia on ethnic lines (so that the German Bohemians could not be outvoted by the Czechs), and imposing German as a 'state language' throughout Cisleithania. On the basis of this uncompromisingly nationalist blueprint, Erasmus Handel at the Ministry of Interior worked out a new constitution, which was taken up by Karl's advisers at the start of the new reign. With Count Heinrich Clam-Martinic as Prime Minister, the new Austrian government was still principally of a German hue (with Handel himself as Minister of Interior) and it spent its first months negotiating with German and Polish politicians in order to pass the 'German solution' by decree before the Reichsrat was reconvened.[36] Even if these efforts came to naught in the short term, they revealed that Karl's new regime was not going to be the watershed that some imagined. Instead, early 1917—a last opportunity perhaps for domestic compromise and a radical restructuring of the Empire—witnessed an Austrian government with a stubbornly nationalist agenda: one wholly indifferent and anathema to the Czechs and Slovenes, who were not consulted.

When the Reichsrat reconvened on 30 May, its complexion was anything but the 'inner unity' which Clam hoped to display to the outside world. The Slav MPs brought complaints from the recent past and their own agenda for the future. The Polish deputies, far from resting content with a special status for Galicia, spoke out for a fully independent Polish state, which after the change of regime in Russia they now envisaged as most auspicious through an Entente victory. The Czech and South Slav clubs presented demands, on the basis of self-determination, for Czechoslovak and South Slav national entities within a federal state structure; even if still under the Habsburg sceptre, these claims were radical in encroaching on Hungarian territory and necessitating the dismantling of Dualism. This parallel Slav stance against any 'German course' put in place that national polarization which would mount steadily in the next eighteen months. In response, Karl's speech from the throne was too vague, simply foreseeing the need for some reorganization of constitutional life (which still left the door open to a German course by decree: indeed, Karl had privately given some assurances to the

German parties). Clam in turn urged all to unite in support of 'Austria', a naive concept in view of his own recent behaviour: not surprisingly it failed, leading to his resignation for he could not secure a majority in the Reichsrat. His successor, Ernst von Seidler, was a bureaucrat well accustomed to government by decree and closely linked to German nationalist circles. Since after a few concessions he hardly deviated from Clam's programme, the Czechs and Slovenes from the summer moved in a more radical direction.

In both the Czech and South Slavs regions there took place from this time a popular civil mobilization with an agenda which was increasingly nationalistic and non-Habsburg. It gained its impetus from calculating nationalist leaders who now exploited the 'constitutional thaw'—their parliamentary immunity, the Emperor's amnesty, the weakening of military power, the greater freedom for press and association. In turn they tapped into grassroots war-weariness and the deteriorating economic situation, illustrated for example by mass strikes in Bohemia from April 1917 and a chronic food crisis in the south. In the Czech lands, what had previously been a small-scale underground network run by a few individuals on instruction from the Czech émigré organization, began to agitate more openly. The authorities could no longer expect expressions of Habsburg loyalty from the provinces as in the past.[37] Newspapers, in the face of an erratic censorship, took more risks; from October, for instance, *Národní Listy* 'wrote uncompromisingly, recklessly in a Czech spirit, as if Austria did not exist'.[38] By 1918, Czech radical politicians were moving into the ascendant in the face of Vienna's obstinacy on the one hand, and rumours about Allied support and the Czech Legion on the other. The celebrations for the Czech national theatre (in May) illustrate well this trend, for they occurred in the wake not only of the Rome Congress but also of the public tightening of Austria-Hungary's alliance with Germany. One Czech journalist noted later that, 'although with the onset of the political spring [the Czech leaders] took off the fur coat of opportunism, they still kept looking nervously at the thermometer'.[39] Yet by July, the temperature was ceasing to fluctuate as the Monarchy's direction seemed ever clearer. Seidler, in one of his last misguided acts as Prime Minister, finally announced that the former 'German course', with all its implications for the Czechs, would be resumed in Austria: he was preparing to implement it by *oktroi*.[40] At the same time a new National Council was formed in Prague, pledged to create 'an independent democratic Czechoslovak state' and to assume control at the right moment.

Nationalist mobilization was perhaps even more striking in the South Slav regions of Austria where in late 1917 a 'declaration movement' took off and spread south from the Slovene lands.[41] The real spark came on 15 September when Bishop Anton Jeglič of Ljubljana, with other clergy and politicians, signed a statement backing the South Slav Club's 'May Declaration'. Jeglič would write later: 'My signature was authoritative and started the movement which made Yugoslavia possible.' Under the guidance of Reichsrat deputies led by Anton Korošec, the agitation moved from parish councils adhering to the declaration, to the mass-gathering of signatures (usually promoted by women and the Catholic clergy) and mass rallies. Recent research has revealed a complex series of motives inspiring those who added their names to the petitions. For some the declaration for Yugoslav unity seemed to offer economic or 'national' security, in the face of rising nationalist threats from inside (the Germans) and outside (Italy). But this did not necessarily mean that most signatories envisaged an independent Yugoslav state. Many long retained a dual loyalty to the Habsburgs and to Yugoslav unity, as evidenced at one mass rally as late as March 1918 when a cry went up: 'We want to be free in a great Habsburg Yugoslavia.' In other words, adherence to the declaration was not simply a 'legal cloak' to protect agitators who had already abandoned the Monarchy. The movement only took a firmly radical turn from May 1918 when Seidler's government declined to concede even Slovene autonomy (let alone any broader Yugoslav unity). Vienna's renewed 'German course' was now on the horizon, and it fully played into the hands of enemy propaganda.

The declaration movement also acted as a catalyst for agitation further south. In Istria and Dalmatia, Slovene or Croat clergy and politicians such as Vjekoslav Spinčić were particularly successful in spreading the message. What was now possible was illustrated on 7 May in the town of Split. The amnestied Dalmatian MP Ante Tresić-Pavičić was welcomed home by a crowd of 2,000, to cries of 'Long live Croatia in a united Yugoslav state' and the unfurling of the Yugoslav tri-colour. Although Vienna began to take a tougher line, officially banning agitation in support of the May Declaration on 12 May, such a ban was unenforceable; rallies continued in the early summer, while local officials turned a blind eye. They culminated in mid-August in Ljubljana's 'Slav days': Korošec and the Slovene radicals took a bold step in launching a National Council for Austria's South Slavs, a forerunner to a broader council which would include representatives from Croatia and Bosnia. As in Prague, the Council now waited on events.

To this fast-emerging Yugoslav option the Habsburg authorities offered no enticing alternative. As General Sarkotić noted wearily from the relative stability of Bosnia, 'a *correct* solution of the South Slav question is only possible in *theory* but not in *practice*'. On the few occasions when the matter was discussed by the Monarchy's leaders in the last months of the war, it was clear that none of them could contemplate a solution outside Dualism. The more perceptive of the elite, such as Sarkotić, sensed that the eleventh hour was at hand and that action, rather than further discussion, was essential. He confided to his diary: 'The South Slav question is a Gordian Knot which can only be untied by someone with intense determination backed by force (the army).' But he knew it was a vain hope, since neither Vienna or Budapest could ever agree on a common strategy.[42]

In Galicia too, even if the breakdown of authority never had the same fatal impact for the Empire as among the Czechs and South Slavs, it was equally apparent and worked in tandem with the latter. True, the Ruthene intelligentsia of Galicia stayed loyal to Vienna, for in February 1918 the Monarchy's peace terms with Ukraine had promised them a separate crownland (as Ruthene MPs had demanded in May 1917). Ruthene clergy now proclaimed the partition of Galicia in their sermons and viewed union with turbulent Ukraine as a second-best option. But Czernin's rash promise to the Ruthenes had a disastrous impact upon the far more crucial Polish question. For the Polish leaders, who had long been weighing the best framework for a united Poland, the idea of splitting Galicia dropped like a bombshell. Most Polish deputies turned against the government (toppling Seidler in July), and there were large-scale demonstrations in Cracow and Lvov. By the summer, even if much of the peasantry was still indifferent or suspicious of the nationalist agitation, most of the Polish educated strata were thinking in terms of an independent Polish state under the auspices of the western Allies.[43]

Thus, in the last months of the war, the image of national polarization in the Monarchy was indeed sharpening, even if it was never as well defined as Italy's propaganda campaign liked to portray.[44] The Czech, Polish and South Slav (especially Slovene) political leaderships had become uncompromising because the Habsburg authorities seemed to offer their national constituencies little future security, and supplied no clear or attractive solutions to meet their quests for greater self-administration. News from the enemy, which slowly filtered into the Monarchy, encouraged many Slav leaders to abandon Vienna in the knowledge that the Allies were about to win the war and seemed ready to support their aspirations. In contrast, the Monarchy's leadership, after being forced to tighten the alliance with Germany in May 1918, was fatally destined to lose the war at Germany's side. The German strait-jacket, which Austria-Hungary at this stage could not remove, was then matched by a rigid domestic 'German-Magyar course'—of commitment to Dualism until the bitter end.

On the Austrian side, although Seidler had resigned, he remained a key advisor to Emperor Karl in the final months. The 'German course' which he had signalled was not, despite appearances, substantially altered by the government of Baron Max von Hussarek (who retained most of Seidler's cabinet). Hussarek might well envisage some form of 'national autonomy' in the Empire, vaguely proclaiming the idea of self-determination in the Reichsrat on 1 October. But it was still within the limits of Dualism and the 'German course'. While hoping vainly that Budapest would arrange some South Slav unity within greater Hungary (a sub-dualist solution which would exclude the Austrian Slovenes), Hussarek pushed forward with his own measures to undermine the Czechs by dividing up Bohemia's administration so that the German Bohemians would gain extra security. The Czechs' hostility, and the increasing signs of Allied recognition for their cause, only made him more determined.[45]

Austria-Hungary entered the final phase of its disintegration on 26 September, when news arrived that Bulgaria had collapsed.[46] As defeat seemed certain, a frantic contest began between emboldened nationalist leaders on the one hand, and the anxious Habsburg authorities on the other. Both wanted to assert their legitimacy in Allied eyes, and pre-empt rival claims to authority in the region. Only now, for instance, did Croatia's ruling coalition agree to enter a 'National Council of Slovenes, Croats and Serbs' in Zagreb with delegates from all the Empire's southern Slav regions; the example was followed a few days later by the Poles in Cracow, with the aim of taking control of Galicia for a united Polish state. In the Reichsrat, František Staněk declared that the defeat of Austria fully matched the wishes of the Czech people who would be represented separately at the peace conference.

At the same time, the outlook of the beleaguered Habsburg elite is clear from the final meetings of the Common Ministerial Council [see Appendix]. Their attention was fixed as much abroad as on the domestic chaos. They desperately hoped that President Wilson would accept peace terms according to his 'Fourteen Points', which would preserve the Monarchy intact. They also finally sensed that some sign of domestic reform was vital, so as to present a 'liberal' image: in Hussarek's words, 'the world will see us, so to speak, at work'. Yet, even at this twelfth hour (2 October) the elite could not agree to force through a South Slav solution: Sándor Wekerle's intransigent stance especially prevented a decision. It was against this background that Emperor Karl issued his Manifesto on 16 October, announcing that the Austrian half of the Empire would be transformed into a 'federal state'. This was not a sincere attempt at domestic reform. It was a 'desperate act' to try to influence Wilson, who had still not replied to Vienna.[47] It also upheld Dualism (since Hungary's integrity was mentioned) and did not banish suspicions of a 'German course' for Austria. As such, it simply emboldened the national councils further, while totally failing in its external impact. On 21 October, Vienna finally received Wilson's reply which rejected national autonomy as a basis for negotiation and effectively approved Czechoslovak and Yugoslav independence. It was the *coup de grâce* for the elite. As the national councils (including the Hungarian) declared independence, and the Italian front collapsed, the authorities in Vienna found themselves without authority or legitimacy. Their world had splintered in different directions.

General Tersztyánszky was correct when he moaned in early 1918 that the war had brought Austria-Hungary 'nothing good'. As in Russia, but also in Italy after the war, the unsatisfactory outcome of the Habsburg state's 'military mission' was a deadly blow to those rulers who had become so identified with it. The Austro-Hungarian Revolution of 1918 meant the disintegration of the Monarchy into 'nationalist components', partly because the collapse of Habsburg authority left chiefly nationalist alternatives. Most of the national leaders were anxious to maintain control and prevent any socialist alternative (achieved except in Budapest). They were also not satisfied with any version of national autonomy which the Habsburg elite were offering, for it made few concessions on the principle of German-Magyar hegemony. Until the end many individuals undoubtedly retained some imperial patriotism, but were swayed by a nationalist vision that offered security in ethnic numbers, against disorder and other competing nationalist threats. Amidst this turmoil, the western Allies' role was significant but secondary. They kept the Monarchy in an interminable struggle, while tightening the economic noose and steadily giving sanction to the notion of nationalist alternatives to the Habsburg mission. Austria-Hungary finally dissolved because the Habsburg authorities lost their legitimacy. And most evidence indicates that this issue of legitimacy had to be resolved before embarking on a lengthy war where it would be put so decisively to the test.

NOTES

1. Arhiv Hrvatske Zagreb [AHZ: Croatian State Archives], Sarkotić papers, Tersztyánszky to Sarkotić, 4 March 1918. In the Empire's final days the same simile was used by the Viennese satirist Karl Kraus: see Edward Timms, *Karl Kraus. Apocalyptic Satirist. Culture and Collapse in Habsburg Vienna* (New Haven and London, 1989) p. 367.
2. The fact that someone of Tersztyánszky's status had to travel by tram was itself symptomatic of the creeping social breakdown in Vienna: see John W. Boyer, *Culture and Political Crisis in Vienna. Christian Socialism in Power, 1897–1918* (Chicago and London, 1995) p. 426.
3. Jean Bérenger, *A History of the Habsburg Empire 1700–1918* (London, 1997) p. 288.
4. Alan Sked, *The Decline and Fall of the Habsburg Empire 1815–1918* (London, 1989) p. 264.
5. Steven Beller, *Francis Joseph* (London and New York, 1996) pp. 179, 229–30.
6. Robin Okey, *The Habsburg Monarchy c.1765–1918* (Basingstoke and London, 2001) p. 390.
7. As one small example, note how Karl agreed to his foreign minister's resignation in late October 1918 and then changed his mind: Ludwig Windischgrätz, *My Memoirs* (London, 1921) p. 312.
8. Peter Broucek (ed.), *Ein General im Zwielicht. Die Erinnerungen Edmund Glaises von Horstenau*, 3 vols (Vienna, 1980–88) I, pp. 394, 398, 405.
9. Manfried Rauchensteiner, *Der Tod des Doppeladlers. Österreich-Ungarn und der Erste Weltkrieg* (Graz, Vienna and Cologne, 1993) pp. 363ff., 392ff.
10. Österreichisches Staatsarchiv [ÖstA: Austrian State Archives], Kriegsarchiv, AOK 1917, Op. Nr 45286, Conrad to AOK Operationsabteilung, 15 September 1917.
11. Sked, *The Decline and Fall of the Habsburg Empire*, p. 261. Sked fails to correct this remark in the second edition of his book (London, 2001); instead he compounds it with another misleading notion, that 'almost all the nationalities fought loyally until the end' (p. 326 note 66).
12. It was naturally an argument popular in Austrian military circles after the war. See the discussions in *Österreichische Wehrzeitung*: for

example, the article by Hugo Kerchnawe in Folge 44, 11 November 1921, pp. 4–5, which reaffirms the *Dolchstoß* theory.

13. Rauchensteiner, *Der Tod des Doppeladlers*, pp. 243–44. An important new study of Conrad in English is: Lawrence Sondhaus, *Franz Conrad von Hötzendorf. Architect of the Apocalypse* (Boston, Leiden and Cologne, 2000).

14. Broucek (ed.), *Ein General im Zwielicht*, I, p. 279.

15. See Mark Cornwall, *The Undermining of Austria-Hungary. The Battle for Hearts and Minds* (Basingstoke and London, 2000), chapters 7 and 9, for the campaign of patriotic instruction.

16. Franz Conrad von Hötzendorf, *Private Aufzeichnungen. Erste Veröffentlichungen aus den Papieren des k.u.k. Generalstabs-Chefs*, ed. Kurt Peball (Vienna and Munich, 1977) p. 78.

17. Rauchensteiner, *Der Tod des Doppeladlers*, p. 372.

18. David Stevenson, *The First World War and International Politics* (Oxford, 1989) pp. 189–98 for a useful summary. When the USA declared war on the Monarchy in December 1917, Wilson stated: 'we do not wish in any way to impair or to rearrange the Austro-Hungarian Empire.'

19. Cornwall, *The Undermining of Austria-Hungary*, pp. 174ff.

20. Ibid., pp. 340–41, 423.

21. Ibid., for a full analysis of the propaganda campaigns by and against the Empire.

22. Max Ronge, *Kriegs- und Industriespionage. Zwölf Jahre Kundschaftsdienst* (Zurich, Leipzig and Vienna, 1930) pp. 327–31.

23. Broucek (ed.), *Ein General im Zwielicht*, I, p. 285; Franz Kafka, *The Diaries of Franz Kafka 1910–1923* (London, 1972) p. 301; Josip Horvat, *Živjeti u Hrvatskoj. Zapisci iz nepovrata 1900–1941* (Zagreb, 1984) pp. 47–48. Horvat's memoirs give a vivid picture of the mood in Zagreb. In Prague in contrast, most evidence confirms that Czechs did not share German enthusiasm: see Jan Galandauer, 'Čeští' vojáci ve Velké Válce a vzájemný obraz Čechů a českých Němců', in Jan Křen and Eva Broklová (eds), *Obraz Němců Rakouska a Německa v české společnosti 19. a 20. století* (Prague, 1998), pp. 78ff.

24. For example, Friedrich Engel-Janosi, *Aber ein stolzer Bettler. Erinnerungen aus einer verlorenen Generation* (Graz, Vienna and Cologne, 1974) p. 46.

25. See Mark Cornwall, 'News, Rumour and the Control of Information in Austria-Hungary 1914–1918', *History*, 77 no. 249 (1992).

26. Cf. Okey, *The Habsburg Monarchy*, p. 379.

27. Quoted in Felix Höglinger, *Ministerpräsident Heinrich Graf Clam-Martinic* (Graz and Cologne, 1964) p. 174.

28. On this subject see Christoph Führ, *Das k.u.k Armeeoberkommando und die Innenpolitik in Österreich 1914–1917* (Graz, Vienna and

Cologne, 1968), who plays down the degree of military influence emphasized in Joseph Redlich, *Österreichische Regierung und Verwaltung im Weltkriege* (Vienna, 1925).

29. Signe Klein, *Freiherr Sarkotić von Lovćen. Die Zeit seiner Verwaltung in Bosnien-Herzegovina von 1914 bis 1918*, (Ph.Diss. Vienna, 1969) pp. 38–39; Hamdija Kapidžić, *Bosna i Hercegovina pod Austro-Ugarskom upravom* (Sarajevo, 1962) pp. 211–13.

30. Rauchensteiner, *Der Tod des Doppeladlers*, p. 270.

31. For a good study of wartime Hungary see József Galántai, *Hungary in the First World War* (Budapest, 1989) and for some concise thoughts: István Deák, 'The Decline and Fall of Habsburg Hungary 1914–1918', in Iván Völgyes (ed.), *Hungary in Revolution 1918–19* (Lincoln, Nebraska, 1971) pp. 10–30.

32. ÖstA, Kriegsarchiv, Evidenzbüro 1918, EvB Nr 16755.

33. Cornwall, *The Undermining of Austria-Hungary*, pp. 24–29, 414.

34. See Eduard März, *Austrian Banking and Financial Policy. Creditanstalt at a Turning Point, 1913–1923* (New York, 1984) pp. 111ff., 205–8.

35. For the economic crisis in Vienna, see Boyer, *Culture and Political Crisis in Vienna*, pp. 419ff.; and in the Yugoslav lands: Mark Cornwall, 'The Experience of Yugoslav Agitation in Austria-Hungary, 1917–1918' in Hugh Cecil and Peter Liddle (eds), *Facing Armageddon: the First World War Experienced* (London, 1996) pp. 659–61.

36. Höglinger, *Clam-Martinic*, pp. 132–57.

37. See the recent analysis of Czech declarations of loyalty by Ivan Šedivý, 'České loajalní projevy 1914–1918', *Český časopis historický*, 97/2 (1999) pp. 293–309. Šedivý has also now submitted the wartime Czechs to a thorough re-evaluation in his new book, *Češi, české země a velká válka 1914–1918* (Prague, 2001).

38. Jan Hajšman, *Mafie v rozmachu. Vzpomínky na odboj doma* (Prague, 1933) pp. 185–86.

39. Ferdinand Peroutka, *Budování státu*, 4 vols (Prague, 1933–38) I, pp. 12–13.

40. Helmut Rumpler, *Max Hussarek. Nationalitäten und Nationalitätenpolitik in Österreich im Sommer des Jahres 1918* (Graz and Cologne, 1965) pp. 25–26.

41. See Cornwall, 'The Experience of Yugoslav Agitation in Austria-Hungary'; and the research of Vlasta Stavbar, 'Izjave v podporo Majniško Deklaracije', *Zgodovinski Časopis*, 46–47 (1992–3). Cf. Bérenger, op. cit., p. 282: 'the national opposition groups . . . remained very unadventurous.'

42. AHZ, Sarkotić diary, entries for 6 March and 30 May 1918.

43. See the comprehensive report by Eduard Fischer, gendarmerie commander of Galicia and Bukovina in: ÖstA, Kriegsarchiv, Evidenzbüro 1918, EvB Nr 23510, 22 July 1918.

44. See Cornwall, *The Undermining of Austria-Hungary*, pp. 353–60, for Czech, Romanian and Polish examples.
45. Rumpler, *Max Hussarek*, pp. 65–77.
46. The expectations of peace during this chaotic period are the subject of chapter 19 in H. Cecil and P. Liddle (eds), *At the Eleventh Hour. Reflections, Hopes and Anxieties at the Closing of the Great War* (London, 1998) pp. 285–300.
47. See Helmut Rumpler, *Das Völkermanifest Kaiser Karls vom 16. Oktober 1918. Letzter Versuch zur Rettung des Habsburgerreiches* (Munich, 1966).

Documents

The Final Meetings of the Common Ministerial Council[1]

[1] Common Ministerial Council, Vienna, 27 September 1918

Protocol of the ministerial council for common business held in Vienna on 27 September 1918 under the chairmanship of His Majesty the Emperor and King.

Present: The k.u.k. Foreign Minister Count Burián, the k.u. Minister-President Dr Wekerle, the k.k. Minister-President Baron von Hussarek, the k.u.k. Minister of War Baron von Stöger-Steiner, the k.u.k. Chief of General Staff Baron Arz, [his deputy] General von Waldstätten.

Subject: To discuss the situation created by Bulgaria's offer of a separate peace.[2] Solution of the South Slav question. Reconstruction of Austria. The question of peace.

His Apostolic Majesty deigns to open the Crown Council by referring to the situation created by Bulgaria's sudden collapse, since this necessitates a discussion of the measures to be taken. In connection with the foreign situation a reconstruction of the interior is absolutely necessary, particularly with regard to the South Slav question which should be a subject for discussion. Finally also some discussion of the question of peace seems to be required. [. . .]

    Burián: The Bulgarian catastrophe has very significantly worsened our situation from every perspective, military and political. It will have immediate consequences and will produce effects which only gradually will be observable. Above all one can reckon on an immediate impact upon the nerves of our population. Already our failure on the Piave,[3] then our—even if temporary—check in Albania, and especially the events on the German Western front have seriously tested the confidence of our war-weary and destitute peoples. The collapse of Bulgaria is the last straw. [Burián notes the special danger now from Romania, all the more so as the peace treaty of March 1918 has still not been ratified, and also that Serbia will now again become a theatre of war which will have domestic repercussions for the Monarchy's South Slavs:] The South Slav danger is approaching in its full magnitude and it urgently requires solution. The treasonable movement, whose most intensive form can be termed the Korošec movement,[4] has recently made its most rapid advances. Today we have no more time to deliberate, we must act as fast as possible, as long as we can avoid the appearance of coercion. We have not a day to lose. We must make decisions, if we want to avoid the peoples themselves taking fate into their own hands and making decisions about their future over the heads of the governments. [. . .] The longer the solution is postponed, the more unfavourable will be the effect of the South Slav movement on other domestic problems. Today, ways of solving the Bohemian question for example are still conceivable. But once a South Slav state has been constituted of its own free will, then the Bohemian question will square the circle. So order must be established quickly, in Croatia and also in Bosnia and Hercegovina. The supreme principle must be: maintenance of the dualist structure of the Monarchy. [The constitutional position of Bosnia, however, has to be settled immediately after peace, and might be left to a final vote by the Bosnian Sabor; while Dalmatia is a matter for Austria, and the same could happen there.] The Slovene question, Count Burián characterizes as recent and artificial, the importance of which cannot be overestimated. [Burián ends by discussing Germany, saying that the first task is for the two allies to establish a new front in the Balkans.] In diplomatic-political terms, the peace threads absolutely must be spun out. It may prove necessary to make a concrete peace offer, which should be launched before 15 October and ought to formulate our peace terms in quite a precise form. In this regard a lively exchange of views is in train with the German government. [Germany will have to make concessions over Alsace-Lorraine, and the Polish question will have to be settled with the end goal of the 'Austro-Polish solution'. Germany is being told that Austria-Hungary definitely cannot continue the war beyond 1918].

Wekerle: [agrees generally with Burián.] He is also convinced that for economic, military and domestic reasons it is out of the question to continue the war any longer. But with regard to domestic reconstruction the maintenance of Dualism absolutely must be the supreme principle. (In connection with this point, Dr Wekerle stresses that regrettably the relationship between the two states of the Monarchy has never been as bad as at present). With regard to peace conditions, the k.u. Minister-President desires that if at all possible the principle of maintaining the integrity of the Monarchy be upheld—and this not only in territorial terms. Above all the Italians must be prevented from establishing themselves on the eastern shore of the Adriatic sea [. . .]

Hussarek: [also agrees generally with Burián's outlook.] As far as Austria's domestic political reconstruction is concerned, he will take the next opportunity to bring his programme before parliament.[5] Referring to a remark of Dr Wekerle, to support the Monarchy's integrity, Baron von Hussarek reflected upon Point 10 of Wilson's January programme,[6] which foresaw a satisfaction of Italian claims within clearly recognizable borders. [. . .] As far as the relationship to Hungary is concerned, Baron von Hussarek stands basically by the principle of Dualism, but he draws attention to the fact that territorial adjustments, for example the incorporation of Poland, could make certain alterations necessary. With regard to the South Slav question, the k.k. Minister-President observes that among the Austrian public, and especially in parliamentary circles, the view prevails that all South Slav regions should be united as a separate entity—an opinion which he personally also might agree with. [He supports Burián's views and notes that political opinion in Dalmatia is already for union with Bosnia and Croatia.] At the moment the other domestic problems of Austria are being most energetically considered and intensively discussed by the k.k. cabinet. First the division of the Bohemian regional administration has to be carried out, whereupon the government plans to enter into negotiations with the parties about its remodelling. Baron von Hussarek does not of course expect much success at first in this, but it will be shown to the world that we are not excluding the need for some reconstruction. The world will see us, so to speak, at work. [With regard to Wekerle's point about bad relations between Austria and Hungary, Hussarek appeals to Wekerle to help Austria with food supplies.]

Arz: [. . .] With regard to morale in the army, it improves visibly with its food provisions. [. . .] The army is very badly supplied with clothing and munitions. It can endure until the end of the year with the current supplies. But from then onwards it will be steadily downhill, so that—if the war does not end earlier—the army could eventually face catastrophe.

[The **Emperor** sums up the key decisions of the meeting which include:
  * that the Austrian and Hungarian governments make an announcement over the South Slav question, with the proviso that a final decision about Bosnia and Dalmatia will be left to their local assemblies;
  * that a start be made on the inner reconstruction of Austria as soon as possible;
  * that the peace of Bucharest with Romania be ratified as soon as possible;
  * that the Polish question should continue to be discussed (with Germany) with a view to implementing the Austro-Polish solution.
  * that energetic pressure be put on Germany over the issue of peace.]

[2] Common Ministerial Council, Vienna, 2 October 1918

Protocol of the ministerial council for common business held in Vienna on 2 October 1918 under the chairmanship of the k.u.k. Foreign Minister Count Burián.

Present: The k.u. Minister-President Dr Wekerle, the k.k. Minister-President Baron von Hussarek, the k.u.k. Minister of War Baron von Stöger-Steiner, the k.u.k. Common Finance Minister Baron von Spitzmüller [responsible for Bosnia-Hercegovina].

Subject: 1. The peace question 2. Solution of the South Slav question.

Burián: [. . .] explains the foreign policy situation. Long before the start of the Bulgarian catastrophe it was clear that we ought to end the war. We certainly ought to be in a position to carry on a defensive fight up to the end of the year, but from then onwards unavoidable decline will lead us irresistibly to complete exhaustion. We would then have to throw ourselves upon the mercy or disfavour of our enemies. In Germany things may be in a better state [. . .] but the final collapse will also be inevitable [there . . .]. We are succumbing to the numerical superiority of our enemies and to the methods of starvation organized by them. We are like a fortress which is bereft of food. The recent peace move of the k.u.k. government has not led to any result,[7] but all future and past considerations, hopes and disappointments, are pointless in view of the collapse of Bulgaria.

Since Bulgaria has been exhausted for some time, it could be foreseen, but it was not too much of a bold hope to depend to some extent on the powers of resistance of the Bulgarians. [He notes that Austria-Hungary had tried to help Bulgaria out with supplies.] Today things stand in such a way that Bulgaria is lost to the Central Powers, while Turkey runs the risk of being cut off from her allies. As a result Turkey in the very near future could be forced into concluding peace at any price. If therefore we have been in agreement for some time on ending the war, today more than ever we must stick to that decision —only now we must seek to accelerate the time-scale of such an action. [Burián notes that as regards peace, the American standpoint offers the best chance for the Monarchy because of Wilson's repeated enunciations:] Germany has herself proposed that we should turn to the Entente with a peace offer through President Wilson as an intermediary—and indeed on the basis of the Fourteen Points and the four additional points. [. . .] The Austrian and Hungarian Minister-Presidents have already agreed to this procedure and His Majesty agrees as well. [. . .]

Wekerle: stresses first with satisfaction that the proposal has been made spontaneously by Germany and has not been a result of pressure from our side. As far as the Fourteen Points are concerned as a basis for negotiation, Dr Wekerle sees in them a great danger for the Monarchy and Hungary. He would welcome the idea of some proviso being formulated, that the Monarchy wants to take care of managing its own internal business. Should foreigners be conceded a say in our internal affairs, then the Monarchy would sink to the level of a state like Turkey—with all the subsequent consequences.

Hussarek: However sad and depressing the revelations of Count Burián, they are not really surprising. The Monarchy for quite a long time has been on a slippery slope and can only be saved by a speedy peace. [Hussarek praises Burián's correct estimation of the situation.] As far as Wilson's Fourteen Points are concerned, these for us are in many ways not so unfavourable—but they give some pause for thought. The critical points are points 9 and 10.[8] [. . .] The point [10] which speaks about some guaranteed autonomy for the peoples of Austria is phrased cautiously and corresponds in many ways to a conception which is now beginning to be recognized here as correct and necessary. In connection with this, Baron von Hussarek discusses the difficulties which obstruct national reconciliation. For example, the Czechs make two irreconcilable claims, since on the one hand they demand the realization of Bohemian state right, on the other hand the union of all Czechs and Slovaks under the slogan of national self-determination. Here there are, according to Baron von Hussarek, the greatest dangers and difficulties. In contrast, the other autonomy movements could lead to a reconstruction, indeed a regeneration of Austria. With regard to the Polish question, here the application of Wilson's principles would mean the complete loss of Galicia. [Hussarek ends by warning against giving up the alliance with Germany—as Wilson demanded in a speech on 27 September—as this would lead to 'German-Austrian irredentism' . . .]

Stöger-Steiner: [. . .] views President Wilson as an ideologue, but he is an honourable champion of his own ideas. [. . .] With regard to sorting out our domestic situation, he [Stöger-Steiner] welcomes the k.u. Minister-President's reservation in accepting the 14 Points. In view of the impact which the Bulgarian events will doubtless have on feeling in our southern territories, Baron von Stöger-Steiner favours immediate action in the work of peace. He expects neither a clear acceptance nor a definite refusal. Probably the enemy will answer first with a demand for occupied territory to be evacuated. [. . .]

Burián: [agrees that] a flat acceptance is certainly not to be expected, but from our move gradually a conversation about the possibility of peace could develop and finally ripen into the desired result. [. . .] Count Burián is determined not to give up the alliance with Germany, but for the moment it is wiser not to give this idea too much publicity nor for the present to renew the alliance, since it could easily be viewed as a provocation, damaging the chances of peace. [He concludes that those present should support his proposal of sending a peace offer to Wilson for they had no other choice and Wilson offered the best hopes. Those present agreed.]

[*Afternoon Session:* The South Slav Question]

Burián: [. . . since speed is of the essence,] proposes that His k.u.k. Apostolic Majesty issue letters to both Minister-Presidents [. . .] giving an assurance that no decision will be made about any regions inhabited by South Slavs without questioning, or against the will or vote of, their people's representative bodies. Count Burián prefers this form of public enunciation to a manifesto issued direct from the Crown—so as not to expose the Crown to any criticism.

All present recognize the necessity and urgency of issuing a pertinent decree on this subject for the general public. They also—with the exception of the k.u. Minister-President—express their basic agreement with the Foreign Minister's suggestion.

Hussarek: [stresses that if Croatia is united with Bosnia and Dalmatia under Hungary in a sub-dualist solution, this will have to be weighed economically so as to ensure parity between Austria and Hungary in the dualist system. In the Emperor's letters, Dualism should not be emphasised so as not to create a bad impression.]

Spitzmüller: [stresses his responsibility for Bosnia and Hercegovina and] says that the sub-dualist solution will no longer satisfy the South Slavs. Therefore, for good or bad we must think of settling it in a trialist sense [and accept Wilson's point 10 in this regard]. The k.u.k. Common Finance Minister is conscious of the dangerous results which such a solution might have for Hungary.

Stöger-Steiner: [. . .] recommends a solution of this question in the sense that the South Slav population which up to now has had to live in six separated states or administrative units, should if possible all be united together in one big political unit. He warns of little jealousies between Austria and Hungary, for it was a question now of the existence of the Monarchy, and he directs a pressing appeal to all responsible elements to take account of the needs of the hour. [. . .]

Wekerle: [speaks out fully against the Emperor issuing any letters.] Particularly, Dr Wekerle warns against promising the South Slavs some kind of reward for staying loyal. Such a move, especially with regard to a trialist solution, would evoke the most distressing sensation and most far-reaching discontent in Hungary. He has to hold absolutely firm to a sub-dualist solution. Dr Wekerle wishes the question to be solved in the sense of the decisions of the Crown Council of 27 September, by pronouncements by the two governments. [. . .] A relevant pronouncement has already been made by the k.k. Minister-President in his policy speech of 1 October [in the Reichsrat]. He himself would use the next available opportunity to set out the position of the Hungarian government. [. . .] In the last few days Dr Wekerle has negotiated with some leaders of the Serb-Croat Coalition and found agreement and understanding from them. [. . .].

[Those present found Wekerle's suggestion—that the two governments should make separate declarations or public speeches—to be 'inadequate and insufficient' to meet the situation. Since no agreement could be reached, Burián proposed that a committee should put together a document summarizing the various arguments which had been made and this would then be used as a basis for another discussion. This proposal was carried.]

[3] Common Ministerial Council, Vienna, 15 October 1918

Protocol of the ministerial council for common business held in Vienna on 15 October 1918 under the chairmanship of His Majesty the Emperor and King.

Present: The k.u.k. Foreign Minister Count Burián, the k.k. Minister-President Baron von Hussarek, the k.u.k. Minister of War Baron von Stöger-Steiner, the k.u.k. Common Finance Minister Baron von Spitzmüller, the Chief of the General Staff Baron Arz, General von Waldstätten, the k.k. Minister of Agriculture Count Silva-Tarouca.

Subject: Manifesto for constitutional reform in Austria

[The protocol of this crucial meeting, which was called to discuss the Emperor's Manifesto, has not survived, but its course can be summarized from notes made by Hussarek and Spitzmüller.[9] **Emperor Karl** opened the meeting and emphasized that because of the domestic situation—the 'frightful political chaos'—and the peace efforts, constitutional reform in Austria was vital. He proposed that a manifesto be issued to this effect. **Hussarek** concurred. **Burián** also approved of the idea for its foreign impact, but stressed that Hungary's integrity must be maintained. **Spitzmüller** however wanted the reform to include Hungary, especially in view of the situation in the southern Slav regions. He warned against Hungary bringing up the idea of a 'personal union' with the rest of the Empire at this stage. The **Emperor** stressed that his coronation oath bound him to uphold Hungary's integrity. But he noted that he would be discussing the matter with Wekerle in the afternoon. He then abruptly adjourned the meeting. **Hussarek** agreed to finalize a text for the manifesto, have it approved by the Austrian government and then brought to the Emperor: this was done on 16 October.]

[4] Common Ministerial Council, Vienna, 22 October 1918

Protocol of the ministerial council for common business held in Vienna on 22 October 1918 under the chairmanship of His Majesty the Emperor and King.

Present: The k.u.k. Foreign Minister Count Burián, the k.u. Minister-President Dr Wekerle, the k.k. Minister-President Baron von Hussarek, the k.u.k. Minister of War Baron von Stöger-Steiner, the k.u.k. Common Finance Minister Baron von Spitzmüller, the k.u.k. Chief of the General Staff Baron Arz.

Subject: Attitude towards the American answer of 18 October 1918.[10]

His k.u.k. Apostolic Majesty deigns to open the Crown Council at 10.30 a.m. [. . .] As far as Austria is concerned [he said] a basis has been laid through the issue of the Imperial Manifesto of 16 October, which makes possible a spinning out of conversations with the President of the United States. As the crowned king of Hungary, His Majesty of course takes the view that he has to preserve the integrity and unity of that kingdom; His Majesty is determined that he will continue to fight to the limit for this principle, to the final collapse, if this corresponds to the will of the people. But His Majesty must also warn the Hungarian government and the political parties which support it, what is at stake, what still could be achieved and saved by giving in quickly, and whether a continuance of the war can be justified before God and the population. In this regard, the decision lies with the Hungarian government. His Majesty directs to the k.k. Minister-President the question whether the moment has not come when one should think of national governments.

Burián: [. . .] The sphinx Wilson has finally spoken, but his messages place us before a new riddle. One must now tread extremely cautiously and pursue for the moment a dilatory tactic. The advantages of Wilson's answer lie particularly in what it conceals; it is not negative and it enables a further spinning of the thread of peace. Our answer must above all be constructed on two basic principles: it must be short and precise, it must not betray any sense of indignation or ill-humour. [...Concerning the content of the reply:] Wilson's whole argument about the Czecho-Slovaks is founded on an extremely weak basis. Neither politically not materially, in everything concerning Czecho-Slovaks, does the Slovak element play any noteworthy role; for example there is not one Slovak in the Czecho-Slovak national council founded abroad,[11] also the Slovaks are far from actually desiring unity with the Czechs. These facts must be made clear in the reply to Wilson. It is also a deliberate lie, which the facts diametrically contradict, for Mr Wilson to say in his introductory remarks that there exists a *de facto* state of war between the Monarchy and the Czecho-Slovak state which he has recognized. Further there is the question, from whom the Czecho-Slovak state has secured its so-called 'authority' (to use Wilson's words). The decision of Mr Wilson and his Entente colleagues is not at all sufficient. If the premises from which Mr Wilson derives his arguments are incorrect, then the conclusions which he has drawn are equally false. Finally it must be remembered that Wilson in his first short answer to the Austro-Hungarian démarche of 16 September 1918 referred expressly to the 14 Points which he now declares to be an insufficient basis for negotiation. All these contradictions and prevarications will have to be suitably pinned down in our answer. Expressly favourable for us is the final sentence of Wilson's note in which the President recognizes the Monarchy as in existence, and urges us to approach the Czechs and South Slavs directly to come to an understanding. [The problem is how the Monarchy should react to Wilson's express points about the Czechoslovak and Yugoslav questions.] In Austria, as his k.u.k. Apostolic Majesty has already stressed, a way forward is the Manifesto, which does not exclude some accommodation with Wilsonian ideas. Far more difficult is the case of Hungary, but also there one cannot ignore either the facts nor the needs of the hour. In this regard two considerations are of the greatest importance: 1. The Slovaks definitely must be mentioned in our answer and, indeed, in a way which takes account of the relevant views of Wilson. [Burián admits that the Slovaks have autonomous tendencies, but denies that they are 'centrifugal' or desiring unity with the Czechs.] 2. At this twelfth hour a clear unambiguous statement must be made about the South Slav question. [The issue here is:] What is to be done in order to set limits on the further proliferation of Great Serbian propaganda, as has been evident in the recent meeting in Zagreb.[12] One cannot go as far as the resolutions approved at that meeting, but one absolutely must advise some far-reaching, very fast concessions, some large-scale revision of our former standpoint. The Hungarian government insists that the integrity and unity of Hungary must be preserved. [. . .] As things stand now, one can only consider uniting all South Slavs 'in the framework of the Monarchy under the Habsburg sceptre'. A reference to Hungary or Austria, or only to the holy crown of St Stephen, does not bring us nearer to the desired goal; indeed such references could unleash dangerous consequences and specifically hinder peace. It would of course be better if we could leave the solution of this thorny question to the peace conference; but this is not possible because Wilson's note requires our views beforehand. Count Burián therefore urgently warns against any intransigence.

Wekerle: [. . .] declares that above all the Serbo-Croat question has to be separated from the nationalities question. As far as the first is concerned, the Hungarian government is willing to make far-reaching concessions. It has declared that South Slav unity depends on these peoples. Of course, this unity can only occur under the holy crown of St Stephen, for the Hungarian government must stick firmly to its rights. He who surrenders his true right surrenders himself, gives the appearance of weakness and contributes towards catastrophe. The more one concedes, the more will be demanded. [. . .] In the question of the nationalities, the Hungarian government is ready to make concessions which even exceed the limits of the nationality law, but here too the pace cannot be pursued too quickly. The spokesman of the Slovaks, MP Juriga,[13] was a few weeks ago still not pushing for autonomy; his demands were limited to the full implementation of the nationality law and to certain concessions over education and the use of the Slovak language. [. . .] The comitats of Pressburg and Trencsen have already spoken out against any unity with the Czechs. [. . .]

Hussarek: [. . .] It seems doubtful that a separation of Czechs and Slovaks can be achieved. [. . .] Individual resolutions, like those mentioned by Dr Wekerle from the comitats of Pressburg and Trencsen, are not sufficient. Only the vote of a large assembly would be of value, and could be used as an argument in the reply to Wilson to show that the Slovaks do not want to unite with the Czechs. [Concerning the South Slav problem, Hussarek agrees with Burián.] The South Slav question will be solved within the framework of the Monarchy: with the simultaneous unity of all South Slavs exclusive of Serbia and Montenegro in a single independent state structure. With regard to His k.u.k. Apostolic Majesty's question about forming special national governments alongside the national assemblies,[14] the k.k. Minister-President observes that he does not feel able to advise such a step out of which precarious developments could occur. [. . .]

Spitzmüller: [opposes Wekerle's views about 'insatiable nationalist aspirations', since Wilson's note still makes possible a compromise of the Monarchy with the South Slavs:] The absolute maintenance of the dualist structure would be a wise policy under certain circumstances, but now it is a matter of the Monarchy's existence, and we must above all be concerned to save it and not try to hang on to Dualism at any price. Surrendering Slovenia to a South Slav land-complex, which the Hungarian government opposes so stubbornly, is a bitter apple which we must bite into. A half-way adequate solution of the South Slav problem will mean clear sacrifices for Hungary, but also Austria will bear great sacrifices. [He mentions 80,000 Germans who would fall into such a Yugoslav unit . . .] Moving on to the issue of the personal union with Hungary,[15] Baron von Spitzmüller strongly advises against introducing such a law at the present critical moment; it would only cause confusion and make peace more difficult. A solution of the South Slav question in the framework of St Stephen's crown is today impossible and therefore Baron von Spitzmüller completely supports the views of Count Burián.

Arz: [notes the effects of domestic circumstances upon the army.] We must conclude peace at any price and as quickly as possible. With the centrifugal tendencies which characterize the political situation, a further holding out by our troops is doubtful. [He warns of Romania entering the war again, coupled with an offensive on the Italian front:] then our powers of resistance would quickly wane.[16]

Burián: [discusses the situation in Romania and the risks at this stage of negotiating with the Marghiloman government, as Arz proposes. **Hussarek** and **Wekerle** also advise waiting on events.]

Arz: [. . .] Any means would be welcome which might deter Romania from an aggressive action [but he defers to Burián's viewpoint. He turns to the military situation in the south:] The Army High Command has done everything possible to counter the advance of the Entente in the Balkans. [He details the military forces currently opposed to the Entente and Romania.] With regard to a remark from the k.u. Minister-President, that there have been loud voices in Hungary which ascribe to the Army High Command anti-Hungarian tendencies—that it would neglect the defence of Hungary—Baron von Arz replies that he must reject this accusation most forcefully. The Army High Command painstakingly strives to meet all demands for the Monarchy's defence in a non-partisan way and purely according to military considerations. [. . .]

[Both **Spitzmüller** and **Hussarek** speak out against Hungary's law for a personal union with the rest of the Empire. **Burián** then advises Wekerle to think seriously of postponing this idea so as not to complicate the approaching peace talks.]

Wekerle: [. . .] replies that the k.u. government is in a tight corner. The law must be introduced in order to take the wind out of the sails of Count M. Károlyi's agitation. But as far as carrying it out is concerned, he [Wekerle] wants to deal with it in a dilatory fashion if possible.

[Emperor Karl sums up:

1. The 'peace action' should be carried out as fast as possible.
2. An answer to Wilson's note should be formulated in such a way that it does not endanger the defensive force of the army.[17]
3. The k.k. and k.u. governments should take the necessary measures, notably in the South Slav question, which seem most suited to halt any further development of centrifugal tendencies. **Wekerle** promises to 'talk about' a solution of the South Slav question in the sense of 'unity of all South Slav regions within the framework of the Monarchy'.][18]

[5] Common Ministerial Council, Vienna, 30 October 1918

The ministerial council for common business held in Vienna on 30 October 1918 under the chairmanship of the k.u.k. Foreign Minister Count Gyula Andrássy.

Present: The k.k. Minister-President Dr Heinrich Lammasch, the k.u.k. Common Finance Minister Baron von Spitzmüller, the k.u.k. Minister of War Baron von Stöger-Steiner, FML Baron von Bardolff, Major Edmund von Glaise-Horstenau [representing Arz], the k.k. Minister of Defence Baron Friedrich von Lehne.

Subject: The army oath.

[No protocol was made of this final meeting, held at 5 p.m. in a dimly lit Ballhausplatz in Vienna. The following summary has been composed from the memoirs of those present.[19]

It was convened by the Emperor, probably after Stöger-Steiner had petitioned him. As the meeting took place there were rowdy demonstrations outside with cries of 'traitor' against the new Foreign Minister, Count Gyula Andrássy, for having agreed to Wilson's peace terms on 28 October. The meeting was also interrupted by telephone calls. Lammasch answered a call from Prague where the National Council had declared Czechoslovak independence on 28 October. Glaise-Horstenau answered a call from Prince Ludwig Windischgrätz from Budapest.

The discussion in the meeting centred on whether the army should now be released from its oath to the Emperor, or whether some compromise formula should be agreed. **Andrássy** and the ministers favoured a compromise: maintaining the oath but allowing soldiers to swear allegiance also to the new national states. **Glaise-Horstenau**, speaking as the representative of the Army High Command, asked whether the Emperor planned to appeal to the army in the current domestic disputes. When **Andrássy** demurred, **Glaise** reminded the meeting of the problems which had emerged in Hungary in 1848 over the oath. He felt the government must take responsibility. If the troops were now assigned to the national states they should be released from their imperial oath; it was dishonourable [*unerhrlich*] to do otherwise and could produce conflicts of allegiance. **Andrássy**, however, was wholly against release from the oath, stating that it was now, when the Empire and Crown were at stake, that it had real meaning. **Glaise** warned of the danger of the Emperor trying to invoke military loyalty to carry out a *putsch*. **Andrássy**: 'Major, a camarilla is required for that; unfortunately we do not have one. If there were still any central authority in the Monarchy, I would join it now without any reservation'.

Andrássy's compromise was carried. The meeting was terminated abruptly because of the commotion in the street outside. Stöger-Steiner and Bardolff were slightly injured on their way back to the War Ministry.]

NOTES

1. Translated by the editor from Miklós Komjáthy (ed.), *Protokolle des Gemeinsamen Ministerrates der Österreichisch-Ungarischen Monarchie (1914–1918)* (Budapest, 1966) pp. 680–703. Material in square parenthesis has been paraphrased.
2. Bulgaria had collapsed on 26 September and requested an armistice.
3. On 15 June 1918 the Austro-Hungarian army had launched its final offensive on the Italian front but had failed to make any breakthrough.
4. Anton Korošec, leader of the Slovene Clerical party and the South Slav club in the Austrian Reichsrat; he was a key figure in the nationalist agitation which swept through Slovenia in 1918.
5. Hussarek did so on 1 October, with a vague speech in the Reichsrat about 'national autonomy'.
6. According to Point 10 of Wilson's programme, the peoples of Austria-Hungary were to 'to be accorded the freest opportunity for autonomous development'.
7. On 14 September, Burián had ignored Germany's protests and gone ahead with a peace offer to the enemy, but by the end of the month it had been rejected (first by the USA).

8. Point 9 proposed the rectification of Italy's borders according to strict principles of nationality; point 10 proposed autonomous development for the peoples of Austria-Hungary without destroying the Monarchy.
9. The following summary is based on Helmut Rumpler, *Das Völker-manifest Kaiser Karls vom 16. Oktober 1918. Letzter Versuch zur Rettung des Habsburgerreiches* (Munich, 1966), pp. 49ff.; and Carvel de Bussy (ed.), *Memoirs of Alexander Spitzmüller* (New York, 1987), pp. 200ff.
10. This was the US reply to Vienna, in response to Germany and Austria-Hungary's peace offer of 4 October. It arrived in Vienna on 21 October.
11. This was erroneous in ignoring the Slovak Milan Štefánik, who was 'Minister of War' in the new Czechoslovak government abroad.
12. In Zagreb on 6 October, a 'National Council of Slovenes, Croats and Serbs' had been established as the basis for a Yugoslav government.
13. Ferdinand Juriga (1874–1950) had co-founded the Slovak People's Party in 1913 and was the only Slovak deputy to serve in the Hungarian parliament throughout the war. On 18 October 1918 he had demanded the right of self-determination for the Slovak nation.
14. In other words, the national councils now springing up.
15. On 16 October, Wekerle had responded to the Emperor's Manifesto by announcing in the Hungarian parliament that Hungary was not now bound by the *Ausgleich* of 1867 but only united to the rest of the Empire by 'personal union': i.e. by the person of the monarch.
16. On 24 October the Italian army launched a final offensive on the Italian front.
17. On 28 October, the new foreign minister Count Gyula Andrássy dispatched a reply to Wilson, accepting his peace terms.
18. In other words, Wekerle only at this final moment conceded the idea of South Slav unity outside the dualist framework.
19. See Peter Broucek (ed.), *Ein General im Zwielicht. Die Erinnerungen Edmund Glaises von Horstenau*, vol. 1 (Vienna, Cologne and Graz, 1980) pp. 506–10; Carl von Bardolff, *Soldat im alten Österreich* (Jena, 1938) pp. 341–43; and Carvel de Bussy (ed.), *Memoirs of Alexander Spitzmüller*, pp. 216–18. Bardolff's memoirs are slightly at variance with the others and propose an exaggerated role for himself rather than for Glaise. Julius Andrássy, *Diplomacy and the War* (London, 1921), does not the mention the meeting. Andrássy termed his brief spell at the Foreign Ministry, 'the most terrible time of my political life. Every minute brought me the news of a new collapse' (p. 290).

Further Reading

(in English)

General

A good entry point for studying the Habsburg Empire in its final decades is Steven Beller, *Francis Joseph* (London, 1996), but readers should then push on to the remarkable new synthesis by Robin Okey, *The Habsburg Monarchy c.1765–1918* (Basingstoke and London, 2001). This is a fine replacement for C.A. Macartney, *The Habsburg Empire 1790–1918* (London, 1968) and its shorter revised version, *The House of Austria. The Later Phase 1790–1918* (Edinburgh, 1978), although they remain packed with useful detail. For the theory of centrifugal versus centripetal forces, the classic study by Oscar Jászi, *The Dissolution of the Habsburg* Monarchy (Chicago, 1929) is essential. For the influential views of two British contemporary experts, *The Times* journalist Henry Wickham Steed sets out an incisive analysis in *The Hapsburg Monarchy* (London, 1913); while R.W. Seton-Watson's personal journey can be followed in Hugh and Christopher Seton-Watson, *The Making of a New Europe. R.W. Seton-Watson and the Last Years of Austria-Hungary* (London, 1981). For the modern debate, the reader should consult the work of Solomon Wank, for example, 'Some Reflections on the Habsburg Empire and its Legacy in the Nationalities Question', *Austrian History Yearbook* vol. 28 (1997). More optimistically, David Good has set out the Empire's 'success story' in *The Economic Rise of the Habsburg Empire 1780–1914* (Berkeley, 1984). Alan Sked in *The Decline and Fall of the Habsburg Empire 1815–1918* (2nd ed., London, 2001) is paradoxically keen to stress the lack of decline, but presents a stimulating historiographical review. Jean Bérenger's *A History of the Habsburg Empire 1700–1918* (London, 1997) in contrast is best avoided, not least because of the bad translation. A.J.P. Taylor, *The Habsburg Monarchy 1809–1918* (London, 1948) provides, as usual, a controversial and lively read for the initiated.

Austrian Politics and Society

The complex pre-war Austrian political scene can be explored through William Jenks, *The Austrian Electoral Reform of 1907* (New York, 1950); and for Viennese politics in particular, John Boyer, *Culture and Political Crisis in Vienna. Christian Socialism in Power, 1897–1918* (Chicago and London, 1995). For the view of a Viennese arch-satirist, see Edward Timms, *Karl Kraus. Apocalyptic Satirist. Culture and Collapse in Habsburg Vienna* (New Haven and London, 1989). And amidst a wealth of literature on the Viennese milieu: Steven Beller, *Vienna and the Jews 1867–1938* (Cambridge, 1989); William Johnston, *The Austrian Mind. An Intellectual and Social History, 1848–1958* (Berkeley, 1972); and Peter Vergo, *Art in Vienna 1898–1918* (London, 1981). Recently in *Austrian History Yearbook*, vol. 29 (1998) Gary Cohen appealed for a fresh assessment of 'popular political engagement' in Austria, as demonstrated in his own *Education and Middle-Class Society in Imperial Austria 1848–1918* (West Lafayette, 1996). A complementary approach has been the work of Pieter Judson who has explored the German Liberal mentality best in articles in *Austrian History Yearbook* (1991 and 1995) but also in *Exclusive Revolutionaries. Liberal Politics, Social Experience and National Identity in the Austrian Empire 1848–1914* (Ann Arbor, 1996). For the rise of the far-right, Andrew Whiteside's work remains essential: *The Socialism of Fools. Georg Ritter von Schönerer and Austrian Pan-Germanism* (Berkeley, 1975) and in his underrated *Austrian National Socialism before 1918* (The Hague, 1962). Further afield, the Poles and Ruthenes are partly accessible through A. Markovits and F. Sysyn (eds), *Nationbuilding and the Politics of Nationalism. Essays on Austrian Galicia* (Cambridge, Mass., 1982); but for the latest approach see Keely Stauter-Halsted, *The Nation in the Village. The Genesis of Peasant National Identity in Austrian Poland 1848–1914* (Ithaca, 2001). The role of the army has been analysed best by István Deák, *Beyond Nationalism. A Social and Political History of the Habsburg Officer Corps 1848–1918* (Oxford, 1992) and Gunther Rothenburg, *The Army of Francis Joseph* (West Lafayette, 1976).

The Czech Question

There is no full and recommendable study of late Habsburg Czech developments in English, but a number of angles have been covered well in the past twenty years. For Czech politics, see especially Bruce

Garver, *The Young Czech Party 1874–1901 and the Emergence of a Multi-Party System* (New Haven, 1978) and Paul Vyšný, *Neo-Slavism and the Czechs 1898–1914* (Cambridge, 1977). Mills Kelly has been researching the Czech National Socialists with the first fruits in *Austrian History Yearbook* vol. 29 (1998). T.G. Masaryk's development is clear from Gordon Skilling, *T.G. Masaryk. Against the Current 1882–1914* (Basingstoke, 1994), and Robert Pynsent et al. (eds), *T.G. Masaryk*, 3 vols (London, 1989). Something of the rich variety of German and Jewish perceptions can be explored through Gary Cohen, *The Politics of Ethnic Survival. Germans in Prague 1861–1914* (Princeton, 1981); Scott Spector, *Prague Territories. National Conflict and Cultural Innovation in Franz Kafka's Fin de Siècle* (Berkeley, 2000); and the work of Hillel Kieval: *The Making of Czech Jewry, 1870–1918* (New York and Oxford, 1988) and his broader study, *Languages of Community. The Jewish Experience in the Czech Lands* (Berkeley, 2000). For the economic side to Czech advancement, see Richard Rudolph, *Banking and Industrialization in Austria-Hungary* (Cambridge, 1976).

Hungarian Politics and Society

Among contemporary accounts, those which caused a scandal at the time are still among the most informative: R.W. Seton-Watson, *Racial Problems in Hungary* (London, 1908) and *Corruption and Reform in Hungary* (London, 1911). To these can be added the memoir on Seton-Watson above, and his edited correspondence: *R.W. Seton-Watson and his Relations with the Czechs and Slovaks. 1905–1951*, 2 vols (Prague and Martin, 1995). An opposite view, possibly prompted by official Magyar sources, is C.M. Knatchbull-Hugessen, *The Political Evolution of the Hungarian Nation*, 2 vols (London, 1908). C.A. Macartney warms to his favourite subject, and the debate over Magyarization, in *Hungary and her Successors 1919–1937* (Oxford, 1937). For Hungarian work, now appearing more readily in English, readers can turn to two books by András Gerő: *Modern Hungarian Society in the Making. The Unfinished Experience* (Budapest, 1995) and *The Hungarian Parliament 1867–1918. A Mirage of Power* (New Jersey, 1997). Most recently Gerő has tackled the Imperial relationship with Budapest, an aspect missing from Beller's study of Franz Joseph: *Emperor Francis Joseph. King of the Hungarians* (New York, 2001). From the USA, Gábor Vermes supplies the most thorough biography of Tisza: *István Tisza.*

The Liberal Vision and Conservative Statecraft of a Magyar Nationalist (New York, 1985); while for the Slovak challenge to the Magyar nation state, see Milan Hodža, *Federation in Central Europe* (London, 1942) and Peter A. Toma and Dušan Kováč (eds), *Slovakia. From Samo to Dzurinda* (Stanford, 2001). A stimulating if slightly conservative survey of life in the Hungarian capital is John Lukacs' *Budapest 1900. A Historical Portrait of a City and its Culture* (New York, 1989). For a more innovative cultural approach, see Alice Freifeld's acclaimed work, *Nationalism and the Crowd in Liberal Hungary 1848–1914* (Washington DC, 2000).

The thorny interpretation of Transylvanian history is the subject of László Peter (ed.), *Historians and the History of Transylvania* (New York, 1992). And if the Romanian nationalist-communist slant is ditched, the essays are still quite rewarding in Miron Constantinescu et al., *Union of the Romanian National State* (Bucharest, 1971). Katherine Verdery, *Transylvanian Villagers* (Berkeley and Los Angeles, 1983) is one example of an anthropological approach to studying peasant society. From the other side, the colour of high society is best glimpsed through Miklós Bánffy's epic novel in three parts: *They were Counted*; *They were Found Wanting*; *They were Divided* (London, 1999–2001).

The South Slav Question

The most accessible introduction for pre-1914 is now John R. Lampe, *Yugoslavia as History. Twice there was a Country* (Cambridge, 1996). A more demanding read is Ivo Banac, *The National Question in Yugoslavia. Origins, History, Politics* (Ithaca and London, 1984). The best study of the Croatian problem remains that of the eye-witness R.W. Seton-Watson, *The Southern Slav Question and the Habsburg Monarchy* (London, 1911) which can be supplemented by his correspondence: *R.W. Seton-Watson and the Yugoslavs 1906–1941*, 2 vols (London and Zagreb, 1976). But for a lively new approach, see Mark Biondich, *Stjepan Radić, the Croat Peasant Party and the Politics of Mass Mobilization, 1904–1928* (Toronto, 2000). The Slovenes are accessible chiefly through Carole Rogel, *The Slovenes and Yugoslavism 1890–1914* (New York, 1977). The context of Bosnia-Hercegovina's fate is set out well in Noel Malcolm, *Bosnia. A Short History* (London, 1994); and in a timeless fashion in Ivo Andrić's novel *The Bridge on the Drina*. For more detail see Peter Sugar, *The Industrialization of Bosnia 1878–1918* (Seattle, 1963);

and, for the Moslems, Robert Donia, *Islam under the Double Eagle 1878–1914* (New York, 1981). The contemporary notes of Joseph Baernreither, *Fragments of a Political Diary* (London, 1930) add the perspective from Vienna. The atmosphere in the Balkan kingdoms is vividly described in M.E. Durham, *Twenty Years of Balkan Tangle* (London, 1920); and in modern studies by Wayne Vucinich, *Serbia between East and West. The Events of 1903–8* (New York, 1968); David MacKenzie, *Apis. The Congenial Conspirator* (New York, 1989), and John D. Treadway, *The Falcon and the Eagle. Montenegro and Austria-Hungary 1908–1914* (West Lafayette, 1983). Vladimir Dedijer, *The Road to Sarajevo* (London, 1996) remains a classic on the Sarajevo assassinations.

Foreign Policy

The best studies of the Monarchy's foreign entanglements are F.R. Bridge, *The Habsburg Monarchy among the Great Powers 1815–1918* (Oxford, 1990) and Samuel Williamson, *Austria-Hungary and the Origins of the First World War* (London, 1991). Bridge's *Great Britain and Austria-Hungary 1906–1914. A Diplomatic History* (London, 1972) has a wider angle than it suggests, while the Hungarian point of view is clearly set out in István Diószegi, *Hungarians in the Ballhausplatz* (Budapest, 1983). For more detailed aspects some older works remain essential: notably Bernadotte D. Schmitt, *The Annexation of Bosnia* (Cambridge, 1937) and E.C. Helmreich, *The Diplomacy of the Balkan Wars 1912–1913* (Cambridge, Mass., 1938). For the decision-making in the July Crisis, James Joll, *The Origins of the First World War* (2nd ed., London, 1992) and Keith Wilson (ed.), *Decisions for War, 1914* (London, 1995) set the Habsburg viewpoint in context. But the key work is by John Leslie, 'The Antecedents of Austria-Hungary's War Aims: Policies and Policy-Makers in Vienna and Budapest before and during 1914', in *Archiv und Forschung. Wiener Beiträge zur Geschichte der Neuzeit*, vol. 20 (Vienna, 1993). For the latest analysis, see William Godsey Jr, *Aristocratic Redoubt. The Austro-Hungarian Foreign Office on the Eve of the First World War* (Purdue, 1999).

Habsburg diplomacy in the war can be followed through Bridge and through David Stevenson, *The First World War and International Politics* (Oxford, 1988). The crucial tensions with Germany are uncovered well in Gary Shanafelt, *The Secret Enemy. Austria-Hungary and the German Alliance 1914–1918* (New York, 1985) and Fritz Fischer's seminal *Germany's Aims in the First World War* (London, 1967). The foreign ministers justify their behaviour in a suitably ponderous fashion: Stephen Burián von Rajecz, *Austria in Dissolution* (London, 1925); Ottokar Czernin, *In the World War* (London, 1920); and—slightly more lively, with a Hungarian angle— Julius Andrássy, *Diplomacy and the War* (London, 1921). The standard work on peace talks in the East (since the author talked to many of those involved) remains John Wheeler-Bennett, *Brest-Litovsk. The Forgotten Peace. March 1918* (London, 1963).

The World War

The fullest introduction to the Empire at war is the heavily written A.J. May, *The Passing of the Hapsburg Monarchy 1914–1918*, 2 vols (Philadelphia, 1966). More accessible and good for its Czech dimension is Z.A.B. Zeman, *The Break-Up of the Habsburg Empire 1914–1918* (Oxford, 1961); while the view from Hungary is best expressed by József Galántai, *Hungary in the First World War* (Budapest, 1989). Leo Valiani, *The End of Austria-Hungary* (London, 1973) is no easy read, but it supplies useful Italian and Hungarian angles. The Monarchy's wartime propaganda struggles and their impact are the subject of Mark Cornwall, *The Undermining of Austria-Hungary. The Battle for Hearts and Minds* (Basingstoke and London, 2000). A range of topics are also explored in the essays in R. Kann, B. Király and P. Fichtner (eds), *The Habsburg Empire in World War I* (New York, 1977) and B. Király and N. Dreisziger (eds), *East Central European Society in World War I* (New York, 1985).

For military events, Holger Herwig, *The First World War. Germany and Austria-Hungary 1914–1918* (London, 1997) is the best new survey. For a shorter analysis see Mark Cornwall, 'Morale and Patriotism in the Austro-Hungarian Army 1914–1918', in John Horne (ed.), *State, Society and Mobilization in Europe during the First World War* (Cambridge, 1997). For more specifics on the front-line experience, see Norman Stone, *The Eastern Front 1914–1917* (London, 1975) and Cornwall, *The Undermining*, for a fresh evaluation of the Italian front. One key protagonist has at last found his biographer in Lawrence Sondhaus: *Franz Conrad von Hötzendorf. Architect of the Apocalypse* (Boston, Leiden and Cologne, 2000).

The wartime regimes can be studied, for Hungary, through Galántai and Vermes' biography of Tisza, and for Austria, through Joseph

Redlich, *Austrian War Government* (New Haven, 1929). Useful thinking on ethnic nationalism is provided in a synthesis by Aviel Roshwald, *Ethnic Nationalism and the Fall of Empires. Central Europe, Russia and the Middle East, 1914–1923* (London and New York, 2001). For regional examples see especially H. Louis Rees, *The Czechs during World War I* (New York, 1992); and Mark Cornwall 'The Experience of Yugoslav Agitation in Austria-Hungary 1917–1918' in Hugh Cecil and Peter Liddle (eds), *Facing Armageddon: The First World War Experienced* (London, 1996). Similar studies in English for Galicia or Transylvania are lacking, but a valuable addition is now Marsha Rozenblit, *Reconstructing a National Identity. The Jews of Habsburg Austria during World War I* (Oxford, 2001). For cultural dimensions, the essays by Claire Nolte and Steven Beller are especially illuminating: in Aviel Roshwald and Richard Stites (eds), *European Culture in the Great War. The Arts, Entertainment and Propaganda* (Cambridge 1999). The economic collapse in all its complexity is unravelled in Eduard März, *Austrian Banking and Financial Policy. Creditanstalt at a Turning Point 1913–1923* (New York, 1984) and Gusztáv Graz and Richard Schüller, *The Economic Policy of Austria-Hungary* (New Haven, 1928).

How western Allied policy evolved is clear: for Britain in Kenneth Calder, *Britain and the Origins of the New Europe 1914–1918* (Cambridge, 1976); for Italy in Cornwall, *The Undermining*; and for the USA in Tibor Glant, *Through the Prism of the Habsburg Monarchy. Hungary in American Diplomacy and Public Opinion in the First World War* (New York, 1998). For the émigré movements see especially, Dimitrije Djordjević (ed.), *The Creation of Yugoslavia 1914–1918* (Santa Barbara and Oxford, 1980), Constantinescu et al. on the Romanians, and (a controversial study) Josef Kalvoda, *The Genesis of Czechoslovakia* (New York, 1986). Memoirs which illuminate the émigré struggle include: T.G. Masaryk, *The Making of a State. Memoirs and Observations* (London, 1929); Edvard Beneš, *My War Memoirs* (London, 1928) and Henry Wickham Steed, *Through Thirty Years 1892–1922*, 2 vols (London, 1924).

Reaching the final collapse, Edmund von Glaise-Horstenau, *The Collapse of the Austro-Hungarian Empire* (London and Toronto, 1930) can still be recommended. The confusion of the last months is vividly portrayed in a range of memoirs: Ludwig Windischgrätz, *My Memoirs* (London, 1921); Carvel de Bussy (ed.), *Memoirs of Alexander Spitzmüller* (New York, 1987); and Michael Károlyi, *Fighting the World. The Struggle for Peace* (New York, 1925). The conflicting emotions, as peace approached, are examined in Mark Cornwall, 'Austria-Hungary', in Hugh Cecil and Peter Liddle (eds), *At the Eleventh Hour. Reflections, Hopes and Anxieties at the Closing of the Great War, 1918* (London, 1998).

Index

(AH is used as an abbreviation for Austria-Hungary)

Conservatives, 53
in Hungary, 105
Pan-Germans, 54, 81, 83, 84
People's Party, 83
Radicals, 51, 62, 68, 119
Social Democrats, *see* Social Democrats
societies, 49, 78, 87–90
Workers' Party (National Socialists), 55
Germany, 8, 13, 14, 17, 19–20, 22, 23–5,
27–34, 66, 68, 83, 90, 91, 113, 122,
151–2, 198, 200–2
wartime tension with AH, 35–43,
155–61, 163, 175–7, 179, 188, 191
Gessmann, Albert, 53
Gladstone, W.E., 18
Glaise-Horstenau, Edmund von, 11, 180,
209–10
Gorizia, 129, 140, 145
Gorlice, 157–8, 176
Grafenauer, Franc, 182
Great Britain, 14, 16, 18, 23, 24–6, 27, 28,
30, 34, 127, 152, 175, 177–8
Greece, 28, 29, 30, 128, 137
Grégr Eduard, 79
Grey, Edward, 32
Gross, Gustav, 51

Hainfeld, congress (1889), 54
Handel, Erasmus, 187
Heinold, Karl, 134
Hindenburg, Field Marshal Paul von, 38,
155, 156, 159, 177
historiography, 2–7, 11n, 12n
Hodža, Milan, 109
Hohenwart, Count Karl, 77, 94
Horvat, Josip, 181
Hoyos, Alexander, 26
Hungarian parliament, 98, 102, 106,
107–8, 110, 124, 183–4
obstruction, 98, 108, 151
standing orders, 98, 108
Hungary (Transleithania), 8, 16, 20, 50,
60, 89, 93, 97–114 *passim*, 124, 135,
140, 183–5, 191, 205–8
constitutional crisis, 13, 97–102
Independence Party, 100, 104, 107, 111
law and order in, 102, 112
local government, 101–2, 109
New Party (Bánffy), 100, 104
non Magyars in, 101, 103–7, 108, 110,
112–14, 116n, 184–5, 207

Party of National Work (Tisza), 104,
107
People's Party, 100, 104
Radicals (Jászi), 107, 112
relations with Austria, 50, 60, 89, 97–8,
100, 105, 114, 115n, 161–2, 167,
183–4, 186, 199, 204
Social Democrats, *see* Social Democrats
Hus, Jan, 92
Hussarek, Baron Max von, 68–9, 191, 192,
199, 201–4, 207–8, 210n

inflation, 66, 112, 186
internment (wartime), 66, 110, 182, 185
Isonzo, river, 123, 139, 160
Istria, 123, 124, 126, 130, 143, 145, 146n,
186, 189
Italian front, 37, 139, 140, 158–9, 160, 162,
163, 167, 176, 179, 192, 208, 211n
Italians (of AH), 49, 59, 61, 123
Italo-Ottoman war, 19, 26, 27, 29
Italy, 9, 14, 16, 18–19, 22, 25, 27–9, 30,
34, 36, 37, 39, 110, 122, 123, 127,
129–30, 134–5, 136, 138–40,
149–50, 152, 156, 173, 175, 177,
178–9, 190, 199
Izvolsky, Alexander, 22–4

Jászi, Oszkár, 3, 107
Jeglič, Bishop Anton, 135, 189
Jelačič, Baron Josip, 146
Jesser, Franz, 90
Jews, 53, 54, 79, 82, 89, 105, 106, 164n
Joseph Ferdinand, Archduke, 159
Judenburg, 143
judicial system, 88
July crisis (1914), 10, 31–3, 34, 109, 133,
147n, 174
Juriga, Ferdinand, 207, 211n
Justh, Gyula, 107

Kafka, Franz, 180–1
Kaizl, Josef, 79, 83
Kalina, Antonín, 92
Kaloušek, Jan, 92–3
Kann, Robert A., 3
Karl, Emperor-King, 10, 38–9, 40, 42, 43,
67–9, 92, 140, 144–5, 159, 169–72,
176–7, 183, 187–8, 191, 192, 193n,
197, 200, 202–3, 204, 205, 206,
209–10